1989

GIVING CHILDREN A CHANCE

GIVING CHILDREN A CHANCE

The Case for More Effective National Policies

GEORGE MILLER
Editor

CENTER FOR NATIONAL POLICY PRESS

WASHINGTON, D.C.

Copyright © 1989 by

Center for National Policy Press

Distributed by arranagement with

UPA, Inc.
4720 Boston Way
Lanham, MD 20706

European Distribution by

Eurospan
3 Henrietta Street
London WC2E 8LU England

Printed in the United States of America

British Cataloging in Publication Information Available

Library of Congress Cataloging–in–Publication Data

Giving children a chance.
Includes bibliographies and index.
1. Child welfare– –United States. 2. Children– –Services for–
–United States. I. Miller, George, 1945-   .
HV741.G53   1989   362.7'0973   88-35188 CIP
ISBN 0–944237–27–4 (alk. paper)
ISBN 0–944237–28–2 (pbk. : alk. paper)

All Center for National Policy Press books are produced on acid-free paper
which exceeds the minimum standards set by the National Historical
Publication and Records Commission

CONTENTS

PREFACE

THIS PUBLICATION is part of a Center for National Policy project called "Investing in Prevention." Under a grant from the Primerica Foundation, the Center conducted a series of private meetings in four metropolitan areas around the country, to seek the views of young corporate and community leaders about the problem of the underclass in the United States, and how this problem relates to the issue of what happens to children born in poverty.

Peter D. Hart, an opinion research specialist, guided these discussions, as participants expressed their views and attitudes on the issues involved. A summary of the results of the four sessions is included here as an appendix to this volume.

Essentially, we found a high degree of concern, strongly contradicting the conventional view of this group of younger leaders, members of the baby boom generation, as self-interested. We also found, however, that there is a lack of information about the problem. New program designs, and the accumulating research results of recent years, especially as they relate to the importance and the effectiveness of early intervention, are not well known or understood. This is a particularly important finding; it has encouraged us to assemble this book of essays as a means of bridging the information gap.

We believe that this issue is at the core of the challenge we face as a nation in ensuring a healthy society and a productive economy in the future. We are most grateful to the Primerica Foundation for its support for the project as a whole, as well as for this publication.

Edmund S. Muskie
Washington, D.C.

INTRODUCTION

George Miller

THE TIME HAS COME for America, as a nation, to invest in the future of our children. As a society, we have traditionally relied on the family and its informal networks of support to provide young children with the nurturing, education and economic sustenance they need. But for many families today, that system of childrearing is under enormous pressure. The sweeping economic and demographic changes of the past 20 years have affected families at every income level, and in every ethnic group and geographic region. Only now are policymakers realizing the extent of the effort that will be necessary to deal with those changes.

Today's parents, many of whom are overburdened in their efforts to provide both care and economic support for their children, are increasingly asking for help in the task of caring for their children. And large numbers of children growing up in poverty—nearly one in four children today—need social, medical and educational services that their parents cannot provide. At the same time, business and labor leaders, local elected officials and national policymakers from both political parties have become increasingly aware that if we are to forge a productive, economically secure future for our country, we must invest now in developing the capacities of the children who will run that future economy. In Washington, D.C., and across the country, the needs of children have become the focus of both political and policy interests, with voters joining the experts to urge that child care and other children's programs be among our highest national priorities.

Underlying an emerging new consensus, but rarely expressed, is the recognition that children matter in their own right—as human beings, as well as future citizens, employees, consumers or taxpayers. All children, regardless of the income level of their parents, deserve and need decent nutrition and health care, a safe place to live and an appropriate education. Today, too many children are not receiving those basic human necessities. It is our moral responsibility, and it is also our national interest, to see that those needs do not go unmet.

Policymakers' growing interest in the problems and needs of their youngest constituents has been paralleled by a new understanding in the academic community of children's early developmental needs, and an outpouring of empirical evidence on the effectiveness of early childhood health and education programs. Since its creation in 1983, the bipartisan Select Committee on Children, Youth and Families of the U.S. House of Representatives has accumulated a vast record of testimony documenting the worth of prenatal and early childhood development programs, particularly for children from low-income or distressed families.

Our challenge now is to translate this convergence of knowledge, political consensus and public need into a national policy best suited to meet the needs of America's children, their families and the needs of the nation as a whole.

AN ERA OF RETRENCHMENT

The early 1980s brought an administration to Washington committed to reducing federal spending and to decreasing the influence of government in private affairs. While President Reagan did not succeed in persuading either the public or Congress that federal activities should be reduced across the board, he did achieve a major reordering of national spending priorities, shifting significant resources out of discretionary domestic spending and programs aiding the poor, and into massive weapons procurement programs.[1]

In agreeing to the President's budget priorities, Congress and the public accepted a number of the administration's arguments about the nature and effectiveness of federal social programs. Those arguments included the notion that people should largely be left alone to help themselves rather than receive any assistance from government; that the antipoverty programs of the 1960s and the 1970s did not help people escape poverty; and, that the entrenched welfare-dependent population was created by welfare itself. These arguments have lingered long after their fundamental premises have been proven false by statistical and scientific analysis.

In fact, a number of federal efforts aimed at reducing the negative effects of poverty on children have been demonstrably successful.[2] These include Medicaid, which has extended the benefits of medical advances in prenatal care and childrearing to women on welfare; Head Start, which has greatly improved children's success rates in school; and nutrition supplementation, provided through programs like WIC, which reduces health risks for pregnant women, nursing mothers and young children.

Although children are the one population group patently unable to improve their own economic status, programs directed at low-income children have suffered severe cutbacks under the Reagan administration. At the same time, the numbers of children in need of services increased, the President's stated commitment to the social safety net notwithstanding. Since 1980, 2.5 million more children have slipped into poverty—a total of almost 13 million children in 1987 lived below the federal poverty line.[3] Today, the richest nation on earth consigns one out of four children to live in poverty by the time they reach 18. Millions of babies, pregnant women and school children go through the day without adequate food, housing or medical care. This is a sad legacy of an era that has conferred great prosperity on many Americans.

It will take years to reverse the negative effects of the past, and the process will be even slower because of the massive budget deficits created during this administration. Fortunately, we have a clearer idea than ever before of what it takes to help lift families out of poverty, and what children need to develop to their full potential. But the task will be formidable.

THE REALITIES FACING TODAY'S FAMILIES

Since the late 1960s, families have been radically affected by several major demographic trends. Women of childbearing age have entered the labor force in record numbers, postponing having children until later and sometimes altogether. The national birthrate has declined steadily, resuming a decades-long downward path that was interrupted by the post-World War II baby-boom phenomenon. Divorce has become commomplace. Medical advances, improved income and healthier lifestyles have contributed to longer lives for the elderly.

As a result of such changes, the basic family unit of popular lore—working father, mother at home, several children—is no longer basic in any real sense. Children are now born into and grow up in smaller families; they are cared for, increasingly, outside their own homes, and they are far less likely than before to remain in the same family situation throughout childhood. They are far likelier now to spend some of their growing up years with just one parent, and they are far likelier now to live in marginal economic circumstances at some point.[4]

These trends, combined with substantial increases in the proportions of teen-age mothers who are unmarried, are increasing the numbers of American children who begin life in significant hardship, and whose future is less hopeful as well. The high levels of skill and educational attainment demanded by a technologically sophisticated society are reducing the prospects for many American youth for making it in the mainstream.

At the same time, the pool of available workers is declining. American corporations have begun to take an aggressive interest in how well our schools are doing in training a work force capable of keeping our nation competitive in tomorrow's tough global economy. Educators and state, local and national officials have proposed a wide array of actions: higher standards in math, science and languages; improved technological competence at the university level; more effective stay-in-school and school-to-work transition efforts, and continued improvement in elementary school curriculum and teaching. As important as any other effort, however, will be a new focus on early childhood.

EARLY CHILDHOOD—KEY TO LATER SUCCESS

Over the past two decades, child development researchers and theoreticians have established beyond all doubt that the logic underlying early childhood education programs such as Head Start is even more critical than originally thought. The interaction between a child and its environment to age five, and even before birth, is crucial in determining whether that child will be able to realize full human potential. From the most basic contribution of adequate nutrition to brain, nerve cell and muscle development, to the most complex application of emotion and understanding to the tasks of learning higher cognitive skills, the environment an infant inherits has an extraordinarily important effect on its future.

American families of vastly different economic and social circumstances are finding that the challenge of providing the right kind of environmental inheritance is not as simple or as straightforward as it once seemed.

Many working parents of newborns have adequate health insurance coverage as a job-related benefit, and can take advantage of essential prenatal care services; yet, large numbers have no such coverage. Early detection of health and developmental problems, regular preventive health care including immunizations and a continuous relationship with a primary caregiver are essential to a very young child's chances for healthy physical, mental and emotional development; yet, access to preventive health care services and to high-quality out-of-home child care is far from universal. Parental leave to care for newborns and sick children is legally mandated in most Western European countries; yet it is only in the discussion phase in the United States.

At present, low-income parents on welfare have little access to quality child care, without which they cannot seek education, training, or work, or establish economic independence. Welfare reform legislation passed by Congress guarantees child care during participation in education and job training programs, and help parents pay for child care during the transition period.

A decade ago, the greatest challenge was identifying which services could effectively address the problems of inadequate nutrition, education, social services and health. Today, we know what works: the challenge is to provide those resources to those in need. The Supplemental Feeding Program for Women, Infants and Children (WIC), Head Start and prenatal care, among all others, are still woefully underfunded. Less than half of the women eligible for WIC services receive them; only 18% of the children eligible for Head Start are enrolled. This lack of funding is especially shortsighted because these programs deliver proven cost savings down the line. For every federal dollar invested in WIC, $3 is saved in avoided hospitalization costs. For every dollar invested in preschool education, $6.00 is saved in reduced crime, special education and welfare expenditures.

The question of access to an adequate preschool program poses significant challenges. Effective preparation for the start of formal, abstract learning is frequently provided by parents and other family members as a natural part of their daily interactions. For children whose families provide an education-oriented atmosphere in the home, organized preschool programs are a useful component of the overall preparation for elementary school. But for parents whose own schooling was weak and who may have neither the time nor the capacity to give their children constantly attentive responses, preschool can be essential. Yet these are children whose parents can rarely afford to pay for such a program. Several states have instituted their own Head Start and preschool programs to fill in the gap left by inadequate federal funding, but much more needs to be done.

Finally, good parenting often requires more help and support than our increasingly mobile and diverse society provides. Many young people begin families when they are living far from their own parents and siblings. Suburban developments are not places where extended families thrive. One can turn to books, magazines, health care providers, neighbors or coworkers for advice and information, but these resources rarely are full substitutes for the help, guidance and emotional support that families traditionally provided. Such support ought to be more widely available to all young parents than it now is, either through community-based family support centers or existing institutions. For the highly stressed, very young, unmarried welfare mother, support and education in parenthood is essential if her children are to have a reasonable chance of healthy development.

Our decades of experience with early childhood programs, as well as new research, have told us what needs to be done. Getting it done will require the investment of large amounts of time, money and imagination by every community, every organization, every business and every level of government. We must not allow the federal budget deficit or lingering inaccurate views about social programs to deter us from investing in comprehensive health and education services for young children in every community and at every income level.

It is far less costly to serve these needs than it is to ignore them, because ultimately we will pay for that ignorance: in hospital bills, in crime, in school dropouts, in poverty, in teenage pregnancy, in unemployment, in homelessness and in welfare dependency.

TOWARD A NATIONAL STRATEGY FOR CHILDREN

We are moving as a nation toward a new view of public responsibility toward families and children. We have seen this first in the child care field, where working parents are actively seeking action to help redress the lack of supply, quality and equity in the child care system. We are now moving, in Congress, at the state level and in communities throughout America, toward creating a flexible, high-quality child care system that is universally available to all families, at prices they can afford.

Work has begun on other pressing needs of children as well. We must assure that new initiatives are not fragmented or haphazard, but are implemented in a coherent, efficient and cost-effective manner, directed by a strategy that addresses the national need. Thus all children, no matter where they live or how much money their parents earn, will have access to the best possible care and education, and the best possible hope for a bright future. The articles in this volume contribute both evidence and argument to this cause.

In the first article, Bernice Weissbourd and Carol Emig lay out in detail an overview of the problem of inadequate attention to child development issues and a strategy for setting out to solve it. James

Garbarino explains the importance of such a strategy, linking the development of intelligence to the more general process of a child's developing person, and the success of this development in turn to the nature of the care-giving environment.

Articles by Eleanor Stokes Szanton and Sara Rosenbaum provide a comprehensive survey of the data on children's health and welfare, and on services in the United States. These articles place in context the difficult task of making a reasonable start in life equitably available to children across the income spectrum in a nation that directly links the availability of basic services to level of family income.

Two articles address the special problems and special needs of children in families outside the mainstream. James Comer addresses the unique experience of the black family in American history and sets out a programmatic strategy for helping underclass minority children and their families prepare to take advantage of educational opportunity.

Stanley Greenspan deals with multi-risk families where parents with severe life stresses and specific psychological problems exhibit behavior toward their children that is likely to be more dysfunctional than helpful. He, too, offers a specific program model to address the problems of such parents.

Finally, articles by Lisbeth Bamberger Schorr and by Judith Musick and Robert Halpern review the concept and practice of "family support" programs that have been established in various communities around the country, along the lines of efforts described by Comer and Greenspan. Schorr stresses the positive, detailing successful experimentation and suggesting guidelines for successful replication, while Musick and Halpern sound a note of caution, identifying the significant challenges that confront us in tackling the most serious and most difficult problems families face.

The unique Peter D. Hart 'focus group' interviews with baby-boom generation corporate and community leaders that appear as an appendix to this volume provide important insights into the nature of the communications challenge facing those who care about this issue. In all, the material in this publication should make a significant contribution to meeting that challenge successfully.

* * * * * *

Fundamentally, Americans value independence and the duty to individual responsibility that accompanies it. Families that need help, be it finding a job, paying for child care, or educating their children, want that help provided in such a way that it enhances their potential for self-sufficiency, rather than diminishing it. It is our duty to help

America's children get a strong start in life, and to do it in such a way that their families are strengthened in the process. At no other time in our history have we had the opportunity to make such a positive difference for an entire generation of children. If we fail to make use of this opportunity, it will be a national tragedy.

NOTES

1. John L. Palmer and Isabel V. Sawhill (Eds.), *The Reagan Record: An Assessment of America's Changing Domestic Priorities.* New York: Ballinger Publishing Co., 1984.

2. Select Committee on Children, Youth, and Families, U.S. House of Representatives, "Opportunities for Success: Cost-Effective Programs for Children," Washington, D.C.: Government Printing Office, 1985.

Select Committee on Children, Youth and Families, U.S. House of Representatives, "Opportunities for Success: Cost-Effective Programs for Children, Update, 1988," Washington, D.C.: Government Printing Office, 1988.

3. $11,612 for a family of four.

4. *See* Frank Levy, *Dollars and Dreams: The Changing American Income Distribution,* New York: Russell Sage Foundation, 1987; and, Select Committee on Children, Youth, and Families, U.S. House of Representatives, "America's Families in Tomorrow's Economy," Washington, D.C.: Government Printing Office, July 1, 1987.

EARLY CHILDHOOD PROGRAMS FOR CHILDREN IN POVERTY: A GOOD PLACE TO START

Bernice Weissbourd
Carol Emig

POOR CHILDREN in the United States have captured the attention of politicians in both parties and policymakers of many persuasions. In the 1988 presidential election child care centers became almost as popular a campaign stop for presidential candidates as senior citizen centers and factory gates. A call for a children's tax credit to help low-income parents pay for child care, and increased funding for Head Start,[1] were countered with support for the Act for Better Child Care, which would provide grants to states to subsidize and upgrade child care, and for early childhood education.

This is just the latest in a series of efforts by politicians and policymakers to focus attention on poor children. Democratic Governor Mario Cuomo of New York used his 1988 State of the State Address to launch the Decade of the Child, proposing preschool programs for all four-year-olds and an extension of Medicaid coverage to poor children who are presently ineligible to participate in the program.[2] One year earlier, Republican Governor James Thompson of Illinois challenged his state to meet the needs of children in poverty, warning that, "if we lose the child, we lose the adult—to mental hospitals, penitentiaries, crime, poverty and ignorance."[3] These gubernatorial declarations were buttressed by policy statements from the National Governors' Association, including a report on welfare prevention which recommends a program of comprehensive services for poor children: prenatal care, nutrition, quality child care and preschool programs and family resource centers.[4]

Congress' recent welfare reform efforts will bring pressure to bear on absent parents who fail to provide adequate child support and

---

Portions of this chapter are taken from Carol Emig, *Caring for America's Children.* Evanston, IL: Family Focus, 1986.

1

would require states to provide some child care and health coverage as parents attempt to become self-sufficient.[5] Liberal Senator Christopher Dodd (D-CT) and conservative Senator Orrin Hatch (R-UT) have introduced competing bills to provide federal support for child care.[6]

Nor have the media been silent on the issue of children in poverty. Several *New York Times* editorials have urged public support for existing early childhood programs as well as for innovative efforts to break the cycle of poverty by supporting children in the earliest years of life.[7] *U.S. News and World Report* and *Newsweek* both highlighted the potential impact of children's issues in the 1988 presidential campaign.[8]

In the political arena, poor children—who cannot vote and whose parents are among those least likely to be involved in the political process—are emerging as a new and generally accepted "special interest." A poll commissioned by KidsPac, the political action committee devoted to children's issues, revealed a surprising depth of support for children. Sixty percent of voters surveyed would find a candidate who gave special attention to issues of early childhood health and education appealing. The same percentage indicated support for full funding of these programs, even in the face of budget deficits.[9]

An earlier poll by Louis Harris reported that almost two-thirds of Americans say that, as a society, we expend too little effort on the problems of children; slightly more than two-thirds said the same about the problems of the poor. Almost 90% wanted government to provide more child care for the children of poor working mothers and to provide health coverage for children who do not have health insurance.[10]

Finally, support for poor children has surfaced in what many would consider an unlikely quarter. The leaders of several of America's largest corporations, under the tutelage of the prestigious Committee for Economic Development, have challenged our political leadership and the rest of the business community to accord "the highest priority to early and sustained intervention in the lives of disadvantaged children."[11]

What's going on here? As the Bible so accurately predicted, the poor *have* always been with us. So why have their children suddenly become the object of such intense and high-level attention? The reasons range from compassion to astute politics, from pragmatism to just plain common sense.

Children in need have always been recognized as deserving of our compassion and charity, even when that concern has not translated into action. Social reformers from Jane Addams to Mother Theresa have admonished us to treat the poor with dignity and to cherish and nurture their children. In the political arena, many advocates for the poor concentrate their efforts on advancing programs for children, at least in part because poor children often evoke more sympathy and support than poor adults, who too often have the unfortunate experience of being blamed for their economic circumstances. It is, after all, hard to accuse an infant of sloth.

Demographic developments in the past decade also have contributed to the public's discovery of childhood poverty. There are simply so many more poor children now—14 million in 1986, accounting for nearly one in four children in the country.[12] This represents the highest child poverty rate since the early 1960s.[13] Children have displaced the elderly as the largest single group living in poverty, comprising about 40% of the poor in this country.[14]

The overwhelming presence of children in what many now regard as a permanent underclass and the seemingly insurmountable barriers erected by a childhood in poverty have left both casual observers and serious students of poverty with a sense that the problem has spun out of our control. Among the indicators that leave even the most determined and optimistic feeling helpless are:

- *A nationwide infant mortality rate in 1985 of 10.6 deaths per 1,000 live births, higher than that of most other western industrialized countries.*[15] Nonwhite children in Chicago, Boston, Detroit, Washington, D.C., Indianapolis, Memphis and Philadelphia had infant mortality rates in 1985 that exceeded 20 per 1,000 live births.[16] Prevention of infant mortality is highly correlated with access to health care which, in the United States, is correlated with family income.
- *Births to teenagers amounting to 13% of all babies born in 1985.*[17] These mothers are at high risk of dropping out of school, face poor employment prospects and often confront a future of long-term dependency for themselves and their children.
- *Nearly one million youngsters failing to complete high school, entering the labor market each year barely literate and lacking in most basic skills.* They are joined by about 700,000 who receive diplomas but who are no more competent than their drop-out counterparts.[18]

In the midst of these profoundly troubling indicators, there is nevertheless reason for hope. A review of anti-poverty policies enacted in the last 25 years reveals a consistent and encouraging fact: *Positive efforts to support children and their families in the first few years of a child's life are among the most effective, and the most cost-effective, methods of breaking the cycle of poverty.* A comprehensive strategy to combat the long-term effects of childhood poverty would include prenatal care;

acute and preventive health care for children; adequate and proper nutrition; family support programs to help parents establish a family environment which nurtures young children and promotes healthy physical, social and emotional development; and quality child care and preschool programs.

Of course, early childhood programs, in the absence of effective policies to promote full employment, safe and affordable housing, adequate health care and a decent minimum standard of living, will not eradicate poverty. What a comprehensive early childhood strategy can do, however, is place a large percentage of poor children on the same physical, social and educational footing as children from more economically advantaged families, thus increasing their chances of succeeding in school and securing a job.

As the following pages indicate, a foundation already exists of successful, cost-effective children's programs, in spite of an erratic federal funding history. The Reagan years brought severe cuts in social programs which benefit children, although a resurgence of legislative interest in children appears to be underway now. Building on this foundation by expanding, improving and refining existing programs will be expensive in the short-term, but will, in relatively quick fashion, yield cost-effective results. Failure to do so will be infinitely more expensive and, ultimately, more damaging to our society.

MATERNAL AND CHILD HEALTH

The health problems of many poor children begin before birth, with inadequate prenatal care for many low-income expectant mothers. Pregnant women who receive no prenatal care are three times as likely to deliver a low birth weight baby as are women who receive adequate prenatal care.[19] Low birth weight, in turn, is highly correlated with infant mortality and morbidity, retardation, developmental problems, cerebral palsy and other disabilities.[20] The Children's Defense Fund estimates that nearly a quarter million children who were low birth weight babies enter school each year at much higher risk of being educationally impaired or of experiencing major problems at school.[21]

Prenatal care which begins early and continues throughout a pregnancy can eliminate or alleviate many of these poor outcomes, reducing the risk of a low weight birth by 25 to 50%.[22] Seventy-five percent of the risks associated with low birth weight can be evaluated in the first prenatal visit and addressed in subsequent interventions.[23]

Comprehensive prenatal care is also among the most cost-effective forms of medical care. The $4,300 average cost of complete prenatal care and a hospital delivery for a healthy mother and baby increases almost threefold when a child is premature and experiences major complications and more than sixfold when an infant is extremely premature.[24] The Institute of Medicine found that every dollar spent on comprehensive prenatal care saved $3.38 in just the first year of a baby's life.[25] In 1986, the estimated cost of delivering comprehensive prenatal care to all poor pregnant women in the United States was about half of the $2.3 billion we paid for hospital care for sick infants in their first year.[26]

Failing to provide prenatal care to expectant teenagers has particularly tragic and costly consequences because very young mothers run the greatest risk of complications during pregnancy and delivery. The younger a pregnant woman is, the less likely she is to receive early prenatal care. While 34% of all pregnant women receive less than adequate prenatal care (e.g., care that does not begin before the second trimester), the figure for pregnant teenagers approaches 60%.[27] One consequence is that teenage mothers account for a disproportionately high percentage of all low birth weight births.

Most children in the United States routinely receive periodic check-ups, immunizations and timely care when illness or accidents occur. Health professionals who work with low-income students, however, report that as many as 80% of their young patients suffer from at least one untreated health problem—including vision, hearing and dental problems; anemia; mental health problems; and developmental disabilities.[28] Routine pediatric care (regular medical check-ups, screening for vision and hearing problems, dental examinations, follow-up treatment when problems are uncovered and timely immunizations) can prevent or ameliorate many of these problems.

Preventive pediatric care is also cost-effective. The Children's Defense Fund reports that preventive health care delivered to Medicaid children reduced overall program costs for these children by almost 10%.[29] Childhood immunizations, an important component of a preventive health regimen, have yielded dramatic and highly cost-effective results. Between 1960 and 1982, for example, there was a more than 99% decline in reported cases of polio, diphtheria and measles.[30] The Centers for Disease Control reported that every dollar spent to immunize children against measles saves more than eight dollars in reduced illness and hospitalization costs.[31] (Severe measles cases can lead to hearing impairment, retardation and other problems.)

Adequate and proper nutrition, especially for young children and pregnant and nursing women, is the third essential component of any preventive health system. Several evaluations of the federal WIC program (which provides supplemental food to low-income pregnant women, nursing mothers and to infants and children up to age five) have provided strong evidence linking nutrition assistance to improved birth weights and growth rates and to decreased rates of anemia. They have also established the cost-effectiveness of nutritional assistance to low-income mothers and children:

- Every dollar invested in the prenatal component of WIC saves approximately three dollars in short-term hospital costs.[32]
- In 1985, it costs $30 a month to provide a WIC nutritional package to a pregnant woman, $35 a month for an infant. In contrast, it costs at least $1,400 *a week* to hospitalize a malnourished infant.[33]

The benefits of a preventive health strategy are well established and widely accepted, both as a sensible course for individuals to follow and as wise public policy. The nation's public record of action in this field, however, has been erratic. The 1960s saw the creation or expansion of several major health programs for poor children, with some continued growth in the 1970s. In the 1980s, however, the federal government's commitment to health services for the poor declined dramatically, ironically at the same time that an abundance of research on these services was producing evidence of both their success and cost-effectiveness.

Access to prenatal care among poor women began to improve in the years following 1965, when Medicaid and federally-funded community health centers were created and maternal and child health services expanded. As a result, infant mortality rates fell precipitously—they dropped almost 50% from 1965 to 1980, compared to only 15% in the 15 years prior to 1965. For black infants, the improvement during this period was even greater. Black infant mortality also fell almost 50% between 1965 and 1980, after declining only five percent during the previous 15 years.[34] Recently, however, progress in reducing infant mortality has slowed. In the 1970s, there was a five percent annual rate of decline in infant mortality. From 1981 to 1983, that annual rate slowed to three percent, the poorest performance in 18 years,[35] and the period between 1984 and 1985 saw no statistically significant decline.[36]

The creation and expansion of public health programs between 1964 and 1975 also resulted in an increase in physician services to poor children of almost 75%.[37] By the late 1970s, poor children participating in public health programs were seeing doctors almost as often as other children.[38] Nevertheless, comprehensive pediatric care remains unavailable to many poor children who lack either public or private health coverage. Medicaid, the major source of health financing for poor families, reached about three-quarters of children in families with incomes below the poverty line in 1986.[39] Nor did private health insurance, which often does not include preventive pediatric care, catch all or even much of the remainder.[40]

The first few years of the 1980s saw a significant reduction in public support for health programs for low-income families. The Medicaid progam in particular came under attack, with the charge led by the Reagan administration and its congressional allies. Medicaid is the nation's largest public health program for children and accounts for 55% of all public health funds spent on children.[41] In general, to qualify for Medicaid, a family cannot have income exceeding AFDC levels, which vary from state to state.[42] In 31 states, upper limits on AFDC income eligiblity (and thus Medicaid eligibility) are less than 50% of the federal poverty level—and in five states, income eligibility is held to less than 30% of the poverty level.[43]

In 1981, Congress accepted Reagan administration proposals to reduce federal funding for both AFDC and Medicaid. As a result of the AFDC cuts, state eligibility levels (never generous to begin with) were tightened further, denying thousands of working poor families access to both AFDC and Medicaid. In addition, some states limited the number of hospital stays or doctor's visits for which they would pay, or limited the reimbursement rates for health professionals treating Medicaid patients.[44] This last step often leads doctors to restrict the number of Medicaid patients they will treat, or to refuse to accept them at all.

Significant expansions in Medicaid eligibility have been enacted since that early retrenchment, largely over the objections of the Reagan administration. Legislation was enacted in 1984 requiring states to provide Medicaid coverage to all pregnant women and children under age five whose family incomes were below state AFDC eligibility levels, regardless of whether their families participated in AFDC. Legislation passed in the fall of 1986 gave states the option to extend coverage further, to include pregnant women and children under age five whose family incomes are below the federal poverty level. Now, states may extend this coverage even more, to include pregnant women and young children with family incomes up to 185% of the federal poverty level. Most states leapt at this opportunity to extend coverage—by mid-1988, 43 states and the District of Columbia

had expanded coverage to at least some of the newly-eligible populations.[45]

The budgets of other federal health programs benefiting poor
children and pregnant women have eroded over the course of the
Reagan administration. In 1981, Congress approved an administration proposal to merge several separately-funded health programs
for poor children and pregnant women into the Maternal and Child
Health Block Grant. However, total funding for the Maternal and
Child Health Block Grant in 1981 was *less* than the sum of the
individual programs it replaced. Although funding has increased
since then, it has not kept pace with inflation or fully restored services
to their 1981 levels.[46] Maternal and child health services therefore
reach only a fraction of the women and children who need them.

The highly successful WIC program has seen funding increases in
recent years, but continues to deliver food and nutrition counseling
to only 44% of the eligible children and pregnant women in the
country.[47] Federal spending for childhood immunizations increased
by about one and two-thirds between 1982 and 1986, but the cost of
immunizing a child increased fivefold, resulting in a steady decrease
in the number of children served by the federal immunization program.[48]

PRESCHOOL

Enrollment of three and four-year olds in nursery school and early
childhood development programs doubled between 1970 and 1983.[49]
Many parents—whether they use out-of-home child care or stay home
to care for their children—view quality preschool programs as important developmental experiences for their children.

An extensive body of research attests to the value of quality preschool programs for children from low-income families. The best
known is a longitudinal study of participants in the Perry Preschool
Program in Ypsilanti, Michigan conducted by the High/Scope Foundation. Perry Preschool was established to examine the long-term
effects of participation in a high-quality early childhood education
program. Participants were low-income black children, ages three and
four, with low IQs. They received two years of center-based preschool
education for two and one-half hours a day from a highly trained
teaching staff. This was supplemented by weekly home visits by the
teachers to work with both mothers and children. The most recent
evaluation, released in 1984, reported on participants at age 19.[50]

Like some Head Start assessments (discussed below), the Perry evaluations found that improvements in IQ attributable to preschool education lasted only about two or three years. This seemingly short-lived boost, however, was enough to help the children perform better in their early school experiences, thus increasing their self-confidence and their teachers' expectations for them, and improving their placements in school. As a result, the Perry children reported a stronger attachment to school than did children from similar backgrounds who had not had a preschool experience.[51]

Additionally, Perry participants were significantly better off on several measures of success than were members of a control group who received no early intervention. Members of the Perry Preschool group:

- spent less time in special education classes;
- had higher high school graduation rates;
- were more likely to enroll in post-secondary education;
- had higher rates of employment at ages 16 to 19;
- scored higher on a test of functional competence;
- had lower pregnancy and birth rates among female participants; and
- were less likely to have been arrested.[52]

The Perry evaluation also included a cost-effectiveness analysis which concluded that the benefits of one year of preschool exceeded costs by seven times. Researchers were able to measure the benefits of reduced special education enrollments and to estimate future savings resulting from higher levels of employment, less reliance on public assistance and fewer arrests.[53]

Studies of the Head Start program yield similar findings. Head Start, one of the most comprehensive early childhood education programs, was established by the federal government in 1965. It provides high quality educational programs for low-income children, along with health, nutrition and other social services. Head Start is also one of the few federally-supported programs for poor children which explicitly builds in parental involvement. One tangible result of this involvement is that 80% of Head Start parents are program volunteers, and 31% of Head Start's paid staff are parents of present or former Head Start children.[54]

Unlike most federally-funded human service programs, Head Start has had *increased* funding, from $820 million in fiscal year 1981 to $1,130 billion in fiscal year 1987.[55] This increase, however, has only enabled the program to keep pace with inflation, not expand services.

In 1986, Head Start served 451,000 children—only 18% of the 2.5 million children who were eligible to participate in the program.[56]

Fortunately for some of the children who cannot get into a Head Start program, many states in recent years have begun to establish early childhood education programs for children from low-income families. By 1985, at least 28 states had enacted early childhood initiatives, many of which were deliberately focused on poor children.[57]

Senator Edward Kennedy (D-MA) introduced legislation in 1988 to expand existing state and local early childhood education programs to full-day, year-round programs to accommodate children of working parents. (Most early childhood education programs, including Head Start, are part-day programs.) Kennedy's proposal, dubbed "Smart Start," would require programs receiving funding to have nutrition, health and social service components, to ensure parental involvement and to provide activities and an environment which are developmentally appropriate for young children Programs receiving Smart Start funding would also have to reserve at least 50% of their slots for children from low-income families, until all low-income children in a locality are served. More affluent families would pay a fee based on a sliding scale for their children to participate in a Smart Start program.[58]

CHILD CARE

The demand for child care among families of all incomes far exceeds the supply. About half of all women with children *under the age of three* work,[59] and that percentage is expected to increase in the coming decade. Sixty-five percent of single mothers with children under the age of three work full-time.[60]

Child care is an essential service for families in which both parents or a single parent must work to support a family. Access to child care enables teenage parents to complete high school and parents with few job skills to participate in training programs. The absence of child care is perhaps the single most important barrier keeping low-income parents out of the workforce.[61]

Child care is a costly service to provide. Full-time care in a child care center can cost from $3,500 to $5,000 a year for children under age five. Several states have begun to realize, however, that an investment in child care for parents seeking to leave welfare and enter the workforce costs them less than the extended AFDC and Medicaid payments that may be incurred if parents remain out of the workforce. In Colorado, for example, the Department of Social Services estimated that providing child care to families who need it in order to remain in the workforce costs about 38% of the total costs of keeping these families on the AFDC and Medicaid rolls.[62]

Unlike most industrialized countries, the United States does little to subsidize, encourage or provide child care. Extensive child care legislation was passed by Congress in 1972, but was vetoed by President Nixon. Since then, no major national child care legislation has succeeded. At present, only two forms of federal assistance are available to families needing child care services—the Dependent Care Tax Credit and the Social Services Block Grant. The first is of little practical value to poor families, while the impact of the second has diminished considerably as a result of Reagan-era budget cuts.

The Dependent Care Tax Credit is the largest federal program providing help to families to defray the cost of child care services. It provides indirect support for child care by granting a tax credit equal to a portion of income spent on care for a dependent family member, including expenditures for child care services. The amount a family can claim for this credit is determined by a sliding scale based on family income, but in no instance does it exceed $2,400 for one child or $4,800 for two or more children.[63] Because the Dependent Care Tax Credit is nonrefundable, families receive credit only up to the amount of their tax liability. Thus, poor families who pay little or no taxes (because their incomes are too low) cannot take advantage of this credit, even though they may have significant child care expenditures.

Some subsidized child care and several other services for families were for years funded through the federal Title XX Social Services Program. In 1982, Congress created the Social Services Block Grant at the behest of the Reagan administration to replace the existing individual Title XX programs. As is true with other block grants created during the Reagan administration, funding for the Social Services Block Grant has never matched the sum of the funding in 1981 for the separate programs which were then subsumed into the block grant. In real terms, funding in 1985 was only 72% of the 1981 level.[64]

Some states have responded to the reduction in federal child care funds by increasing their own funding or creating new programs to provide child care to low-income families. According to the Children's Defense Fund, 30 states increased funding for child care for low-income families between fiscal years 1985 and 1986.[65] In real terms, however, child care budgets in 29 states were still below 1981 levels.[66] As a result, by fiscal year 1986, 23 states were providing publicly subsidized child care services to fewer children from low-income families than had received services in fiscal year 1981, even though the number of poor children had increased over the same time period.[67]

The immediate problem caused by reduced Social Services Block Grant funding is the further limiting of decent, affordable child care for low-income families. A longer-term problem is the potential this holds for the further development of a two-tier system of child care. As subsidies disappear for lower-income families, these families will increasingly turn to less expensive and often lower quality care for their children. Middle and upper-income families, in contrast, will continue to demand (and to varying degrees be able to afford) higher quality care for their children.

Ensuring poor families access to child care is only a partial step in an anti-poverty strategy which focuses on young children. If the care is of low quality, it will not benefit children and may very well harm them. Publicly subsidized child care for poor families is a less than optimal investment if it does not include measures to ensure that that care meets high standards.

The 1980s have seen an explosion of research on the importance of the early years, yet we have largely failed to incorporate that knowledge into policy, particularly child care policies. Quality child care depends on skilled providers with whom children and parents are comfortable; small groups of children and appropriate staff-to-child ratios; clean, safe surroundings; and a family resource component to provide parents with information on parenting and child development and to promote trusting relationships between parents and child care staff.

One way to ensure that poor families are not limited to substandard child care is to establish and enforce standards for all child care providers. In 1979, the fedeal government took some tentative steps in that direction. The Department of Health and Human Services commissioned a National Day Care Study and issued regulations for federally subsidized child care based on the Commission's recommendations. The regulations included staff/child ratios of one to three for children under age two and one to four for children between ages two and three; small group sizes; and staff training in child development.[68] Congressional action in 1981, however, prevented the implementation of these regulations, and HHS withdrew them. Since then, the regulation of child care services has been primarily the responsibility of individual states.

State licensing has been limited in both scope and enforcement. Child care centers, which account for about 23% of all child care provided,[69] are licensed in every state, but the standards in place fall far short of those recommended by professionals in early childhood development.[70] Only three states (Kansas, Massachusetts and Maryland) meet the standard generally recommended by child development experts that no caregiver should care for more than three infants at one time, and many states allow ratios as high as eight to one.[71] The federal funding cuts initiated in 1981, moreover, induced a majority of states to cut back on their efforts to regulate child care providers or enforce standards for quality care. By 1985, 33 states had lowered standards for child care centers receiving Title XX funding; 32 states had reduced their licensing and monitoring efforts.[72] Family day care, the form of care used by about 40% of families needing out-of-home care and most often found in poor communities, is largely unlicensed.[73]

High-quality child care also depends on well-trained staff who are knowledgeable about and responsive to the rapidly changing needs and abilities of young children. Unfortunately, child care workers are the lowest paid of all human service providers.[74] In 1986, the average child care teacher working full-time in a center earned less than $10,000 a year. (The poverty line for a family of four that year was $11,203.) Family day care providers, on average, earn less than half that.[75]

Low wages for child care workers adversely affect children in several ways. In some cases, low wages force skilled staff to drop out of the profession or discourage talented individuals from entering. Frequent turnovers in staff prevent children from forming the kind of stable and long-term relationships with caregivers that enhance the quality of care. Low wages also make it difficult for individual providers to afford additional training, and low rates for child care services make it difficult for many centers to offer training to their staffs.

Recent congressional debate on welfare reform revealed a strong national consensus in favor of moving AFDC parents—including mothers of very young children—into the workforce. The Family Welfare Reform Act of 1988 requires parents of children over the age of three to work, to be in school or to participate in a training program, and gives states the option of requiring parents of children older than one year to participate. The bill also requires states to provide child care to these parents for 12 months after parents begin working.[76]

These child care provisions are a welcome indication that policymakers recognize the importance of child care to poor parents seeking to support their families, but several concerns remain. Any genuine welfare reform must include safeguards to ensure that the children of poor parents moving into the workforce receive high quality care. Two steps are critical to bringing this about: sufficient reimbursement rates to permit parents to purchase good quality care, and provisions to strengthen standards for child care providers. Without these, we risk placing the children of the poor in sub-standard care which could cause both short and long-term harm.

Child care for both poor and middle-income families became a prominent political issue in 1988. Republicans generally advocated various tax credits and refunds to help parents pay for child care or to compensate them for lost income when one parent stays out of the workforce to care for a child. Democrats generally preferred the approach taken by the Act for Better Child Care (the ABC bill) which calls for financial assistance to states to increase the availability of affordable child care and to improve the quality of care. Specifically, the ABC bill would provide funding to states to do the following:

- provide child care assistance to families with incomes up to 115% of a state's median family income, with subsidies based on a sliding income scale;
- provide funds to start and expand child care programs and to train new family day care providers;
- train and provide technical assistance to child care providers, supplement salaries for child care workers, and establish programs to help parents to make informed child care decisions; and
- improve standard licensing standards and hire sufficient staff to enforce those standards.[77]

FAMILY RESOURCE PROGRAMS[78]

Whether poor families live in high-density, high-crime urban neighborhoods or in remote rural communities, the stress, frustration and isolation of everyday life can overwhelm even the most mature and confident parents. Parents in poor communities know better than anyone else that their children are at risk every day of an array of serious problems, including school failure, poor health and nutrition, child abuse and neglect, teenage pregnancy, delinquency and substance abuse.

Unfortunately, there are virtually no supportive services to help families of any income cope with the stresses of daily life *before* a crisis erupts. This is particularly true for families with very young children, even though research and experience indicate strongly that much of a child's important physical, social and intellectual development occurs in these early years. This is the period in which positive support to parents in the form of parenting education, child development information, peer support and links to other community services can increase parents' confidence and competence in their parenting abilities. Their children, in turn, benefit from a more secure and nurturing home environment.

In some communities across the country, families and voluntary community-based organizations are beginning to respond to this lack of supportive services by organizing family resource programs which are significantly and deliberately different from traditional social service programs. Rather than focusing primarily on a limited and carefully circumscribed group of families who are in the midst of severe problems, family resource programs reach out to a wide range of families, with the goal of helping them function better so as to enhance their quality of life and avoid or lessen problems which might develop later.

Family resource programs exist in a range of settings, including community centers, schools, the workplace, or wherever it is convenient for families to meet. In some cases, "traditional" social service agencies—child care centers, community mental health centers, Head Start programs or health clinics, for example—have added family resource components to their existing programs.

While the specific services provided by family resource programs vary from program to program, depending on the needs of the community and the financial and human resources available to the program, one or more of the following services are generally found at a family resource program:

- parent education and support groups for parents;
- parent/child joint activities which focus on child development and promote healthy parent/child relationships;
- classes and discussion groups on issues of concern to parents— e.g., family budgeting, dealing with stress in families, health and nutrition, etc.;
- a drop-in center, which offers unstructured time for families to be with other families and with program staff on an informal basis and which lessens the isolation many families experience;
- child care while parents are engaged in activities offered by the family resource program;
- information and referral to other services in the community,

including child care, health care, nutrition programs and counseling services;
• home visits, generally designed to introduce hard-to-reach families to family resource programs; and
• health and nutrition education for parents and developmental
exams or health screening for infants and children.

While a few well-established family resource programs may receive
some federal funding for specialized projects, the federal government
and most state governments currently provide no funding for these
programs. Two notable exceptions are Maryland, whose network of
family resource programs reaches mainly adolescent parents, but
extends to other parents as well, and Minnesota, which assists local
communities wishing to establish Early Childhood Family Education
programs through their school systems for all families with children
under the age of six.

As a result of the general lack of public financing, most programs
depend on local—generally private—support. Many are struggling to
keep their doors open, some have been forced to close and others are
unable to expand or to reach families most in need of services. The
most troubling consequence of a lack of funding, however, is that it
prevents family resource programs from developing or expanding in
poor communities, where families are most in need of the innovative
support services they offer. Any effective anti-poverty effort which
focuses on children must include generous support for family resource programs.

CONCLUSION

With the exception of family resource programs, most of the
elements of a comprehensive attack on childhood poverty are already
recognized parts of our social welfare policy. Medicaid provides some
pregnant women and some poor children with the health care they
need. Child nutrition programs supplement the diets of a fraction of
children in low-income families. Head Start prepares a handful of
disadvantaged children for school. The federal Social Services Block
Grant helps a few poor parents afford out-of-home care for their
children while they work or complete their education.[79]

What is missing is a deliberate and sustained effort to ensure that
every poor child receives every service he or she needs to prevent long-
term problems from developing. If poor children are to have a
fighting chance of succeeding, they need access to *all* of the services

discussed above. One or two is not enough. Preschool programs for children in poor health will not be effective; a well-fed child in a chaotic or neglectful family will not thrive. Unfortunately, our present system of delivering services—characterized by fragmentation and insufficient funding—virtually eliminates the possibility that most poor children will receive anything close to a comprehensive set of services.

A successful approach to combatting childhood poverty also needs to recognize and reinforce the importance of the family. Traditionally, Americans have resisted governmental involvement in family life, except under extreme circumstances such as instances of child abuse and neglect. While respect for the privacy of families should not be taken lightly, it also should not discourage policymakers from considering ways in which government can support the efforts of parents to raise healthy children. Our present policies too often overlook the fact that children thrive or don't thrive in families and that a parent's influence can have lasting effects on a child. Family resource programs offer an important model to policymakers searching for positive ways to support and assist the parents of poor children in their efforts to raise healthy children.

While early childhood programs alone will not eliminate poverty, research and practical experience indicate strongly that they are among the most effective weapons we have for combatting the long-term effects of poverty. We know, for example, that children who receive preventive health care from the prenatal period and beyond are less likely to suffer from undetected health problems and disabilities which will hinder their development and jeopardize their ability to succeed in school. We know that children with supportive adult care—both from parents and from other care providers—are less likely to lack confidence, feel alienated and distrustful, or suffer from long-term learning and behavioral problems. We know that adults who feel supported and valued in their role as parents will pass their security and self-esteem on to their children.

Yet we continue to tolerate a situation in which millions of poor children exist without the basic health, nutritional and developmental supports which middle and upper-income families routinely provide to their children. We cannot accept this on moral grounds, and—as the evidence in this chapter and elsewhere in this book indicates—we cannot accept it on fiscal grounds. Preventive health care for poor children and pregnant women saves the public money, often within just a few years. Quality preschool programs for poor children save the public money, with the savings recognized both during the time a child is in school and in the years beyond. Access to decent child care enables parents to work to support their families. Family support programs lessen the isolation and insecurity of many poor families and increase parents' confidence and competence in their parenting skills, resulting in more stable families and more secure children.

Expanding and extending these services to every family in need is a costly proposition only if one thinks (as many of our policymakers regrettably do) exclusively in the short-term. This penny-wise and pound-foolish attitude toward the children of the poor has overburdened our schools, our welfare system, our mental health facilities and our prisons. It robs us of productive, creative citizens. For our sake, and for our children's, it must stop.

NOTES

1. Gerald M. Boyd, "$1,000 Tax Refund Proposed by Bush in Child Care Plan," *The New York Times*, 25 July 1988, p. 1.

2. Jeffrey Schmalz, "Cuomo Urges Expansion of Efforts to Aid Children," *The New York Times*, 7 January 1988, p. 14.

3. Inaugural Address by Governor James R. Thompson, Prairie Capitol Convention Center, Springfield, Illinois, January 12, 1987.

4. National Governors' Association, *Bringing Down the Barriers*, (Washington, D.C.: National Governors' Association, 1987), p. XI. See also, *The First Sixty Months*, (Washington, D.C.: National Governors' Association, 1987).

5. U.S. Congress, House, *Family Welfare Reform Act of 1987*, H.R. 1720, 100th Congress, 1st session, 1987, and Senate *Family Security Act of 1987*, S. 1511, 100th Congress, 1st session, 1987.

6. Cindy Skrzycki and Frank Swoboda, "Child Care Emerges as Focus of Legislative Efforts," *Washington Post*, 8 February 1988, p. A19.

7. "Head Start on Head Start," *The New York Times*, 13 January 1987, p. 22. "The President and the Children," *The New York Times*, 18 October 1987, p. E26. "Rescue the Future, At Birth," *The New York Times*, 1 January 1988, p. 16. "The State of Children," *The New York Times*, 7 January 1988, p. 22.

8. Andy Plattner, "Crusading for Kids on the Hustings," *U.S. News and World Report*, 14 September 1987, pp. 29–30. Mickey Kaus, "Playing Politics With Children," *Newsweek*, 13 June 1988, pp. 26–27.

9. KidsPac press release, July 2, 1988, Cambridge, MA. Poll conducted by Peter D. Hart and Associates.

10. Louis Harris, Address to the Child Welfare League of America's National Conference, Washington, D.C., March 18, 1987.

11. Committee for Economic Development, *Children in Need: Investment Strategies for the Educationally Disadvantaged*. New York: Committee for Economic Development, 1987, p. 3.

12. U.S. Congress, House Committee on Education and Labor, *The Chairman's Report on Children in America: A Strategy for the 100th Congress*. Vol. 1, 99th Congress, 2nd session, p. 1.

13. Children's Defense Fund, *A Children's Defense Budget, FY 1988*. Washington, D.C.: Children's Defense Fund, 1987, p. 85.

14. Harold L. Hodgkinson, *All One System: Demographics of Education, Kindergarten Through Graduate School*. Washington, D.C.: Institute for Educational Leadership, 1985, p. 8.

15. Dana Hughes, *et al., The Health of America's Children: Maternal and Child Health Data Book*. Washington, D.C.: Children's Defense Fund, 1987, p. 8.

16. *Ibid.*, p. 253.

17. *Ibid.*, p. 221.

18. Committee for Economic Development, p. 3.

19. Economic Policy Council of UNA-USA, *Work and Family in the United States: A Policy Initiative*. New York: United Nations Association of the United States, 1985, p. 35.

20. National Center for Clinical Infant Programs, *Infants Can't Wait: The Numbers*, Washington, D.C.: National Center for Clinical Infant Programs, p. 18.

21. Children's Defense Fund, *A Children's Defense Budget: An Analysis of FY 1987 Federal Budget and Children*. Washington, D.C.: Children's Defense Fund, 1986, p. 221.

22. Children's Defense Fund, *A Children's Defense Budget: FY 1989*. Washington, D.C.: Children's Defense Fund, 1988, p. 62.

23. Kay Johnson and Sara Rosenbaum, "Maternal and Child Health: Exemplary State Initiatives," Washington, D.C.: Children's Defense Fund, 1986, p. 3.

24. Rachel Benson Gold, Asta-Maria Kenney and Susheela Singh, *Blessed Events and the Bottom Line: Financing Maternity Care in the United States*. New York: The Alan Guttmacher Institute, 1987, p. 18.

25. Institute of Medicine, *Preventing Low Birthweight*. Washington, D.C.: National Academy Press, 1985, p. 232.

26. Children's Defense Fund, "Questions and Answers About Prenatal Care," Washington, D.C.: CDF Adolescent Pregnancy Prevention: Prenatal Care Campaign, 1986, p. 6.

27. Gold, *et al.*, p. 14.

28. Children's Defense Fund, *A Children's Defense Budget: An Analysis of the FY 1987 Federal Budget and Children*, p. 101.

29. Children's Defense Fund, *A Children's Defense Budget: FY 1989*, p. 76.

30. U.S. Congress, Select Committee on Children, Youth, and Families, *Opportunities for Success: Cost-Effective Programs for Children Update, 1988*, 100th Congress, 2nd Session, 1988, p. 31.

31. *Ibid.*

32. *Ibid.*, p. 6.

33. Economic Policy Council of UNA-USA, *Work and Family in the United States: A Policy Initiative*. New York: United Nations Association of the United States, 1985, p. 37.

34. Children's Defense Fund, *A Children's Defense Budget: An Analysis of the FY 1987 Federal Budget and Children*, p. 109.

35. *Ibid.*, p. 9.

36. Dana Hughes, *et al.*, p. 3.

37. Children's Defense Fund, *A Children's Budget: An Analysis of the FY 1987 Federal Budget and Children*, p. 9.

38. *Ibid.*

39. U.S. Congress, House Select Committee on Children, Youth, and Families, *Opportunities for Success: Cost-Effective Programs for Children Update, 1988*, p. 25.

40. Children's Defense Fund, *A Children's Defense Budget: FY 1988*, pp. 71–73.

41. *Ibid.* Medicaid is administered by the states, although the federal government funds 50 to 75% of a state's Medicaid program, depending on the state's per capita income.

42. Elizabeth Wehr, "States Expand Health Care for Poor Children, Mothers to Cut Down Future Costs," *Congressional Quarterly*, November 19, 1983, p. 2415.

43. Dana Hughes, *et al.*, p. x.

44. Children's Defense Fund, *A Children's Defense Budget: An Analysis of the FY 1987 Federal Budget and Children*, p. 110.

45. Children's Defense Fund, July 25, 1988 memorandum from Health Division, "News from Washington, D.C."

46. Children's Defense Fund, *A Children's Defense Budget: An Analysis of the FY 1987 Federal Budget and Children*, p. 109.

47. U.S. Congress, *Opportunities for Success: Cost-Effective Programs for Children Update, 1988*, p. 9.

48. Children's Defense Fund, *A Children's Defense Budget: FY 1988*, p. 75.

49. U.S. Congress, House Select Committee on Children, Youth, and Families, *Families and Child Care: Improving the Options*, 98th Congress, 2nd session, Sept. 1984, p. 14.

50. John R. Berrueta-Clement, *et al.*, *Changed Lives: The Effects of the Perry Preschool Program on Youths Through Age 19*. Ypsilanti: High/Scope Educational Research Foundation, 1984.

51. *Ibid.*, pp. 23–24.

52. *Ibid.*, p. 2.

53. *Ibid.*, p. 90.

54. Children's Defense Fund, *A Children's Defense Budget: An Analysis of the FY 1987 Federal Budget and Children*, p. 300.

55. Children's Defense Fund, *A Children's Defense Budget, FY 1988*, p. 225.

56. *Ibid.*, p. 221.

57. Anne Bridgman, "Early Childhood Education: States Already on the Move," *Education Week*, Oct. 16, 1985.

58. "Kennedy Early Childhood Education Initiative" fact sheet, U.S. Senate Labor and Human Resources Committee, Washington, D.C., 1988.

59. National Center for Clinical Infant Programs, p. 30.

60. *Ibid.*

61. Children's Defense Fund, *A Children's Defense Budget, FY 1988*, p. 205.

62. *Ibid.*

63. U.S. Congress, House Select Committee on Children, Youth, and Families, *Federal Programs Affecting Children*, p. 244.

64. Children's Defense Fund, *A Children's Defense Budget: An Analysis of the FY 1987 Federal Budget and Children*, p. 94.

65. Helen Blank and Amy Wilkins, *State Child Care Fact Book 1986*. Washington, D.C.: Children's Defense Fund, 1986, p. 11.

66. *Ibid.*

67. *Ibid.*, p. 14.

68. Ad Hoc Day Care Coalition, *The Crisis in Infant and Toddler Care.* Washington, D.C.: Ad Hoc Day Care Coalition, 1985, p. 11.

69. Robert J. Trotter, "Project Day Care," *Psychology Today*, December 1987, p. 36.

70. Select Committee on Children, Youth, and Families, *Families and Child Care: Improving the Options*, p. 93.

71. Trotter, p. 36.

72. Select Committee on Children, Youth and Families, *Families and Child Care: Improving the Options*, p. 95.

73. *Ibid.*, p. 94.

74. National Center for Clinical Infant Programs, *Who Will Mind the Babies?* Washington, D.C.: National Center for Clinical Infant Programs, p. 12.

75. National Association for the Education of Young Children, Washington, D.C., 1986.

76. U.S. Congress, House, *Family Welfare Reform Act of 1987*, H.R. 1720, and Senate, *Family Security Act of 1987*, S. 1511. The Family Welfare Reform Act of 1988.

77. Legislative summary provided by Alliance for Better Child Care, Washington, D.C.

78. For a complete discussion of family resource programs, see Kagan, Powell, Weissbourd and Zigler, *America's Family Support Programs*. New Haven and London: Yale University Press, 1987.

79. Title XX, Social Security Act.

EARLY INTERVENTION IN COGNITIVE DEVELOPMENT AS A STRATEGY FOR REDUCING POVERTY

James Garbarino

WHEN WE SPEAK of cognitive development, we are talking about the way children acquire and use knowledge. There are two major themes in the study of cognitive development. Both have something to say about the way a child's mind works and the way it changes and grows.

The first is concerned primarily with measuring the speed and power of the child's capacity as an information processor. Why and how are some children more effective and efficient in processing, storing and discerning patterns in the information available from their senses? This has been the organizing question for traditional intelligence testing. The second theme, in contrast, emphasizes the *styles* of knowing that people exhibit in their ideas about the world. How do ideas, or abstract concepts, and the ability to generate and use ideas, arise? This is the second theme's central question.

A concern with the whole child incorporates both themes: ideas without calculation are chaotic; calculation without substance is sterile. Research and theory about cognitive development have matured substantially in recent decades, in both thematic areas.

The nineteenth century saw the development of tests to measure an individual's intellect. In the late 1800s, Sir Francis Galton prepared a battery of tests designed to determine how effective different individuals were in discriminating among sights, sounds and other sensory input. Within a few decades, derivatives of these tests were being used by the military and other institutions to categorize and classify people, and to place them in different jobs or schools. In the 20th century researchers and testers have placed great emphasis on an individual's score on such tests in relation to standardized expectations for a given age—the Intelligence Quotient (IQ score). The IQ score is constructed so that 100 indicates a match of performance with age—the average around which scores are distributed. This distribution means that most scores are found between 90 and 110.

One of the important issues in research and theory dealing with intelligence has been the degree to which intelligence is a more or less single general characteristic or attribute, or whether it is not in fact a collection of different abilities. This is an area in which the field has shown a great deal of maturing in recent years. Early in the twentieth century the dominant view was that intelligence consisted of an inherited "general factor" that characterized a person's ability to think abstractly and to verbalize. Louis Terman proposed this view and labelled this factor "g," for general. Later Charles Spearman hypothesized that a second factor exists ("s") that accounts for mathematical and spatial reasoning. As the decades have passed, "g" and "s" have been the subject of many empirical studies, and subject to theoretical critique.

Today, most experts believe that intelligence includes many different abilities, abilities that may develop independently of each other. Intelligence is thus "multidimensional." While at some level there may be a foundation for learning and intellectual function that is general, the best picture of the human intellect portrays a large set of characteristics and abilities, not just one or two.

Perhaps the most highly evolved among current efforts to understand intelligence is the work of Robert Sternberg.[1] Sternberg's approach takes the concept of intelligence from an abstract quality to a feature of real life situations, and in so doing postulates that there must be several different kinds of ability brought to bear in the process of making sense of the world. He believes that the best model of how the mind works posits three basic kinds of intelligence, each one depending to an extent upon the others. He calls this a "triarchic" theory of human intelligence.

The first type of capacity Sternberg calls *componential* intelligence. This is raw analytic power. It comprises the whole set of "components" contained in traditional thinking about intelligence. It describes what goes on in the brain in making sense of perceptions, solving abstract problems, assessing and criticizing hypotheses, etc. This is information processing, somewhat in the image of a computer.

The second capacity identified by Sternberg is called *experiential* intelligence. This is the ability to combine knowledge and ideas creatively and insightfully. The emphasis here is on creating new arrangements of what one has experienced or learned, and bringing those new arrangements to bear as a way of understanding and mastering the world at hand. Sternberg finds that three sub-categories of ability comprise experiential intelligence. These are: being able to see the relevant information in a puzzling situation; being able to put facts together in a consistent way; and being able to see analogies between objects or events previously thought to be unconnected or dissimilar.

Sternberg's third basic capacity is *contextual* intelligence. This is the ability to understand a particular situation—in effect, to know what the environment's expectations are, and to arrange to meet or to change those expectations. The emphasis is on the ability to read social realities and to master them as a way to reach objectives or solve problems. Sternberg's approach here is based on how well people understand possible matches, or see mismatches, between a given situation and what the individual thinks or wants—between situation and self. It involves the ability to perceive accurately how social realities are organized (who wants me to do what? why? how much control do they have? how much control do I have? etc.) and understanding how to make these realities work towards one's own goals, a process that might include working to reshape or redirect the environment.

One important implication of Sternberg's view is this: you only know as much about a person's intelligence as you permit yourself to know by the range of assessments you make.

A narrow test of information-processing capacity may only permit expression of componential intelligence, just as an examination of creativity and insight will only be good for uncovering experiential abilities. Similarly, assessing situationally-defined competence (be it on the streets or in school) will measure only contextual intelligence.

Sternberg points out that conventional tests of "intelligence" play almost strictly to the first theme, componential intelligence. Modern assessments of IQ do a pretty good job of discriminating among individuals with respect to basic perceptual and analytic problem-solving abilities. For those individuals of average or better IQ, however—100 or higher—measured IQ differences do not seem to account very effectively for differences in real life success. Psychologist James Guildford has developed a conception of multiple intellectual abilities that, with the addition of creativity, allows the identification of experiential intelligence, but "life" is what presents the ultimate opportunity for assessing contextual intelligence.[2]

An essential thrust of Sternberg's approach is to argue that each person needs to do as much as possible to enhance all three types of capacity, and to arrange life to play to strengths and shield weaknesses. In a diverse and positive environment, there normally are many opportunities to accomplish this. The keys are to avoid a debilitating deficiency of componential, or information-processing, intelligence; to be encouraged to develop experiential intelligence; and to have access to opportunities to learn "the ropes" of social realities, to experience those important material and psychic rewards and resources that motivate learning about the community's major social contexts—i.e., contextual intelligence. The major threats are early physical and sensory deprivations that suppress componential intelligence; repressive environments that stultify creativity and foster rigid thinking; and being sidetracked or dead-ended into social settings that are lacking in opportunities for dynamic and positive interaction.

The purpose of early intervention programs to improve cognitive development is to deal with these problems in the lives of children whose environments tend not to provide a very good set of intelligence-promoting experiences, environments that in many cases are outright debilitating. The underpinning for such intervention is part of a concept that argues for attention to "the whole child." This concept assumes that cognitive development is rooted in the success of the child's overall progress, and in turn, contributes to that progress, in a dynamic of reinforcement.

If this is cognitive development, what, then, is *child* development? In the broadest sense, of course, it is the process of becoming a fully-functioning human being. A child's experience combines with a child's biological givens, and from this mixture emerges an adult person, one who will face the challenges of day-to-day life—as student, worker, friend, family member and citizen. If they are to succeed in these roles as adults, children need to be rooted in the basic skills of modern life. They need to become socially competent. They must come to know who they are. They must have acquired a secure and positive sense of their own identity. In addition, they must become proficient in thinking and in speaking clearly. They must learn to understand the many ways people communicate with one another. It is in the context of this broad conception of the process of child development that we must understand cognitive development. Sternberg's three-part model complements this view.

UNDERSTANDING THE PROCESS OF DEVELOPMENT

Much of our thinking about how children develop intellectually relies upon the pioneering work of the Swiss psychologist Jean Piaget. Piaget's view of development is based upon the idea that children form concepts that represent reality. As their brains mature and they experience the world, they either fit these experiences into existing concepts (a process that Piaget called "assimilation") or they adjust or change the concepts to make sense of new or incongruous ideas (a process that Piaget labelled "accommodation"). Thus, for example, the child develops a scheme, "dog," to cover four-legged furry creatures, and is able to assimilate the fact that German shepherds, collies, and dachshunds are all dogs. But the child must alter his or her concept of "dog" to accommodate the fact that some four-legged furry creatures are not dogs, but rather are horses, cows, cats, or llamas.

But Piaget is not the whole story. As children develop, their intellectual, physical and emotional *potentials* change. The range of what is possible increases and alters. These changes in a child's capacity are the basis of the developmental process. Many experts believe these changes take place in a regular sequence, in which the child faces first one, then another issue. Erik Erikson, for example, described eight "stages" of development of the person, beginning in infancy and extending through old age. Figure 1 outlines the first four, the stages that apply to childhood in Erikson's approach and the key developmental issues that the child faces at each stage along the way. Confronting the tasks of overall development is a process in which the development of intelligence is bound up.

The child's capacity to experience "trust" depends upon an ability to recognize continuity and regularity in care and caregivers. To *feel* the world is a regular and safe place the child must be able to *know* who she or he is—and who not. To become confident about fantasy and reality the child must *know* the basic behaviors required for mastery. The point in all this is that the processes of knowing are inextricably bound to the processes of feeling. Children develop as organic beings, not as mechanical processors of data being programmed as new software becomes available.

Beyond the demands of everyday social competence, children need a sense of curiosity to sustain cognitive development. They need to appreciate the full experience of being alive. They should do more than just learn to read; they should be able to understand and to enjoy literature, to take pleasure in reading, to want to read. They need to do more than just cope with human relationships. They should learn about a range of positive feelings, including love and friendship, as well as competition, anger, fear or dislike. In sum, they need to be able to do more than just exist. It is not impossible for any child to experience the emotions and perceptions associated with success, with creativity, with the sight of a blue sky, or the sound of a poem, with the rush of dance, or the peace of reflection, or the satisfaction of helping someone else. To know all this, to have even a

FIGURE 1
STAGES OF CHILD DEVELOPMENT

Stage I: Infancy   Basic Trust vs. Mistrust (birth to 18 months)

The infant needs to develop a sense of security, feeling that the world is a trustworthy place. This comes from establishing a safe and nurturing relationship with primary caregivers—most notably parents (and usually the mother). This period emphasizes basic sensory and intellectual growth.

Stage II: Toddler   Autonomy vs. Shame (18 to 36 months)

The toddler needs to develop a sense of being able to do things on his or her own. This includes walking well alone and beginning to master basic communication through words and gestures. Relationships with parents, brothers and sisters, and caregivers are important in providing opportunities for learning and demonstrating these basic skills. Learning to control bodily functions is very important. Piaget observed the emergence of basic intellectual operations through the senses of touch, sight, smell, and hearing in this period.

Stage III: Preschool   Initiative vs.Guilt (3 to 5½ years)

The preschooler needs to become confident about testing the limits of individual freedom and group responsibility, of fantasy and reality, of what feels good and what is permissible. Intellectual skills become more sophisticated and language matures rapidly. There is need to come to terms with social reality in a significant way, but in a manner that does not frighten the child from believing in self worth.

Stage IV: Elementary School   Industry vs. Inferiority (5½ to 12 years)

This is the time when children take up the important tasks of becoming an active participant in the culture beyond the family. School means learning basic academic skills, basic skills in making and keeping friends, and learning how to live in groups with adult guidance. Children develop their characteristic style for working on projects and for presenting themselves to the world. This is a time of consolidating the child's inner life in preparation for the special challenges that adolescence brings. Piaget identified important maturing of the child's ability to think and reason, thus laying the foundation for more fully adult-like reasoning, the task to be mastered in adolescence. Freud called this period the Latency Stage, to indicate that the powerful urges of infancy and early childhood were under control, while the sexual impulses of puberty were yet to come to the surface.

Source: Erik Erikson, *Childhood and Society*

chance to develop fully, children need to spread their wings and fly, as much as they need to take root and live socially responsible lives. They need to develop in all three domains of intelligence.

How is all this to happen? First and foremost, we must recognize that it is not going to happen automatically. If it is going to happen, it is going to because the adults who care for children approach children "developmentally."

A child does not, will not, cannot develop in a social vacuum. There is more to development than simple physical maturation. Development is a social process, for it is through relationships with people that the child learns about the world and how it works. Who points out that this four-legged furry creature is not a dog but is, rather, a cat? Who reassures the child when he or she is frightened? Who affirms the child's need to play and daydream? Who guides and helps the child in learning society's rules and beliefs? Who encourages the child to think creatively—to engage in selective encoding, selective combination and selective comparison?

Child development proceeds through and because of social relationships. The earliest and most important of these are the social relationships between infant and parents (and others who care for the child in the first months and years). These "attachment" relationships are the training ground and the foundation for subsequent social relationships. Problems in early attachments tend to translate into general social problems, cognitive deficiencies and emotional difficulties. Deprive the child of crucial social relationships and the child will not thrive and move forward developmentally, but will fall back, regress, stop.

The child needs responses that are *emotionally validating but developmentally challenging*. This is what moves development forward. When the young child says, "car go," he or she needs a person who responds with a smile and with encouragement, "Yes, honey. That's right, the car is going. And where do you think the car is going?" The child needs people to teach her or him how to be patient, how to follow through, how to behave responsibly, as well as how to tell dogs from cats, A's from B's and 1's from 2's. A child needs people who care for *that* child emotionally.

In addressing this critical requirement of the developmental process, the psychologist Lev Vygotsky emphasized the role of the adult as a teacher in the child's development. A good teacher understands the distance between what a child can accomplish alone and what the child can do when helped by an adult or a more competent peer. Vygotsky called this "the zone of proximal development."[3] It is the critical territory for interventions that seek to stimulate and support the child's cognitive development. When a child's environment does not do these things "naturally," intervention is needed to change that fact, most desirably by changing the child's permanent environment rather than by trying to inoculate the child against that environment (a strategy of dubious validity and very limited success). The key is to shift the child's environment toward operating effectively in the zone of proximal development. This means shaping the behavior of adults in the child's life.

Indeed, it is not so much our capacity for learning that distinguishes humans from other species, but rather our capacity to teach. All animals can learn. But only humans appear to set out to teach consciously, as a way of facilitating the development of the young. Indeed, human beings construct elaborate and sophisticated cultures and teach them to children in ways that are a marvel to behold. It is because we teach that, as a society, we do not need to reinvent the wheel each generation or discover fire over and over again, even though each individual child is inventing and discovering these things. Children learn from adults in many ways, some of which are inadvertent on the adult's part. Deliberate teaching plays a special role in this learning process, however.

What does all this mean for understanding child development in general, and cognitive development in particular? The primary point is that children's development is neither automatic nor subject to rigid conduct. It will not move forward most efficiently if we simply turn them loose with the message "go forth and learn," nor if we totally plan every detail in their experience. If it is to be successful, it requires constant interaction with other people, preferably people who approach children developmentally.

What does it mean to approach children developmentally? It means that we recognize the child's changing capacities, and that we recognize that a child has the capacity for change.

A child's life is not fixed in some unalterable genetic code that entirely predetermines what and who the child will be. Each child contains the potential to be many different children, and caring adults can do much to shape which of those children will come to life. The worst we can do is to assume that all is fixed.

When genetically identical twins are raised together or in very similar communities, they grow up to be very similar, even to the extent of having very similar IQ scores. However, when genetically identical twins grow up in very different environments, their IQ scores are likely to be much less similar. One study reported a correlation of .85 for identical twins reared separately but in similar communities, but only .26 for identical twins reared in dissimilar communities—about the same degree of similarity noted for siblings growing up the same family.[4]

While recognizing that genetic heritage can (and usually does) make an important contribution to cognitive development, we have come to realize that other biological influences can be powerful as well—for example, nutrition, which affects brain growth. What is more, we *must* recognize that the social environment a community provides will go a long way toward determining whether biological potential will bloom or wither, whether the biological underpinnings of cognitive development will be fulfilled or denied by experience.

Approaching children developmentally also means that we recognize that development is the process by which a child forms a picture or draws a map of the world and his or her place in it.

The developmental process reflects the effects of a mixture of forces and influences, some conscious, some not. Unconscious forces play an important role in the child's life. Early evidence of unconscious processes comes from a toddler's sudden resistance to going to sleep, acquiring imaginary playmates, having nightmares and the invention of monsters, ghosts, witches and boogeymen. Fantasy and play (and particularly "pretending" play) are vital to a child's development. Through them, children have a chance to explore the meaning of the world around and *inside* them. In this sense, play is the child's vocation. It serves both the need to work through unconscious forces and the need to practice basic life skills.

In effect, children draw maps, and then they move forward on the paths they believe exist. If a child develops a map of the world which depicts people and places as unremittingly hostile, and the child as an insignificant speck relegated to one small corner, we must expect troubled development of one sort or another: a life of suspicion, low-self esteem, self-denigration and perhaps violence and rage. We can also expect a diminution of cognitive development, most likely in the experiential and contextual domains.

What does it take for a child to form a realistic and positive map of the world, a map that will lead outward into the world with confidence, love, trust, social responsibility and an appreciation for beauty? Ideally, children would come into a world that offers to the child's family the means to meet his or her basic developmental needs. Basic needs include access to health care as well as adequate nutrition so that children can grow strong and healthy. Early deprivation (including malnutrition) can suppress brain development and cognitive functioning. For physical and psychic reasons, the child needs a family that has access to adequate employment and income. This provides the basis for *pro-social* contextual intelligence. And, it provides day-to-day stability in important caregiving relationships for the child. Such stability is crucial, in the early years most of all.

Whether or not children experience these essential ingredients is critical to their development. Threats to the physical health of a child can jeopardize mental and emotional development. Poverty can stunt intellectual development and impose stress that undermines social development. Instability of child care arrangements can threaten the child's sense of security and continuity.

Beyond these roots, what does the child need to develop experiential intelligence? It takes adults—parents, teachers, caregivers—who recognize the processes of development at work in the life of the child and who seize upon occasions to interact with the child and thus to create an environment in which the development of creativity can go forward, so that experiential intelligence can flourish.

DEVELOPMENT IN AN IMPOVERISHED ENVIRONMENT

Having provided a brief sketch of what is meant by child development, we can turn to the matter of early intervention in a more systematic way. We do so in an attempt to set forth some principles to guide early investment in children as a way of promoting cognitive development and reducing the social problems associated with poverty.

Early intervention to contribute to better cognitive development opportunities for children at risk, particularly in low-income families, became a national policy issue more than twenty years ago with the creation of Head Start. The assumptions underlying the enactment of Head Start remain valid. They are that

- the life circumstances of children living in poverty tend to restrict cognitive development;
- deficient cognitive development in early childhood is a serious obstacle to later success in school;
- school failure perpetuates the cycle of poverty; and that
- early intervention with children and with adults (as parents) can override the negative effects of poverty on cognitive development.

All four of these assumptions have been subject to criticism, refinement and elaboration on empirical and theoretical grounds. What exactly is it about poverty that undermines cognitive development? Research has identified a wide range of factors—malnutrition and health care deficiencies, violence, lack of stimulation, lack of responsiveness to the child's exploratory and early verbal behavior, etc. How do deficiencies in cognitive development impede school success? Many poor children start school below the minimum level of componential intelligence (with IQs of less than 90), but the biggest problem seems to be cultural, in the sense that many poor children have not been immersed in the "academic culture" because they don't see people reading, do not have models of success in school, are not familiar with the kinds of things that happen in school. Being thus out of sync with school, they fall behind more and more as the years pass and their path of cognitive development (often in all three domains) become less and less attuned to school success.

How does school failure perpetuate the cycle of poverty? Being "unschooled" does not automatically make for poverty. But in contemporary life in the United States, school failure means lacking one very important set of the credentials that are used to screen entrants to the work force. It means that individuals are likely to have experienced a pattern of socialization that makes them out of touch with the style needed on the job, and thus deficient in the contextual intelligence relevant to job success (no matter how useful it is "on the streets"). It even means, frequently, some deficiencies in conventional (i.e. componential) intelligence. Thus, school failure perpetuates the cycle of poverty in several ways, with cognitive development being directly involved, particularly from a perspective informed by the triarchic model of intelligence.

THE IMPORTANCE OF EARLY INTERVENTION

How can early intervention override the negative effects of poverty on cognitive development? Most early intervention programs make no claim to eliminate poverty directly. Rather they seek to sever the links between low income and deficient cognitive development. That at least some negative effects can be prevented is unarguable, with respect to certain important issues, as the experience of many programs in the prevention of infant mortality have demonstrated. Is it possible to apply the same logic successfully to cognitive development? The results of Head Start suggest the answer is "yes" (at least if we define success as reducing, if not eliminating, the links).

Experimental programs, like High/Scope's preschool education curriculum[5] and Missouri's birth-to-three parent education program[6] are very encouraging in their ability to reduce special education placements (a measure of cognitive impairment broadly defined) and raise IQ scores. Programs like the Erikson Institute Early Literacy Project[7] show great promise in being able to socialize poor children into the school culture (particularly the "culture of literacy"). Programs like the Home Health Visitor Program[8] that begins with pre-natal visits seems to work in reducing many of dangerous early life circumstances for children in poverty (e.g. low birth weight, neglect, child abuse, negative attitudes toward young children, etc.)

In one of the most ambitious efforts to date, the Center for Successful Child Development[9] in Chicago is seeking to bring all these elements together in a comprehensive early intervention program, the goal of which is to prevent deficiencies in cognitive development.

All the indications are that early intervention can do a great deal to reduce the negative consequences of poverty for cognitive development. But to make these programs a matter of policy, we must heed the following lessons learned over the last 20 years:

Those who bring the most to learning, learn the most: When early childhood intervention programs, such as Head Start, were offered in a community, not everyone participated and not everyone bene-fited equally. It has been the more highly motivated, the people who already had their heads a bit above water, who made use of these opportunities and whose children gained the most.

The greater the challenge, the greater the payoffs. Each instance in which a child is protected from developmental delays and educational failure can mean a savings of many thousands of dollars in later costs to society. These savings flow from more productive employ-ment, better health, less delinquency and less welfare dependency. But, as we move along the path from the easiest to the hardest cases, we experience a simultaneous increase in both program costs and program benefits. Providing effective early childhood educa-tion centers for very poor children, the children of the "under-class," is and will be a very challenging proposition.

We cannot inoculate children against future failure. Effective early intervention programs cannot prevent later failure. What they can do is prepare children to take advantage of later opportunities in school and in the world of work. Without this preparation, many children are bound to fail. Investing in powerful early childhood intervention programs is, therefore, a necessary condition for pro-grams later in life to work—it is not a guarantee.

Earlier is better. Programs that wait until kindergarten are generally not as effective as programs that begin in the preschool period. And programs that start at age three are generally not as effective as programs that start in infancy. The point is that the earlier intervention begins, the better are its chances of succeeding.

No program can do it alone. For early childhood intervention programs to succeed, they have to be part of a well-coordinated campaign to prevent early developmental delays, to prevent health problems that disproportionately affect and inhibit the development of poor children, and to upgrade the conditions of life in high-risk social environments.

If parents are not part of the solution, they are part of the problem. Our 20 years of experience with early childhood intervention has taught us that we must collaborate with parents. This means that poor parents must be brought into the process of intervention as much as children.

Doing the job well requires well-trained professionals. Developing and running good early childhood intervention programs requires a high level of professional expertise. Managing a nursery school, for example, for middle-class children who come from stable, highly-motivated families with resources to spare is difficult enough, but successfully operating an early childhood education program for children of the "underclass" is light years away in the level of challenge it presents for the staff. They cannot be trained or hired cheaply.

Have we as a nation the intelligence to learn and live by these lessons in making policy about early intervention? That is the big unanswered question. Most observers agree that the cost of ignoring these lessons is staggering—lost economic productivity, crime and delinquency, suffering. How smart a nation are we?

Notes

1. Robert Sternberg, *Beyond IQ*. New York: Cambridge University Press, 1985.

2. James P. Guilford, "Creativity," *American Psychologist*. Vol. 5, 1950, pp. 444–454.

3. Lev Vygotsky, *Thought and Language*. London: MIT Press, 1934.

4. Urie Bronfenbrenner, Phyllis Moen and James Garbarino, "Families and

Communities." In Ross Parke (Ed.) *Review of Child Development Research.* Chicago: University of Chicago Press, 1984.

5. "High-Scope's Preschool Education Curriculum." In David Weikart (Ed.) *Prevention Strategies For Healthy Babies and Healthy Children.* Testimony before the Select Committee on Children, Youth, and Families. U.S. House of Representatives, June 30, 1983.

6. Parents As Teachers: The National Center. Missouri Department of Elementary and Secondary Education. Jefferson City, Missouri.

7. Joan McLane and Gillian McNamee, *Early Literacy.* Cambridge: Harvard University Press, (in press).

8. David Olds, Charles Henderson, Jr., R. Chamberlin and Robert Tatelbaum, "Preventing Child Abuse and Neglect: A Randomized Trial of Nurse Home Visitation." *Pediatrics,* Vol. 78, 1986, pp. 65–78.

9. Gina Barclay, *Center for Successful Child Development.* Chicago, 1987.

OUR NATION'S YOUNGEST CHILDREN: WHO THEY ARE AND HOW THEY ARE CARED FOR

Eleanor Stokes Szanton

THIS CHAPTER summarizes U.S. national statistics kept on children before they reach school age. The figures are perhaps as eloquent in what they fail to record as in what they report. By and large, in this country children between birth and school age fall out of any systematic or periodic review of their physical health, mental health or developmental status. Our knowledge of the incidence of disability and developmental risk comes largely from inference based on statistics collected at school age. Even the prevalence of the most basic preventive health program, immunization against childhood disease, is calculated on the basis of incomplete data.[1]

Although in some important areas, such as the incidence of infant mortality, the past 25 years have seen major improvement, figures on the status of infants and young children nonetheless portray a population many members of which experience significant problems, not just in one area but in several at once. This is particularly disturbing, since research has shown that children who are subject to multiple problems are likely to suffer devastating cumulative developmental effects.[2]

The areas in which data indicate recent improvements in the health and welfare of, and services for, U.S. children include the following:

- though our infant mortality rate is high and demographically uneven, it has been cut by one third in the past 15 years;
- only 60% as many children aged one to four are dying now as died 15 years ago. A major area of decrease is in motor accidents;
- the number of children in nursery school and kindergarten has

Prepared with major assistance from Penny Anderson, Research Associate, and Judy McLean, typist, NCCIP.

increased by almost 50% in 15 years. For black children the number has increased by more than 60%;

- the resources available to low-income pregnant women and young children through the federal WIC and Supplemental Feeding programs have increased by a factor of ten;
- the new legislation passed by Congress allowing states to offer Medicaid to working poor pregnant women and their young children, will shortly begin to have an impact in those states which have chosen to accept it; and
- new legislation (PL 99-457) has been enacted mandating services to children who are handicapped at age three and giving states strong incentives to plan services from birth.

In spite of the good news, however, nearly one in four children under six years of age were living in poverty in 1985, a highly disproportionate share compared with the population as a whole. They receive a much smaller share of the Medicaid dollar than the elderly and that share has been decreasing over time. A higher percentage of poor children under age six have physical and health limitations than do their wealthier peers. A far higher percent have high levels of lead in their blood. They are more likely to have poor nutritional status. Yet, the majority of them do not receive supplemental feeding, and programs to control lead poisoning have diminished in recent years.

Children under age six are much more likely to be living with only one parent than were their counterparts of 20 years ago; yet in many instances, their families lack formal or informal social supports.[3]

The incidence of low birth weight and premature babies remains very high for some segments of the population; yet almost one quarter of all babies born between 1979 and 1985 were born to women who had had no prenatal care in the first three months of their pregnancy, in spite of the fact that the amount of prenatal care is highly correlated with successful outcomes in pregnancy. Close to 200,000 per year are treated in neonatal intensive care units.

Children under age six need regular preventive health care, yet a smaller proportion of children under age six have access to private insurance than do other segments of the population. 15% of their mothers had no insurance, public or private, at time of delivery. Only two-thirds as many preschool age children are immunized against the major childhood diseases as are their school age brothers and sisters. 70% of them have never visited a dentist.

Considerable numbers of them are born with actual or potentially handicapping conditions; yet, for many these conditions are not identified until they reach school and even fewer are treated.

A significant number of infants are compromised *in utero* by mothers who smoke or who have alcohol or drug dependencies. A small but rapidly increasing number are born with AIDS.

An increasing number of children under age six are reported maltreated, yet programs to prevent and deal with the effects of child abuse have decreased in the past five years.

More than 50% of all infants and preschool children are now in families in which the mother is in the labor force. Their families by and large have less access to parental leave at time of child birth than do their counterparts in 80 Western and Third World countries. The supply and quality of infant and child care has failed to keep up with this trend.[4]

Children are enrolled in preschool in inverse proportion to the level of education of their mothers, so that those who might benefit most from early education programs are least likely to receive them.

Finally, infants born in this country are more likely to die in the first year than are their counterparts in 11 other Western countries. Black infant mortality is almost twice as high as white.

HOW MANY CHILDREN AND WHAT KIND OF FAMILIES?

In 1985 there were 18,037,000 children in the United States under the age of five, 2 million fewer than in 1960[5] and probably about half a million more than there will be in the year 2000.[6] Roughly 14.6 million were white; 2.7 million were black; 1.8 million were Hispanic.[7]

Of the total, 3,749,000 were newborns, representing a birth rate of 15.7 per 1,000.[8] They were born to women who, as a group, were having only a little more than half as many babies as their counterparts of 25 years ago. In 1986 the *fertility* rate, 64.9 births per 1,000 women aged 15–44 years, was the lowest ever observed in the United States, two percent lower than in 1985. The fertility rate has dropped most drastically among black women, to 81.4 per 1,000 in 1984 (53% of what it was in 1960). However, it has dropped greatly among whites as well, to 62.2/1,000 (55% in 1984 of what it was in 1960).[9,10]

The birth rate among Hispanics was about 50% higher than among non-Hispanics.[11] Hispanics tend to begin childbearing earlier. They continue to have children longer and have larger families.[12] The birth rate among Hispanics has shown a slight decline in the 1980s (from 23.9 in 1982 to 22.7 in 1984). It is hard to see how much of a long-term trend this represents, since the government did not collect separate data on Hispanic births until 1980.[13] Hispanic children are highly concentrated in eight states, which account for 87% of the Hispanic population: Arizona, California, Florida, Illinois, New Jersey, New Mexico, New York and Texas.[14]

Fewer children are born to young women. Births to teenagers fell drastically over the last quarter century, as did births to women 20–24 years.[15]

	1960	1984
Teenagers	89 per 1,000	51 per 1,000 (a 43% decline)
Women 20–24 years old	258 per 1,000	107 per 1,000 (a 58% decline)

In 1985, 480,000 teenage women gave birth. Approximately 10,000 of these births were to young women less than 15 years old. 167,000 were to young women 15–17 years old.[16,17]

A much higher percentage of children are born to women who are unmarried. The increase in the proportion of teenage mothers who

TABLE 1
PERCENTAGE OF TEENAGE WOMEN MARRIED AT TIME OF FIRST BIRTH

1964–66	76%
1972	60%
1980	50%

Source: National Center for Health Statistics, S. J. Ventura: Trends in Marital Status of Mothers at Conception and Birth of First Child: United States, 1964–66, 1972, and 1980. *Monthly Vital Statistics Report*, Vol. 36, No. 2, Supp. DHHS Pub. No. 87-1120. Public Health Service, Hyattsville, Md., May 29, 1987, p. 1.

TABLE 2
BIRTHS PER 1,000 UNMARRIED WOMEN 1970–85

	Ages 15–19		Ages 20–24	
	White	Black	White	Black
1970	10.9	96.9	22.5	131.5
1980	16.2	89.2	24.4	115.1
1984	19.0	87.1	27.8	110.7
1985	20.5	88.8	30.9	116.1

Source: National Center for Health Statistics: Advance report of final natality statistics, 1985. *Monthly Vital Statistics Report*, Vol. 36, No. 4. Supp. DHHS Pub. No. 87-1120. Public Health Service, Hyattsville, Md., July 17, 1987, pp. 32–33, Table 19.

are unmarried has been particularly dramatic in the past 15 years. In 1985 more than half of all births to teenagers were to unmarried teenagers. 145,500 children were born to unmarried white teenagers; 126,000 to unmarried black teenagers and 8,600 to unmarried teenagers of other backgrounds. The rate has been increasing more for whites than for blacks and has sometimes even decreased for blacks.[18]

The phenomenon of increasing births to unmarried women is by no means limited to teenagers. In 1985, the rate rose eight percent over the previous year; in all, the incidence of births to unmarried women rose 24% between 1980 and 1985.[19]

Though the percentage of unmarried black women giving birth declined somewhat over the past 15 years, the rate for black teenagers still stands at more than four times the rate for white teenagers and almost four times that of white women ages 20–24.[20] Nonetheless, because there are so many more in the population, white women accounted for almost all of the increase in births to unmarried women.[21,22] In 1984, about 86% of the unmarried teenagers who gave birth had not finished high school; about 15% had some college.[23]

Poverty. 4,170,000 children, or almost one quarter of all children under five years of age, were living in poverty in 1985. They were disproportionately poor compared to other age groups: 23% of those under five are living in poverty; in contrast, only 14% of individuals of all ages were living in poverty in 1985.[24] This is not surprising, since birth rates for low income families (under $10,000 annual income) are twice as high as for families with incomes of $25,000 to $29,000 and five times as high as for those with incomes over

TABLE 3

PERCENTAGE OF THOSE FAMILIES WITH CHILDREN
THAT ARE FEMALE-HEADED

	1960	1970	1980	1984	1986
Total	7%	10%	18%	19%	19%
White	6	8	13	15	14
Black	21	31	47	49	48

Source: U.S. Bureau of the Census, *Statistical Abstract of the United States, 1985* (for 1960–1980), Table 66; U.S. Bureau of the Census, *Current Population Reports*, Series P-20, No. 411, "Household and Family Characteristics: March 1985" and earlier reports; and unpublished data from the Current Population Survey, U.S. Bureau of the Census. Reported in *U.S. Children & Their Families: Current Conditions & Recent Trends, 1987*; "A Report Together With Additional Views of the Select Committee on Children, Youth, and Families," U.S. House of Representatives, 100th Congress, 1st Session. Washington, D.C.: U.S. Government Printing Office, March, 1987. p. 9.

$35,000.[25] Though poverty *per se* does not inevitably mean that an infant or a young child will have health risks or poor developmental outcomes, it is statistically a very strong correlate of risk factors such as a high degree of family stress, a single parent family, compromised maternal health, mental health or education.

Female-headed households are more than three times as likely to be impoverished as are all families; consequently, young children under six in female-headed, single-parent families are more likely to be poor. In 1980, 15.4% of all children under six lived with their mother alone; in 1985, that number had increased to 20%. The numbers were 11% in 1980 and 13.9% in 1985 for white children; 39.5% in 1980 and 54.1% in 1985 for black children; and 18.2% in 1980 and 24.8% in 1985 in families of Spanish origin[26] (See Table 3).

However the family is constituted, moreover, the spread in average income between the poorest quintile and the richest quintile is increasing. The income of the three lowest quintiles of American families has fallen in real terms since the 1970s.[27]

At Risk From the Start. Many of our nation's children are already "at risk" during their fetal development and for an important percentage, these are multiple risks. Some of the most serious problems are caused by too close spacing of births; the fact that a conception is unwanted; and by smoking, alcohol or drug abuse.

To be born less than 18 months after a sibling is to increase the likelihood of being born low birth weight or with other health prob-

TABLE 4
PERCENTAGE OF BIRTHS UNWANTED AT CONCEPTION

	1976	1982
By Race		
Total	12.0%	10.5%
White	9.5	8.0
Black	25.8	23.7
By Education level		
<12 yrs.	16.1	16.5
12 yrs.	11.2	9.7
>12 yrs.	7.4	6.8

Source: National Center for Health Statistics, *Advance Data*, No. 56, January 24, 1980, "Wanted and Unwanted Births Reported by Mothers 15–44 Years of Age: United States, 1976," by E. Eckard and "Fertility Patterns: The Number, Timing and Wantedness of Births, United States, 1982," *Vital and Health Statistics Report*, Series 23, Data from the National Survey of Family Growth.

TABLE 5
DEATHS DUE TO SMOKING 1984
(children under one year)

	number of deaths	% attributable to smoking
Prematurity, low birth weight	3,262	18
Respiratory distress syndrome	3,557	18
Other respiratory conditions	3,497	18
Sudden Infant Death Syndrome	5,245	13

Source: Centers for Disease Control weekly bulletin, Friday, October 30, 1987.

lems. Yet 36% of births to young women 15–19 years old come less than 18 months after the previous birth.[28]

Infants unwanted at conception are more likely to be at risk for later problems. According to self-reports of mothers at birth, unwanted conceptions are almost three times as prevalent among blacks as among whites, and more than twice as frequent among young women with less than 12 years of schooling than among women who have begun college. These disparities are increasing.

Infants born to women who smoke regularly are at greater risk of low birth weight. And though there appear to be no current figures on the number of women who smoke during pregnancy, we know that though the percentage is going down, almost one-third of all women ages 20–44 currently do smoke, and that in 1980, more than a quarter of married mothers of live-born infants smoked during their pregnancy.[29] It is estimated that in 1984 more than 2,500 deaths of infants under one year old could be attributed to smoking by the mother. Various studies have shown that smoking increases the frequency of low birth weight infants, premature births, lung disorders in the newborn period and Sudden Infant Death Syndrome.

Infants born to women who consume alcohol on a regular basis are at greater risk of disability. Infants born to heavy drinkers are more likely to suffer fetal alcohol syndrome, a cluster of congenital defects including nervous system dysfunction. Thirteen percent of women age 20 and older consume alcohol three or more times per week; and 30% have five or more drinks at least once a year.[30] It is estimated that between 1500 and 2000 children are born each year with fetal alcohol syndrome.[31]

The incidence of babies exposed to drugs *in utero* is rising sharply. A 1988 survey of 36 U.S. hospitals found that, on average, 11 percent were exposing their unborn babies to illegal drugs, with cocaine the most common.[32]

CONDITIONS OF BIRTH, INFANCY AND EARLY CHILDHOOD

Generally, infant mortality and the two conditions most closely associated with it, prematurity and low birth weight, have all declined significantly over the past quarter century, a decline found across population groups. Our rates remain higher than the rates of most other Western countries. To a greater extent than is desirable the reduction in infant mortality has resulted from the development of intensive-use, high-technology, costly in-hospital neonatal care, and not from the extension of appropriate nutrition and prenatal care to all pregnant women.

TABLE 6
LOW BIRTH WEIGHT RATE OF SELECTED EUROPEAN COUNTRIES IN COMPARISON TO THE UNITED STATES, 1982–1983

	(percent)
Belgium	5
France	5
Fed. Rep. of Germany	5
Ireland	4
Netherlands	4
Norway	4
Switzerland	5
United Kingdom	7
U.S.	7

Source: C. Arden Miller, *Maternal Health & Infant Survival,* Washington, D.C. National Center for Clinical Infant Programs, 1987, p. 16.

TABLE 7
MEAN DAYS IN NEONATAL INTENSIVE CARE FOR SURVIVING INFANTS

Number of grams at birth	Mean number of days
>2500	3.5
2001–2500	7
1501–2000	24
<1500	57
<1000	89

Source: Preventing Low Birth Weight. Committee to Study the Prevention of Low Birth Weight, Institute of Medicine, Washington, D.C., 1985, p. 34.

TABLE 8

PERCENTAGE OF LOW BIRTH WEIGHT INFANTS PRODUCED
BY VARIOUS SUBSECTIONS OF THE POPULATION IN 1984

White non-Hispanics:	5.5*
Black non-Hispanics:	12.4
Hispanics:	6.2
Women under age 15:	12.8
Women 15–19 years:	9.3
Women over 40 years:	8.1
Women of all ages:	6.8

*of all births by women in this category.

Source: National Center for Health Statistics, S. J. Ventura: Births of Hispanic Parentage, 1983 and 1984, *Monthly Vital Statistics Report*, Vol. 36, No. 4, Supp. (2). DHHS Pub. No. (PHS) 87-1120. Public Health Service. Hyattsville, Md., July 24, 1987, p. 17, Table 12 and National Center for Health Statistics, S. Taffel: Characteristics of American Indian and Alaska native births, United States, 1984. *Monthly Vital Statistics Report*, Vol. 36, No. 3, Supp. DHHS Pub. No. (PHS) 87-1120. Public Health Service, Hyattsville, Md., June 19, 1987, p. 11, Table 9.

TABLE 9

BABIES BORN WEIGHING 1500 GRAMS OR LESS

	1970	1976	1980	1984
All	1.2%	1.2	1.2	1.2
White	1.0	.9	.9	.9
Black	2.4	2.4	2.4	2.6

Source: National Center for Health Statistics, *Health*, United States, 1982, Table 24; Monthly Vital Statistics Report, Vol. 31, No. 8 Supplement, Nov., 1982, Tables 13 & 20; Vol. 35, No. 4 Supplement, July 1986, Table 25; and unpublished data. Reported in *U.S. Children and Their Families: Current Conditions and Recent Trends, 1987*, "A Report Together With Additional Views of the Select Committee on Children, Youth, and Families," U.S. House of Representatives, 100th Congress, 1st Session, Washington, D.C.; U.S. Government Printing Office, March 1987, p. 45.

A. Low birth weight. Almost seven percent of all babies born in the U.S. in 1985 weighed less than 2500 grams (5 pounds, 8 ounces).[33] Our incidence of low birth weight is higher than that of almost all other Western countries.[34] More than 60% of all deaths in the neonatal period (first 28 days), and 20% of deaths between 28 days and one year are of low birth weight babies. Low birth weight babies have a 40 times greater risk of death in the neonatal period than infants weighing more than 2500 grams at birth.[35] Surviving low birth weight infants often spend weeks or months in costly neonatal intensive care. Very low birth weight infants also are at serious risk of disabilities. 42% have some neurological handicap or congenital anomaly.[36]

Some kinds of mothers are at higher risk of producing a low birth weight baby than others. Black teenagers produce more than one-quarter of all low birth weight infants born to blacks,[37] and the racial disparity in birth weight is increasing. Between 1973 and 1983, the rate of low birth weight decreased more among whites than blacks, and the rate of very low birth weight increased among blacks but slightly decreased among whites.[38]

The incidence of very low birth weight babies since 1970 has declined slightly for whites, increased for blacks. The chances of being born low birth weight if one is black and born in Michigan are

CHART 1
Sample Variation in Low Birth Weight, By State, 1985

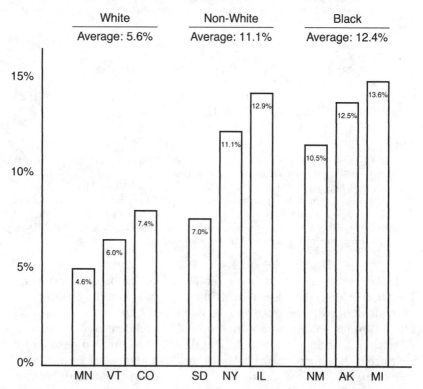

Source: National Center for Health Statistics; calculations by Children's Defense Fund. Reported in *The Health of America's Children: Maternal and Child Health Data Book.* Dana Hughes, *et al.* Wash., D.C.: Children's Defense Fund. 1988, pp. 68 & 69, Tables 2.5A-2.5D.

more than three times as great as the chances of being born low birth weight if one is white and born in Minnesota.

The significantly lower incidence of low birth weight among Hispanics and American Indians when compared with blacks of similar income level, age, onset of prenatal care and number of years of education is a mystery. A more fine-grained analysis of the components of maternal diets and fetal environments among one cultural group as compared to another may help to illuminate our ignorance as to the causes of low birth weight.

Surviving low birth weight infants often spend weeks or months in costly neonatal intensive care.

B. Premature births. Prematurity, or birth before the normal full term of nine months, is highly correlated with later risk and also varies from one population subgroup to another. The rate has been increasing over the past five years.[39]

	1980	1984	1985
All	8.9	9.4	9.8
White		7.9	8.2
Black		16.8	17.5

Teenagers, women over 40 and low income blacks are at especially high risk of prematurity.[40]

C. Infant mortality.[41] The infant mortality rate in the United States is still higher than that of 16 other industrialized countries. However, it has decreased markedly in the past 12 years. The disparity between

TABLE 10
INFANT MORTALITY RATE PER 1,000 BIRTHS—1982

Sweden	7
Japan	7
Finland	7
Switzerland	8
Norway	8
Netherlands	8
Denmark	8
France	9
Canada	9
Spain	10
Australia	10
U.S.A.	11

Source: *The State of the World's Children 1985*. United Nations Children's Fund, p. 921.

CAESARIAN SECTIONS

The number of infants born with Caesarian sections has increased significantly over the past five years.

Caesarian births over time: Percent of all deliveries to total number.

1979: 16.4%
1982: 18.5
1984: 21.1

U.S. National Center for Health Statistics, unpublished data, published in U.S. Bureau of the Census, *Statistical Abstract of the United States: 1987,* 107th edition, Washington, D.c., 1986, p. 62, Table 88.

APGAR SCORES

Apgar scores are a general measure of the health and viability of newborn babies, applied as a standard assessment by all U.S. hospitals. They measure 10 indicators, such as heart rate, respiratory effort, muscle tone, irritability, and color. Apgar tests are made at one minute after birth and at five minutes after birth. The five-minute Apgar has more predictive value with respect to later developmental measures than the one-minute Apgar. A score of less than seven indicates that there may be cause for worry. A score of 9 or 10 is considered excellent.

PERCENTAGE OF INFANTS BORN IN 1984 WITH A
1-MINUTE AND A 5-MINUTE APGAR SCORE
OF LESS THAN 7.

	1-minute	5-minute
White	9.3%	1.7%
Black	12.4	3.3
Indian	11.0	2.0
All infants	9.9	2.0

National Center for Health Statistics, S. Taffel: Charactristics of American Indian and Alaska native births, United States, 1984. *Monthly Vital Statistics Report,* Vol. 36, No. 3, Supp. DHHS Pub. No. (PHS) 87-1120. Public Health Service, Hyattsville, Md., June 19, 1987, p. 13, Table 12, and National Center for Health Statistics, S. J. Ventura: Births of Hispanic parentage, 1983 and 1984, *Monthly Vital Statistics Report,* Vol. 36, No. 4, Supp. (2). DHHS Pub. No. (PHS) 87-1120. Public Health Service. Hyattsville, Md., July 24, 1987, p. 17, Table. 13.

the chances for survival of black babies and white is very great, and because the rate for blacks has been improving less, the difference is increasing. Black infant mortality is now almost twice as high as white. The growing disparity between races over time is most strongly reflected in the neonatal mortality rates.

Postneonatal mortality rates for black infants are twice as high as for white. Nonetheless, the disparity is shrinking somewhat. Finally, the odds against living to one's first birthday vary greatly by state as well as by race. To be white and born in North Dakota is to have more than three times as great a chance to survive as a child who is non-white and born in Delaware.

D. Deaths of young children. Deaths of children under five years of age are, of course, much more frequent in the first year than in the

TABLE 11
INFANT MORTALITY RATES BY RACE OVER TIME

	All races	White	Black
1972–74	17.6	15.7	28.2
1977–79	13.6	11.9	22.8
1982–84	11.2	9.8	19.1

Source: National Center for Health Statistics: Data computed by the Division of Analysis from data compiled by the Division of Vital Statistics, reported in National Center for Health Statistics: Prevention profile, by P. M. Golden. *Health, United States, 1986.* DHHS Pub. No. (PHS) 87-1232. Public Health Service. Washington. U.S. Government Printing Office, December 1986, p. 86, Table 14.

TABLE 12
NEONATAL MORTALITY RATES BY RACE OVER TIME

	All races	White	Black
1972–74	13.0	11.8	19.6
1977–79	9.4	8.3	15.3
1982–84	7.3	6.5	12.4

Source: National Center for Health Statistics, (see Table 11), p. 88, Table 15.

TABLE 13
POSTNEONATAL MORTALITY RATES BY RACE OVER TIME

	All races	White	Black
1972–74	4.7	3.9	8.6
1977–79	4.2	3.6	7.6
1982–84	3.8	3.3	6.6

Source: National Center for Health Statistics, (see Table 11), p. 90, Table 16.

next four. The number of deaths due to all causes has significantly declined between 1970 and 1984, so that only 60% as many children aged one through four are dying now as died 15 years ago.

But, though the risk of death is lower for all, it remains spread unevenly across sex and race: in 1984, white females age one through four were only four-fifths as likely to die as white males and less than half as likely to die as black males in that age range.

The most important cause for the decline in mortality among young children appears to be the lower rate of death by motor vehicle accident.

Infants up to age one are at significantly higher risk of dying due

CHART 2
Sample Variation of Infant Mortality Rate, By State, 1985

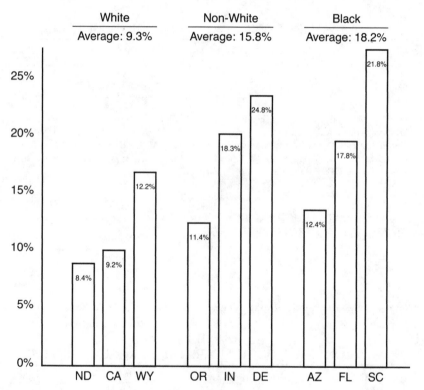

White	Non-White	Black
Average: 9.3%	Average: 15.8%	Average: 18.2%

Source: National Center for Health Statistics; calculations by the Children's Defense Fund. Reported in *The Health of America's Children: Maternal and Child Health Data Book*. Dana Hughes, et al. Wash., D.C.: The Children's Defense Fund, 1988. Tables 2.1A, 2.2A, 2.3A, 2.4A, pp. 42, 60, 62, 64, 66.

TABLE 14
ESTIMATED INFANT MORTALITY RATES,
BY AGE AND FOR 10 SELECTED CAUSES:
UNITED STATES JANUARY–DECEMBER 1986

Age and cause of death	Rate/1,000 live births
Total, under one year	10.4
Under 28 days	6.7
28 days to 11 months	3.7
Certain gastrointestinal diseases	0.1
Pneumonia and influenza	0.2
Congenital anomalies	2.2
Disorders relating to short gestation and unspecified low birthweight	0.9
Birth trauma	0.1
Intrauterine hypoxia and birth asphyxia	0.2
Respiratory distress syndrome	0.9
Other conditions originating in the perinatal period	2.7
Sudden Infant Death Syndrome	1.4
All other causes	
Residual	1.8

In 1985, 9,000 infants died due to birth defects, accounting for 23.7% of all infant deaths.

Source: Ninth International Classification of Diseases, 1987.

Source: National Center for Health Statistics: Births, Marriages, Divorces, and Deaths for January 1987. *Monthly Vital Statistics Report*, Vol. 36, No. 1, DHHS Pub. No. (PHS) 87-1120. Public Health Service. Hyattsville, Md., April 29, 1987, p. 10, Table 8.

TABLE 15
DEATH RATES PER 1,000 POPULATION

Age of Child	1970	1980	1982	1984
<1	21.4	12.9	11.6	10.9
1–4	.85	.64	.58	.52

Source: Death rates are derived by dividing the number of deaths in a population in a given period by the resident population at the middle of that period. It is expressed as the number of deaths per 1000 or 100,000 population. It may be restricted to deaths in specific age, race, sex, or geographic groups, or it may be related to the entire population. National Center for Health Statistics: *Health United States*, 1986. DHHS Pub. No. (PHS) 87-1232. Public Health Service. Washington, D.C., U.S. Government Printing Office, December 1986, p. 230. For a definition of infant mortality, see footnote 40, pp. 75–76.

Source: National Center for Health Statistics: *Vital Statistics of United States*, Vol. 11, Mortality, Part A, 1950–84. Public Health Service. Washington, D.C., U.S. Government Printing Office; Data compiled by the Division of Analysis from data compiled by the Division of Vital Statistics and from Table 1.

to homicide, accident, poisoning or undetermined injury than older children.

E. Handicapping conditions, developmental delays and chronic health problems. It is estimated that 150,000 to 250,000 babies born each year have birth defects.[42] The wide range of this estimate is not

TALE 16
DEATH RATES PER 1,000 IN 1984 BY SEX AND RACE

Age of Child	White Male	White Female	Black Male	Black Female
1–4	.52	.42	.85	.72

Source: National Center for Health Statistics: *Vital Statistics of United States*, Vol. II, Mortality, Part A, 1950–84. Public Health Service. Washington. U.S. Government Printing Office; Data computed by the Division of Analysis from data compiled by the division of Vital Statistics and from Table 1.

TABLE 17
TOTAL DEATHS IN 1984 OF CHILDREN BETWEEN ONE AND FOUR YEARS AND RATE PER 1,000

Age of Child	Number			Rate/1,000		
	All races	White	Black	All races	White	Black
1–4	7,372	5,413	1,679	.52	.47	.79

Source: Calculated by Child Trends, Inc. from unpublished data furnished by the Statistical Resources Branch, National Center for Health Statistics. The data are from the Vital Registration System, which reports cause of death as recorded on the death certificates of each state. Report in *U.S. Children and Their Families: Current Conditions and Recent Trends, 1987,* "A Report Together with Additional Views of the Select Committee on Children, Youth, and Families," U.S. House of Representatives, 100th Congress, 1st Session, U.S. Government Printing Office, March 1987, p. 50.

TABLE 18
DEATH RATES PER 1,000 DUE TO MOTOR VEHICLE ACCIDENTS

Age of Child	1970	1980	1982	1984
1–4	.115	.09	.08	.07

Source: National Center for Health Statistics: *Vital Statistics of United States*, Vol. II, Mortality, part A, 1950–84. Public Health Service. Washington. U.S. Government Printing Office; Data computed by the Division of Analysis from data compiled by the division of Vital Statistics and from Table 1. Reported in *Health*, U.S., 1986. National Center for Health Statistics. DHHS Pub. No. (PHS) 87-1232. Public Health Service. Washington, D.C. U.S. Government Printing Office. December 1986. p. 112, Table 30.

TABLE 19

DEATHS DUE TO ACCIDENT, POISONING OR VIOLENCE— NUMBER & RATE

Age of Child	Number			Rate/1,000		
	All races	White	Black	All races	White	Black
1–4	2,814	2,066	625	.20	.18	.29

Source: Calculated by Child Trends, Inc. from unpublished data furnished by the Statistical Resources Branch, National Center for Health Statistics. The data are from the Vital Registration System, which reports cause of death as recorded on the death certificates of each State. Report in *U.S. Children and Their Families: Current Conditions and Recent Trends, 1987*, "A Report Together with Additional Views of the Select Committee on Children, Youth, and Families," U.S. House of Representatives, 100th Congress, 1st Session, U.S. Government Printing Office, March 1987, p. 50.

TABLE 20

DEATHS DUE TO DISEASE AND HEALTH CONDITIONS— NUMBER & RATE

Age of Child	Number			Rate/1,000		
	All races	White	Black	All races	White	Black
1–4	4,558	3,347	1,054	.32	.29	.49

Source: Calculated by Child Trends, Inc. from unpublished data furnished by the Statistical Resources Branch, National Center for Health Statistics. The data are from the Vital Registration System, which reports cause of death as recorded on the death certificates of each state. Report in *U.S. Children and Their Families: Current Conditions and Recent Trends, 1987*, "A Report Together with Additional Views of the Select Committee on Children, Youth, and Families," U.S. House of Representatives, 100th Congress, 1st Session, U.S. Government Printing Office, March 1987, p. 50.

TABLE 21

NUMBER OF DEATHS OF INFANTS AND YOUNG CHILDREN DUE TO HOMICIDE AND UNDETERMINED INJURY (RATE/100,000)

	1970	1975	1980	1984
Children 1–4	3.2	3.6	3.3	2.8

Source: Philip J. Cook and John H. Laub, "Trends in Child Abuse and Juvenile Delinquency," unpublished manuscript, May 1985, citing the Public Health Service, National Center for Health Statistics, *Vital Statistics of the United States, Vol. II Mortality*, Part A, various years; and unpublished data provided by the National Center for Health Statistics, reported in *U.S. Children and Their Families: Current Conditions and Recent Trends, 1987*, "A Report Together with Additional Views of the Select Committee on Children, Youth, and Families," U.S. House of Representatives, 100th Congress, 1st Session, U.S. Government Printing Office, March 1987, p. 50.

TABLE 22
INCIDENCE OF CERTAIN DISABILITIES AT BIRTH

	incidence/1,000 live births
Cleft Lip/Palate	1.6
Congenital Heart Disorders	9.0
Severe Heart Disease	2.6
Cystic Fibrosis	0.27
Down's Syndrome	1.4
Muscular Dystrophy	0.11
Neutral Tube Defect:	
Spina Bifida	0.7
Encephalocele	0.15

Source: Steven L. Gortmaker and William Sappenfield, "Chronic Childhood Disorders: Prevalence and Impact," *Pediatric Clinics of North America,* Vol. 31, No. 1, February 1984, pp. 3–18.

surprising. Many defects are not or cannot be detected at birth and are only identified later. The reporting of handicapping conditions—as with the general assessment of the health of young children—is highly unsystematic. Here, however, the inability to predict and identify problems is especially costly, because it means that necessary care cannot be given when it might be most effective.

F. Limitations on young children's activity. In 1985, 2.6% of children under six were physically limited in their level of activity, an increase of 0.2% over 1983. The increase appeared to be for all but the most severely limited.[43] And, though there are not breakdowns between sexes, races and income levels specifically for children under six, there are breakdowns among children of all ages with physical limitations. In 1985 4% more boys than girls were physically limited, 24% more black than white children suffered physical limitations, and almost three times as many children with physical limitations came from families who earned less than $10,000 a year as came from families earning $35,000 a year or more. The greater number of very young children with health problems coming from among black and low-income families is statistically recorded in parental ratings of their children's health status.

Almost one-third of all families earning less than $10,000 a year believed their young children's health to be less than very good. That was more than three times as many as in families earning $35,000 a year or more. The ratio of high quality to low quality health of children under five was assessed by their parents as not much more than two to one for lowest income families. For high income families it was almost nine to one.

TABLE 23

PARENT RATINGS OF THE HEALTH STATUS OF THEIR
CHILDREN UNDER 5 YEARS OF AGE–1985. (Percent.)

	All	White	Black
Excellent	54.7	57.2	42.4
Very Good	25.8	26.3	24.8
Good	17.2	14.8	28.6
Fair or Poor	2.3	1.8	4.2

Source: National Center for Health Statistics, "Current Estimates From the National Health Interview Survey: United States, 1983;" " . . . , 1984;" and " . . . 1985;" *Vital and Health Statistics, Series 10, Nos. 154, 156, and 160, Table 70 in each volume.*

TABLE 24

PERCENT OF FAMILIES EARNING

	under $10,000	10,000– 19,999	20,000– 34,999	35,000– or more
Excellent	41.7	50.3	58.3	65.3
Very good	27.3	29.4	25.1	24.3
Good	26.8	18.0	14.7	8.6
Fair or Poor	4.2	2.4	1.8	1.6
Excellent or Very good	69.0	79.7	83.4	89.6
Good or Fair/Poor	31.0	20.4	16.5	10.2

Source: National Center for Health Statistics (see Table 23).

G. Unsafe lead levels. Through there is disagreement over what constitutes an unhealthy blood level of lead, there is consensus that some children are much more likely to have elevated blood lead than others. (See Tables 25 and 26, p. 56).

H. Children who are abused or neglected. The number of young children reported to be suffering abuse and neglect (including denial of basic necessities and minor injuries) continues to increase significantly, having almost tripled since the mid-1970s. The increased openness in reporting sexual abuse accounts for some of this increase. For obvious reasons, children under six experience a disproportionate share of maltreatment of all children.

The lack of standard reporting in this area is a major problem. Many states do not keep standard figures or report them to the federal government. Those states which do report them vary in how they do so—whether or not they include unsubstantiated reports, how they count multiple reports on one family, and whether they count children or families.[44] Breakdowns by age and type of maltreatment do not exist, but there is data indicating that very young children are more vulnerable than are their older peers. Children from birth to age five nationally made up 28% of the population but accounted for 74% of maltreatment fatalities in 1979.[45] The average age of fatalities from child maltreatment is 2.0.[46]

I. Children with mental health disorders. Statistics kept on young children with mental health problems are extremely sketchy, and

TABLE 25
PERCENT OF CHILDREN WITH ELEVATED BLOOD LEAD
AGES ONE–THREE, 1980

	One year old	Two years old	Three years old
White	2.8	2.8	2.9
Black	18.2	16.8	18.1

Source: J. L. Ames and K. Mahaffey. *Blood Lead Levels for Persons Ages 6 Months–74 years.* Vital and Health Statistics, Series 11, No. 233, U.S. Department of Health and Human Services, August, 1984, as reported in *Infants Can't Wait: The Numbers.* National Center for Clinical Infant Programs, Washington, D.C., 1986. p. 36. By definition, an elevated blood lead level, known to lead to damage, is > 30 micrograms/decaliter. It is suspected that brain cell and other damage appears even at levels of 20 and 25 mg/dl.

TABLE 26
PERCENT OF CHILDREN, SIX MONTHS–FIVE YEARS WITH
ELEVATED BLOOD LEAD, BY FAMILY INCOME, 1980

	All races	White	Black
Income:			
< $6,000	10.9	5.9	18.5
$6,000–14,999	4.2	2.2	12.1
>$15,000	1.2	0.7	2.8

Source: J. L. Ames and K. Mahaffey, *Blood Lead Levels for Persons 6 Months–74 Years.* (see Table 25).

TABLE 27
REPORTED CASES OF CHILD MALTREATMENT FOR
CHILDREN OF ALL AGES (RATE PER 1,000 CHILDREN)

	1976	1980	1982	1984	1985
Number	669,000	1,154,000	1,262,000	1,727,000	1,928,000
Rate	10.1	18.1	20.1	27.3	30.6

Source: American Association for Protecting Children, Inc., *Highlights of Official Child Neglect and Abuse Reporting, 1985,* Denver, Colorado: The American Humane Association, 1987. pp. 3–4, Figures 1 and 2.

TABLE 28
THE HIGHER RATE OF ABUSE OF YOUNG CHILDREN—1985

Age	% of all U.S. children	% who are abused or neglected
0–5	34	43
6–11	31	33
12–17	35	24

Source: American Association for Protecting Children, Inc., *Highlights of Official Child Neglect and Abuse Reporting, 1985,* Denver, Colorado: The American Humane Association, 1987. p. 15, Table 5.

TABLE 29

Type of maltreatment	% of all maltreatments
Physical injury:	
Major	2.2
Minor	15.4
Unspecified	4.1
Neglect (deprivation of necessities)	55.7
Sexual maltreatment	11.7
Emotional maltreatment	8.9
Other maltreatment	10.2

Source: American Association for Protection Children, Inc., *Highlights of Official Child Neglect and Abuse Reporting, 1985,* Denver, Colorado: The American Humane Association, 1987. p. 16, Table 6. The distribution for 1985 is based on a special intensive sampling of four states constituting 24 percent of the U.S. Child Population—Illinois, Florida, New York, and Texas.

SMALL CHILDREN WITH AIDS

An increasing number of children under five have AIDS. Though the numbers remain small—over 900 as of July 1988—80% are children of parents with AIDS or at risk of AIDS, many of whom are in no position to care for their children. The needs of these children for public support for health and daily care are massive. The number has almost doubled in the past year.

Source: AIDS Weekly Surveillance Report—United States AIDS Program, Center for Infectious Diseases, Centers for Disease Control, July 1988.

provide almost no useful information. There is a small amount of data on the number of children in mental health facilities. However, there are no official estimates of the number of children under six who require mental health services. A major recommendation of a recent study by the U.S. Congress Office of Technology Assessment is that the federal government develop a more informed estimate of the number of children who require mental health services.[47]

HOW ARE OUR NATION'S YOUNGEST CHILDREN CARED FOR?

Prenatal care. Almost one quarter of all babies born between 1979 and 1985 were to women who had had no prenatal care in the first three months of their pregnancy. Between five and six percent were born to mothers who had prenatal care only in the last three months before they gave birth or who had no prenatal care whatever. Roughly double that percentage of black and Hispanic infants were born to women who had either no prenatal care or care only in the last trimester.[48]

Proportions of mothers with delayed care or no care were six times higher among mothers who did not finish high school compared with mothers who had at least one year of college.[49] There remains a very strong negative correlation between low birth weight and the commencement of prenatal care.

Proportions of mothers who receive early care vs. late or no prenatal care varies greatly from state to state. A child born in New Mexico is six times as likely to have had late or no prenatal care than a child born in Iowa or Rhode Island.

The United States spends a higher percentage of its gross national product on health care than any European country. Yet the percentages of its pregnant women receiving prenatal care compares unfa-

TABLE 30
PERCENT OF INFANTS BORN AT LOW BIRTH WEIGHT BY
AMOUNT OF PRENATAL CARE RECEIVED

Type of care	Percent low birth weight
No prenatal care	27%
Some prenatal care	7%

Source: *Blessed Events and the Bottom Line: Financing Maternity Care in the United States.* Washington, D.C.: The Alan Guttmacher Institute. 1987, p. 16.

vorably with that in other countries. Many European countries, even those with a lower per capita income than the United States as well as those with health care systems as pluralistic as ours, use a system of incentives to encourage early registration for prenatal care.[50]

Medical Care After Birth. As noted above, in the attempt to save the lives and promote the healthy development of infants born low birth weight and/or with birth defects, United States hospitals treat between 150,000 and 200,000 infants annually in neonatal intensive care units (NICU's). This represents four to six percent of all newborns. Treatment of low birth weight babies in NICU's costs on average between $12,000 and $39,000. Very low birth weight babies' costs range between $31,000 and $71,000; and costs for the very tiniest go as high

CHART 3
PERCENT OF BIRTHS BY TIMING OF MOTHER'S ENTRY INTO
PRENATAL CARE,
SAMPLE VARIATION BY STATE, 1984

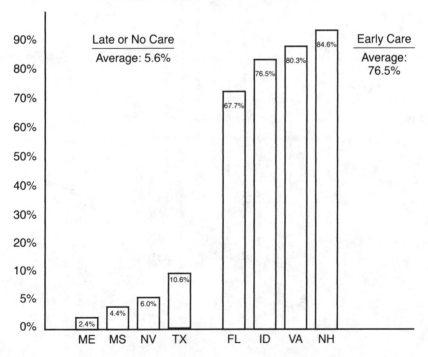

Source: National Center for Health Statistics. Calculation by the Children's Defense Fund. Reported in *The Health of America's Children: Maternal and Child Health Data Book*. Dana Hughes, *et al.* Washington, D.C.: The Children's Defense Fund. 1987. p. 51.

CHART 4
DURATION OF PAID MATERNITY LEAVE (IN WEEKS)

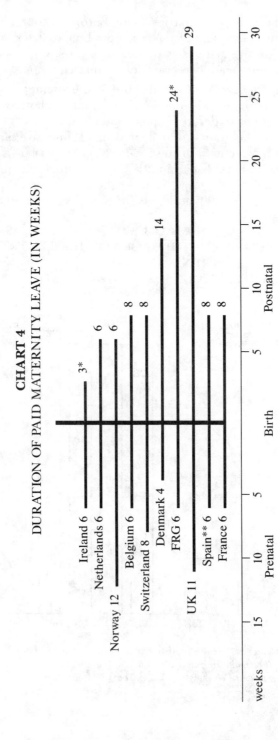

*Leave is extended for premature delivery
Source: Children's Defense Fund, *The Health of America's Children*, 1987.

as $150,000 per child.[51] There seems to be virtually no way, however, for families with less severe problems to receive help outside the hospital setting. For example, the United States has no system for postnatal home visits, unlike most European countries.[52]

Parental leave at time of childbirth. At present, only about 40% of new mothers in the United States receive parental leave which allows them a six-week leave without severe financial penalty.[53] Six states provide paid temporary disability benefits for employed women who give birth. No fathers of newborns receive paid leave. This is in contrast to standard practice in many other nations, including many developing countries, and every other industrialized country, all of which provide some variation of a statutory maternity leave or parental benefit.[54]

TABLE 31
MARRIED, SEPARATED AND DIVORCED WOMEN IN LABOR FORCE WHO HAVE CHILDREN UNDER AGE SIX

	Married		Separated		Divorced	
	number (million)	percent	number (million)	percent	number (million)	percent
1960	2.5	18.6	n/a	n/a	n/a	n/a
1970	3.9	30.3	.3	45.4	.3	63.3
1980	5.2	45.1	.4	52.2	.5	68.3
1985	6.4	53.4	.4	53.2	.6	67.5
1986	6.6	53.8	.5	57.4	.7	73.8

Source: U.S. Bureau of Labor Statistics, *Special Labor Force Reports*, Nos. 13, 130 & 134, Bulletin 2163, and unpublished data. Reported in *Statistical Abstract of the United States: 1987*. 107th edition. U.S. Bureau of the Census. Washington, D.C. 1986. P. 383, Table 654.

TABLE 32
CHILDREN BY MOTHER'S EMPLOYMENT IN 1984
(percent distribution)

Age of Child	Full time	Part time	Not in labor force
0-5	20%	38%	39%

Source: Analysis by Child Trends, Inc., of public use data from the Census Bureau's March 1985 Current Population Survey. Tabulations produced by Technical Support Staff, Office of the Assistant Secretary for Planning and Evaluation, U.S. Department of Health and Human Services. Reported in *U.S. Children and Their Families: Current Conditions and Recent Trends, 1987*, "A Report Together With Additional Views of the Select Committee on Children, Youth and Families." U.S. House of Representatives, 100th Congress, 1st Session. Washington, D.C.: U.S. Government Printing Office, March, 1987. p. 17.

TABLE 33
PRIMARY CHILD CARE ARRANGEMENTS USED BY EMPLOYED MOTHERS FOR THEIR CHILDREN UNDER FIVE, BY AGE, DECEMBER, 1984 THROUGH MARCH, 1985

	Under 1	1–2	3–4
Care in her home	+	+	+
by father	18.2%	16.2%	14.3%
by grandparent	7.4	6.4	4.5
	>37.3	>32.8	>27.1
by other relative	3.2	4.5	3.3
by non-relative	8.5	5.7	5.0
	–	–	–
Care in other home	+	+	+
by grandparent	12.6	11.0	8.5
by other relative	5.1 >40.7	4.0 >41.8	4.7 >30.9
by non-relative	23.0	26.8	17.7
	–	–	–
Group care	+	+	+
day care center	8.4	12.3	17.8
nursery school	5.7 >14.1	5.0 >17.3	14.4 >33.9
kindergarten/grade school	—	—	1.7
	–	–	–
Mother cares for child while working	8.1	8.2	8.1

Source: U.S. Bureau of the Census, Current Population Reports, Series P-70, No. 9, *Who's Minding the Kids? Childcare Arrangements: 1984–85,* Washington, D.C.: U.S. Government Printing Office, 1987, p. 5, Table D.

Child Care. More than half of all U.S. children under age six now have mothers in the labor force. That percentage represents a dramatic change over the past 25 years. The pattern of increase in working mothers holds for those who are married, separated and divorced, but the rate is almost half again as high for children whose mothers are divorced as it is for children whose mothers are married.

Almost twice as many mothers of children five years old and younger work part-time as work full-time. (Part-time includes "part-time, full-year," "full-time, part-year" and "part-time, part-year.")

Almost four-fifths of families with children two and under where the mother works choose child care in a home setting (either the child's own home or another home). By age three, the number choosing group care more than doubles. Nineteen percent of family day care providers have an eighth grade education or less. Ninety-four percent of family day care is informal and unregulated.[55] Only three states comply with the proposed 1979 federal regulations for adult:child ratios in center based care.[56] There is a trend toward greater use of group care for very young children. The percentage of working women using group care for children under one year of age almost tripled from 1982 to 1985.

Children in preschool and kindergarten. Paralleling increases in use of child care, the number of children three to five years of age who are enrolled in nursery school and kindergarten has increased by almost 50% in 15 years. The increase has been most striking for black children. The increase in nursery school enrollment, though still much less than kindergarten, has grown the fastest. An important contributor to pre-primary enrollment is the increase in children being served by Head Start. Unfortunately, however, overall the children who probably could benefit most from early education are

TABLE 34

COMPARISON OF PRIMARY CHILD CARE ARRANGEMENTS BY WORKING WOMEN FOR THEIR CHILDREN UNDER ONE YEAR OF AGE

(PERCENT)

	June 1982	December 1984–March 1985
Care in our own home:		
by father	13.9%	18.2%
by grandparent	8.9	7.4
by other relative	5.1	3.2
by non-relative	6.4	8.5
Care in other home:		
by grandparent	13.5	12.6
by other relative	6.2	5.1
by non-relative	23.0	23.0
Group care:	+	+
nursery school	1.7% >5.3	57.0% >14.1
day care center	3.6	8.4
Mother cares for child while working	9.2	8.1
Don't know/no answer	8.6	not included

Source: Martin O'Connell and Carolyn C. Rogers, "Child Care Arrangements of Working Mothers: June 1982." *Current Population Reports.* Series P.23, No. 129. Bureau of the Census, November, 1983, p. 22.

Source: U.S. Bureau of the Census, Current Population Reports, Series P-70, No. 9, *Who's Minding the Kids? Childcare Arrangements: 1984–85,* U.S. Government Printing Office, Washington, D.C., 1987, p. 5, Table D.

less likely to be receiving it. Pre-primary enrollment is higher when parents' education is greater.

Nutrition assistance for impoverished pregnant women and for children. There has been a significant increase in federal expenditures on nutrition supplements for women who are pregnant and for

TABLE 35
PRE-PRIMARY SCHOOL ENROLLMENT 3–5 YRS. (1970–85)
(millions)

	1970	1975	1980	1985
	4.1	5.0	4.9	5.9
White	3.4	4.1	4.0	4.8
Black	.58	.73	.72	.92
All-Nursery School	1.1	1.7	2.0	2.5
All Kindergarten	3.0	3.2	2.9	3.4

Source: U.S. Bureau of the Census, *Current Population Reports*, series P-20, No. 318; and unpublished data, reported in *Statistical Abstract of the United States: 1987*, 107th edition, U.S. Bureau of the census, Washington, D.C., 1986, p. 119.

TABLE 36
PERCENT CHANGE IN ENROLLMENT 1970–86

Age	Percent Change
Three–Six year olds	+ 48%
Three year olds	+144
Four year olds	+ 85

Source: U.S. Department of Education, Center for Education Statistics, *The Condition of Education, 1985 Edition*, 1986. Table 1.3. For details of projection methodology, see *Projections of Education Statistics to 1992–1993*, 1985.

TABLE 37
HEAD START ENROLLMENT 1970–1985
(thousands)

	1970	1975	1980	1982	1985
Enrollment	229	292	362	396	452
Federal appropriation:					
Current $	326 mill.	441 mill.	735 mill.	912 mill	1.075 mill.

Source: U.S. Bureau of the Census, *Statistical Abstract of the United States, 1982–83*, Table 563; and *U.S. Children and Their Families: Current Conditions and Recent Trends, 1987*, "A Report Together with Additional Views of the Select Committee on Children, Youth, and Families," U.S. House of Representatives, 100th Congress, 1st Session, U.S. Government Printing Office, March 1987, p. 91.

young children who are poor. The research data correlating improved nutrition with a lower incidence of low birth weight births and infant mortality has affected both federal and state appropriations for these programs. Thus funding increased for both the Special Supplemental Feeding Program for Women, Infants and Children

TABLE 38
ENROLLMENT RATE IN 1985 IN NURSERY SCHOOL OR KINDERGARTEN, BASED ON MOTHER'S LEVEL OF EDUCATION

	White	Black	Hispanic
<8 Years	40.9	42.4	39.0
One–Three Years HS	40.4	53.1	41.0
High School Graduate	52.9	56.8	41.8
College One–Three years	61.8	59.7	62.6
College graduate (4 years or more)	67.8	63.2	too small to be counted

Source: U.S. Bureau of the Census, *Current Population Reports*, series P-20, No. 318; and unpublished data, reported in U.S. Bureau of the Census, *Statistical Abstract of the United States: 1987*, 107th edition, Washington, D.C., 1986, p. 119.

YOUNG CHILDREN IN FOSTER CARE

In 1984 more than one quarter of a million children were in foster care. 3.3% of these were under one year of age. 21.2% were between the ages of one and five.

Source: Toshi Tatara. *Characteristics of Children in Substitute and Adoptive Care*. Washington, D.C.: American Public Welfare Association. June, 1987. pp. 62–63.

TABLE 39
NUMBER OF PEOPLE FED AND DOLLARS SPENT THROUGH WIC AND RELATED PROGRAMS
(millions)

	1975	1980	1985
Number participating	.5	2.0	3.3
$ expended	$94	$603	$1,235 billion

Source: U.S. Department of Agriculture, Food and Nutrition Service. In *Agricultural Statistics*, annual; and unpublished data, reported in *Statistical Abstract of the United States: 1987*, 107th edition, U.S. Bureau of the Census, Washington, D.C., 1986, p. 111.

TABLE 40
NUMBER OF CHILDREN FED AND DOLLARS SPENT
THROUGH CHILD CARE FOOD PROGRAMS

	1970	1980	1985
Number Participating	.1 million	.7 million	1.0 million
$ Expended	$6 million	$210 million	$389 million

Source: U.S. Department of Agriculture, Food and Nutrition Service. In *Agricultural Statistics*, annual; and unpublished data, reported in *Statistical Abstract of the United States: 1987*, 107th edition, U.S. Bureau of the Census, Washington, D.C., 1986, p. 111.

TABLE 41

PERCENT BREASTFED	1983
all infants	61.4
white infants	64
Hispanic infants	54
black infants	32
all infants born into families earning less than $10,000	44
black infants born into families earning less than $10,000	20

Source: *Report of the Surgeon General's Workshop on Breastfeeding and Human Lactation.* U.S. Department of Health and Human Services, June, 1984. Data from the National Center for Health Statistics and the Ross Laboratory Mothers Survey.

(WIC) and the Commodity Supplemental Food Program since 1975. Nonetheless, appropriations barely kept even with inflation. In 1986, according to Children's Defense Fund estimates, WIC served only 40% of eligible women and children. In 11 states, fewer than one-third of eligible women and children were served. The Child Care Food Program, a program which provides year-round subsidies to feed preschool children in child care centers and family day care homes, has also increased substantially in the past ten years. Even accounting for inflation, it is clear that not only the numbers of children but the amount spent on each child has increased. In 1985 the Department of Agriculture provided 22.9 million meals to day care homes and 37.1 million meals to child care centers.[57]

Availability of the healthiest nutritional start for infants at birth and in the earliest months of life—breastfeeding—varies by race and income.

Immunization of young children. Statistics on the percentage of infants and preschool children who are immunized against the major childhood diseases are difficult to assess. The federal government has not resolved exactly how best to estimate, and it has made changes in how the estimate is made in the past few years. Currently it is a measure based on those who can produce written shot records. One fact is clear: the requirement that children have a full set of immunizations before entering school has greatly improved the percentages of children immunized at age six or above. Younger children (including those with written shot records and those without) appear to have

TABLE 42
IMMUNIZATION OF CHILDREN ENTERING SCHOOL

	DPT	Polio	Measles	Rubella	Mumps
1980–81 school year	96	95	96	96	92
1984–85 school year	97	96	98	98	97

Source: U.S. Public Health Service, Centers for Disease Control, Division of Immunization. Data from Annual School Entered Assessment. Reported in *U.S. Children and Their Families: Current Conditions and Recent Trends, 1987*, "A Report Together with Additional Views of the Select Committee on Children, Youth, and Families," U.S. House of Representatives, 100th Congress, 1st Session, U.S. Government Printing Office, March 1987, p. 57.

TABLE 43
CHILDREN AGED ONE–FOUR: PERCENT IMMUNIZED

	DPT	Polio	Measles	Rubella	Mumps
1980	66.3	58.8	63.5	63.5	56.6
1984	65.7	54.8	62.8	60.9	58.7
1985	64.9	55.3	60.8	58.9	58.9

Source: U.S. Center for Disease Control, Atlanta, GA, United States Immunization Survey, annual. Reported in *Statistical Abstracts of the United States: 1987*, 107th Edition. Washington, D.C., U.S. Bureau of the Census, 1986. p. 102, Table 162.

TABLE 44
CHILDREN AGED ONE–FOUR: PERCENT IMMUNIZED 1985
BY RACE

	DPT	Polio	Measles	Rubella	Mumps
White	68.7	58.9	63.6	61.6	61.8
Black and other	48.7	40.1	48.8	47.7	47.0

Source: Division of Immunization, Center for Prevention Services, Centers for Disease Control: Unpublished data from the United States Immunization Survey, reported in *Health, United States, 1986*. National Center for Health Statistics: DHHS Pub. No. (PHS) 87-1232. Public Health Service. Washington. U.S. Government Printing Office, December 1986, p. 119.

TABLE 45

CHILDREN AGED ONE–FOUR: Percent Immunized, 1985,
By Location

	DPT	Polio	Measles	Rubella	Mumps
Central City	55.5	47.1	55.5	53.9	52.4
Metropolitan areas					
(not central city)	68.4	58.4	63.3	61.0	61.0
Rural	67.9	58.0	61.9	60.3	61.4

Source: Center for Prevention Services, Centers for Disease Control, (see Table 43).

TABLE 46

COMPARISON OF NUMBER AND DOLLARS SPENT ON AFDC
CHILDREN BY MEDICAID, 1972–1985

	1972	1975	1980	1983	1985
% Recipients	44.5	43.7	43.2	43.8	44.7
% $ Spent	18.1	17.9	13.4	11.8	11.8

Source: Bureau of Data Management and Strategy, Health Care Financing Administration: Unpublished data, reported in National Center for Health Statistics: Prevention profile, by P. M. Golden. *Health, United States, 1986.* DHHS Pub. No. (PHS) 87-1232. Public Health Service. Washington. U.S. Government Printing Office, December 1986, p. 207.

a much lower incidence of immunization. Furthermore, the percent has been decreasing for almost all kinds of immunizations. The percentages of white children immunized are significantly higher than percentages of non-white children, and suburban children have higher immunization rates than do inner city or rural children of preschool age.

Health Insurance for small children. In 1985, 15% of all women who gave birth did so with no public or private insurance coverage at time of delivery. Those who were eligible for public coverage represented a smaller percentage of the Medicaid dollar than might be expected.[58] Also in 1985, children on welfare comprised 44.7% of Medicaid recipients; yet only 11.8% of Medicaid dollars spent were spent on them. This percentage has gone down over the past decade. Thus, though the percentage of children receiving Medicaid benefits has remained quite constant, the percent of Medicaid dollars has fallen by one third.

In fact, health insurance of any kind fails to cover almost one fifth of our nation's youngest children. It covers significantly fewer children under age six than older children. Recent legislation for the first time allows Medicaid coverage for young children in families that are below the federal poverty line but not necessarily on AFDC, in states which choose to adopt it. Its impact will be watched closely.

Visits to physicians. Most children under five years of age do see a physician with some frequency. In 1985 only a small percent (1.9%) under age six had not visited a physician in two years, though 6.2%

TABLE 47
HEALTH CARE ACCORDING TO TYPE OF COVERAGE AND AGE OF CHILD
(Percent of Population)

	Private Insurance	Medicaid (AFDC & SSI)	Not Covered (By private or public insurance of any kind)
1980:			
Children under 6 years	71.0	12.0	14.7
Children 6–16 years	77.3	8.7	11.8
1982:			
Children under 6 years	70.1	11.2	16.9
Children 6–16 years	74.9	8.4	15.0
1984:			
Children under 6 years	67.5	13.0	17.3
Children 6–16 years	74.2	8.5	14.7

Note: Persons with both private insurance and Medicaid appear in both columns.
Source: National Center for Health Statistics. *Health, United States, 1986*. DHHS Pub. No. (PHS) 87-1232. Public Health Service. Washington, D.C.: U.S. Government Printing Office, December, 1986, p. 202.

TABLE 48
AVERAGE NUMBER OF ANNUAL PHYSICIAN VISITS IN 1985, BY AGE

Under Five Years of Age	6.7 per child
Ages 5–17 years	3.3 per child

Source: Calculated from: National Center for Health Statistics. "Current Estimates from the National Health Interview Survey, United States, 1985," *Vital and Health Statistics*, Series 10, No. 160, Table 71 and 72, by Select Committee on Children, Youth, and Families, U.S. House of Representatives, 100th Congress, and reported in *U.S. Children and Their Families: Current Conditions and Recent Trends, 1987*. Washington, D.C.: U.S. Government Printing Office, 1987. p. 62.

TABLE 49

PERCENTAGE OF CHILDREN UNDER SIX YEARS CONTACT
WITH PHYSICIANS, BY TYPE OF CONTACT

	1983	1985
Doctor's Office	54.3	57.0
Hospital Outpatient (clinic, emergency room)	12.8	13.6
Phone	20.6	18.3

Source: Division of Health Interview Statistics, National Center for Health Statistics: Data from the National Health Interview Survey. Reported in *Health, U.S., 1986*. National Center for Health Statistics. DHHS Pub. No. (PHS) 87-1232. Public Health Service. Washington, D.C.: U.S. Government Printing Office. December 1986. p. 137, Table 52.

TABLE 50

PERCENTAGE OF CHILDREN UNDER AGE SIX WHO HAVE
NEVER VISITED A DENTIST

1964	1978	1983
80.4	74.3	70.5

Source: National Center for Health Statistics, (see Table 49), p. 141, Table 56.

TABLE 51

STATE HEALTH AGENCY ASSESSMENTS FOR INFANTS AND
PRESCHOOLERS IN 1984

	Infants
Physical assessments (23 states)	373,700
Developmental Assessments (12 states)	168,000
Nutritional Assessments	186,000

Source: Public Health Foundation, *Public Health Agencies 1984: Services for Mothers and Children*, Vol. 3, January 1987, pp. 8 & 10.

under five had not visited a physician for more than a year. The majority of children under six years see physicians in their own offices, though a significant number have visits in hospital clinics or by phone consultation. Dentistry, however, remains a luxury for most of America's children under age six.

State public health activities. States vary greatly in the amount and type of screening and assessment they do for needy children. Twice as many states screen for phenylketonuria, for example, as for sickle cell anemia, even though the incidence of the latter is much higher.

In general, however, states have become more and more active in developing public programs to support neonatal screening for selected genetic and metabolic disorders. Programs to screen for lead poisoning have been much reduced, since they have lost federal funding.

Care for handicapping conditions. Though there has been an enormous increase in interest within state health departments in tracking infants born with known defects and other risk factors, there is no

TABLE 52
STATE AGENCIES WHICH PROVIDED SCREENING FOR
SELECTED GENETIC AND METABOLIC DISEASES IN 1984

Phenylketonuria	47
Hypothyroidism	47
Galactosemia	34
Thalassemia	13
Maple Syrup Urine Disease	22
Honeystinuria	23
Sickle Cell Anemia	27
Tyrosinemia	14

Source: Public Health Foundation, (see Table 51), p. 9, Fig. E.

TABLE 53
CHILDREN SERVED BY CRIPPLED CHILDREN'S SERVICES—
1984 (35 STATE AGENCIES REPORTING)

	# children served	% of total served
birth to 1 year	36,833	7.6%
1–4 years	141,647	29.3%

Source: Public Health Foundation, *Public Health Agencies 1984: Services for Mothers and Children*, Vol. 3, January 1987, pp. 18–19.

TABLE 54
ENROLLMENT IN PRESCHOOL PROGRAMS FOR CHILDREN
WITH HANDICAPPING CONDITIONS

	number of children served
1976–77	196,223
1980–81	233,793
1984–85	259,483
1985–86	260,513

Source: U.S. Dept. of Education, *Eighth Annual Report to Congress on the Implementation of the Education of the Handicapped Act*, 1986; *Ninth Annual Report*, 1987, pp. E-5—E-22.

uniform system of follow up. Some states have several systems, operating regionally and tracking different risks. 42 states either have
some kind of system or are developing one. However, only in six states
is the system tied to follow-up service delivery.[59]

The record of the number and percent of children with handicapping conditions served by Title V or Crippled Children's Services in
1984 is incomplete. Only 35 states have reported these services.[60] The
higher proportion in percent of children served between ages one
and four indicates that relatively few handicapping conditions are
found and treated during the first years.

The number of preschool children with handicaps served by education programs for the handicapped has risen sharply in the past
ten years. With the passage of PL 99-457, the amendment to the
Education for the Handicapped Act which mandates services to
preschool children and offers states funds for services for children
from birth, the number is likely to continue to rise dramatically over
the next few years. Present figures represent an increase of more
than 33% over the figures of a decade ago.[61]

Services to children who are abused or neglected. Whereas the
number of children reported to have been abused or neglected rose
over 50% between 1981 and 1985, total resources to serve abused and
neglected children increased, in real terms, by less than two percent
between 1981 and 1985.[62] And, despite recorded increases in child
abuse and family disruption, there is no data kept by the federal
government on use of psychological services by children under three
years of age, undoubtedly because very few exist.

Of children three to five years, 208,000 had received psychological
services in 1981, out of a population of 10.4 million children. This
represented two percent of all children age three–five and six percent
of all children who received psychological help.[63]

NOTES

1. The most notable gap in data is information on the mental health status
of very young children. We have virtually no idea how many are experiencing
major compromises to their mental health before age four or five. Our only
evidence comes from figures on child abuse, undoubtedly long after a child's
social and emotional health is endangered; and even abuse figures are kept
in a highly unsystematic way.

2. Arnold J. Sameroff, Ronald Seifer, Ralph Barocas, Melvin Zax and
Stanley Greenspan: "Intelligence Quotient Scores of 4 Year Old Children:
Socioenvironmental Risk Factors," *Pediatrics*, Vol. 79, No. 3, March 1987.

3. For example, the U.S. compares unfavorably to most European countries in home visiting services after birth.

4. Only three states comply with a recommended child staff ratio for caring for infants.

5. U.S. Bureau of the Census, *Current Population Reports,* Series P-25. Reported *in* Statistical Abstract of the United States: 1987 (107th edition), Washington, D.C.: U.S. Bureau of the Census, 1986, p. 14.

6. They made up 6.6% of the population in the Northeast; 7.6% in the Midwest and South; and 8.4% of the population in the West. U.S. Bureau of the census, *Current Population Reports,* Series P-25, No. 952 and U.S. Bureau of the Census, *Current Population Reports,* Series P-25, forthcoming report.

7. U.S. Bureau of the Census, *Current Population Reports,* P-60, Nos. 149, 151, 152, and P-20, No. 403.

8. 3,731,000 infants are estimated to have been born in 1986, a birth rate of 15.5 per 1,000. This increase occurred because the total number of women of childbearing age increased by one percent in 1986. National Center for Health Statistics: Annual summary of births, marriages, divorces, and deaths, United States, 1986. *Monthly Vital Statistics Report,* Vol. 35, No. 13. DHHS Pub. No. (PHS) 87-1120. Hyattsville, MD., Public Health Service, Aug. 24, 1987, p. 1.

9. National Center for Health Statistics: Advance Report of Final Natality Statistics, 1985. *Monthly Vital Statistics Report,* Vol. 36, No. 4. Supp. DHHS Pub. No. 87-1120. Hyattsville, MD., Public Health Service, July 17, 1987, p. 13, Table 1.

10. Births to American Indians have increased by 54% since 1970. National Center for Health Statistics, S. Taffel: Characteristics of American Indian and Alaska Native Births, United States, 1984. *Monthly Vital Statistics Report,* Vol. 36, No. 3, Supp. DHHS Pub. No. (PHS) 87-1120. Hyattsville, MD., Public Health Service, June 19, 1987, p. 1.

11. Births to Chinese, Japanese, Filipinos and other Asian and Pacific Islanders all rose in the 1980s. In 1982 the fertility rate of Hispanics was 96 per 1,000 live births; the fertility rate of non-Hispanics was 65 per 1,000 live births. U.S. House of Representatives, 100th Congress, 1st Session, *U.S. Children and Their Families: Current Conditions and Recent Trends, 1987,* "A Report together with Additional Views of the Select Committee on Children, Youth, and Families," Washington, D.C.: U.S. Government Printing Office, March 1987, p. 5.

12. In 1984, 17% of Hispanic births were to teenager mothers; 12% of non-Hispanic births were to teenager mothers. National Center for Health Statistics, S. J. Ventura: Births of Hispanic parentage, 1983 and 1984, *Monthly Vital Statistics Report,* Vol. 36, No. 4, Supp. (2). DHHS Pub. No. (PHS) 87-1120. Hyattsville, MD., Public Health Service, July 24, 1987, p. 2.

13. U.S.-born Hispanics are most likely to give birth as teenagers than are foreign born Hispanics but less likely to have fourth or fifth children. *Ibid,* pp. 1–2.

14. National Center for Health Statistics, S. J. Ventura: Births of Hispanic Parentage, 1983 and 1984, *Monthly Vital Statistics Report,* Vol. 36, No. 4, Supp.

(2). DHHS Pub. No. (PHS) 87-1120. Hyattsville, MD., Public Health Service, July 24, 1987, p. 1.

15. NCHS, *Advance Natality Statistics, Monthly Vital Statistics Report 1984*, Vol. 35, Supp. 4, July 1986, p. 17 and earlier reports.

16. Approximately one million abortions were performed annually to women ages 15–24 in the early 1980s. Abortions terminated 45% of all teenage pregnancies and 31% of all pregnancies to women 20–24 years old. The birth rate fell faster for black teenagers than for white. National Center for Health Statistics: Advance report of final natality statistics, 1985. *Monthly Vital Statistics Report*, Vol. 36, No. 4, Supp. DHHS Pub. No. 87-1120. Hyattsville, MD., Public Health Service, July 17,1987, p. 14, Table 2.

17. 25% of all births in 1985 were to women age 30 and over. *Ibid.*, p. 1.

18. National Center for Health Statistics: Advance Report of Final Natality Statistics, 1985. *Monthly Vital Statistics Report*, Vol. 36, No. 4, Supp. DHHS Pub. No. (PHS) 87-1120. Public Health Service, Hyattsville, Md., July 17, 1987, pp. 31–33, Tables 18 & 19.

19. National Center for Health Statistics: Advance Report of Final Natality Statistics, 1985. *Monthly Vital Statistics Report*, Vol. 36, No. 4, Supp. DHHS, Pub. No. 87-1120. Public Health Service, Hyattsville, MD., July 17, 1987, p. 7.

20. *Ibid.*, pp. 32–33, Table 19.

21. *Ibid.*, p. 7.

22. The percentage of unmarried Hispanic women giving birth varies greatly with the country of derivation: In 1984, it ranged from:

• 51% of births among women of Puerto Rican extraction
• 34% of births to Central and South American women
• 24% of births to Mexican women
• 16% of births to Cuban women

National Center for Health Statistics, S. J. Ventura: Births of Hispanic Parentage, 1983 and 1984, *Monthly Vital Statistics Report*, Vol. 36, No. 4. Supp. (2). DHHS Pub. No. (PHS) 87-1120. Public Health Service, Hyattsville, Md., July 24, 1987, p. 3.

23. U.S. Bureau of the Census, Dept. of Commerce. *Fertility of American Women: June 1985*, Washington, D.C., Government Printing Office, 1986, Series P-20, No. 406, pp. 13–14.

24. U.S. Bureau of the Census, Current Population Reports, Series P-60, No. 158, *Poverty in the United States: 1985*, Washington, D.C.: U.S. Government Printing Office, 1987, p. 3. Table B.

25. Bureau of Commerce, *Fertility of American Women: June 1985*, Washington, D.C., Government Printing Office, 1986, Series P-20, No. 406, p. 8.

26. U.S. Bureau of the Census, *Current Population Reports*, Series P-20, No. 411, and earlier reports.

27. Sheldon Danziger and Peter Gottschalk, "How Have Families with Children Been Fairing?" Discussion Paper No. 801-86, Madison, Wisconsin: Institute for Research on Poverty, University of Wisconsin, 1986, Table 5.

28. National Center for Health Statistics: Advance Report of Final Natality

Statistics, 1985. *Monthly Vital Statistics Report*, Vol. 36, No. 4. Supp. DHHS Pub. No. 87-1120. Public Health Service, Hyattsville, Md., July 17, 1987, p. 8.

29. Kate Prager, *et al.*, "Maternal Smoking and Drinking Behavior Before and During Pregnancy," *Health: United States and Prevention Profile*, 1983, U.S. Department of Health and Human Services. Public Health Service. Data taken from 1980 Natality Survey. p. 20.

30. Medical Research Institute of San Francisco, Alcohol Research Group, Berkeley, CA, unpublished data, reported in U.S. Bureau of the Census, *Statistical Abstract of the United States: 1987*, 107th edition, Washington, D.C., 1986, p. 106, Table 173.

31. "Public Information Campaign," *National Institute on Alcohol Abuse and Alcoholism*, p. 1. Data from the Centers for Disease Control.

32. Ira J. Chasnoff, Director, Perinatal Center for Chemical Dependence, Northwestern Memorial Hospital, Chicago, IL., 1988.

33. National Center for Health Statistics: Advance Report of Final Natality Statistics, 1985. *Monthly Vital Statistics Report*, Vol. 36, No. 4. Supp. DHHS Pub. No. 87-1120. Public Health Service, Hyattsville, Md., July 17, 1987, p. 27, Table 15.

34. *The State of the World's Children 1985*. United Nations Children's Fund, p. 115.

35. *Preventing Low Birth Weight*. Committee to Study the Prevention of Low Birth Weight, Institute of Medicine, Washington, D.C., 1985, p. 29.

36. Marie McCormick, M.D. "The Contribution of Low Birth Weight to Infant Mortality and Childhood Morbidity." *New England Journal of Medicine*, V. 312, No. 2, January 10, 1985, p. 84. Data from the Robert Wood Johnson Foundation.

37. National Center for Health Statistics: Advance Report of Final Natality Statistics, 1985. *Monthly Vital Statistics Report*, Vol. 36, No. 4, Supp. DHHS Pub. No. 87-1120. Public Health Service, Hyattsville, MD., July 17, 1987, p. 28, Table 15.

38. Joel C. Kleinman & Samuel S. Kessel, "Racial Differences in Low Birth Weight." *New England Journal of Medicine*, Vol. 317, September 17, 1987, pp. 749–753.

39. McCormack, *op cit.*

40. *Percent of Infants Born Premature in 1984*

All	9.6%
All Hispanics	10.4%
Non-Hispanic Whites	7.6%
Non-Hispanic Blacks	16.8%

National Center for Health Statistics, S. J. Ventura: Births of Hispanic Parentage, 1983 and 1984, *Monthly Vital Statistics Report*, Vol. 36, No. 4, Supp. (2). DHHS Pub. No. (PHS) 87-1120. Public Health Service. Hyattsville, Md., July 24, 1987, p. 17, Table 13.

41. "Infant mortality" is the death of live-born children who have not reached their first birthday and is usually expressed as a rate (i.e., the number

of infant deaths during a year per 1,000 live births reported in the year). This is frequently broken down into "neonatal mortality"—death before 28 days of life; and "postneonatal mortality"—from 28 days to one year. National Center for Health Statistics: *Health United States, 1986.* DHHS Pub. No. (PHS) 87-1232. Public Health Service. Washington, D.C., U.S. Government Printing Office, December 1986. p. 230.

42. J. William Flynt, M.D., *et al., State Surveillance of Birth Defects and Other Adverse Reproductive Effects,* Washington, D.C.: U.S. Dept. of Health & Human Services, April 1987, p. 1.

43. Division of Health Interview Statistics, National Center for Health Statistics: Data from the National Health Interview Survey. Reported in National Center for Health Statistics: Health, United States, 1986. DHHS Pub. No. (PHS) 87-1232. Public Health Service. Washington, D.C.: U.S. Government Printing Office, December 1986, p. 123, Table 38; and *U.S. Children and Their Families: Current Conditions and Recent Trends, 1987,* "A Report Together with Additional Views of the Select Committee on Children, Youth, and Families," U.S. House of Representatives, 100th Congress, 1st Session, U.S. Government Printing Office, March 1987, p. 3.

PERCENTAGE OF CHILDREN UNDER SIX YEARS OLD WITH SOME KIND OF PHYSICAL LIMITATION OF ACTIVITY, 1983 & 1985

	Total with limit	Limited but not in major activity	Limited in amount or kind of major activity	Unable to carry on major activity
1983	2.4	0.6	1.3	0.5
1985	2.6	0.7	1.4	0.5

44. The American Humane Association, under contract to the federal government's National Center for Child Abuse and Neglect has sampled five states' reporting in depth. They have found that only 52.9% of all reported cases of child abuse and neglect were substantiated. (Nonetheless, a significant portion of the remaining 47.1% unsubstantiated could be actual, unverified cases. Other actual cases go unreported.)

In addition, the National Center for Child Abuse and Neglect has funded a National Incidence Study (NIS-2), just published (*Study of National Incidence and Prevalence of Child Abuse and Neglect: 1988,* Washington, D.C.) This study uses different methodology, eliminating duplicate reports and relying on voluntary responses. Though the reported incidence estimates are lower by this sampling procedure, they reflect a significant increase over 1980. They also confirm the fact that abuse of very young children is more likely to be fatal.

45. *Everything You Always Wanted to Know About Child Abuse and Neglect.* Washington, D.C.: Clearinghouse on Child Abuse and Neglect Information.

46. American Association for Protecting Children, Inc., *Highlights of Official Child Neglect and Abuse Reporting, 1985,* Denver, Colorado: The American Humane Association, 1987, p. 20.

47. And, as the recent study of the Office of Technology Assessment points out,

"Although defining and establishing criteria for mental disorders is useful, it can mean that children with subclinical mental health problems, or those in danger of developing a disorder, may not be considered to be in need of mental health services."

U.S. Congress, Office of Technology Assessment, *Children's Mental Health: Problems and Services—A Background Paper*, OTA-BP-H-33, Washington, DC: U.S. Government Printing Office, December 1986, p. 49.

48. National Center for Health Statistics: Advance Report of Final Natality Statistics, 1985. *Monthly Vital Statistics Report*, Vol. 36, No. 4. Supp. DHHS Pub. No. 87-1120. Public Health Service, Hyattsville, Md., July 17, 1987, p. 9 and p. 38, Table 25; and National Center for Health Statistics, S. J. Ventura: Births of Hispanic parentage, 1983 and 1984, *Monthly Vital Statistics Report*, Vol. 36, No. 4, Supp. (2). DHHS Pub. No. (PHS) 87-1120. Public Health Service. Hyattsville, Md., July 24, 1987, p. 4.

49. National Center for Health Statistics: Advance Report of Final Natality Statistics, 1985. *Monthly Vital Statistics Report*, Vol. 36, No. 4. Supp. DHHS Pub. No. 87-1120. Public Health Service, Hyattsville, Md., July 17, 1987, p. 9.

50. These include transport privileges, early booking for delivery, paid maternity leave, birthing bonuses, family allowances and home visitors. (Two countries actually withhold benefits from women who have *not* preregistered for early prenatal care.) C. Arden Miller, *Maternal Health & Infant Survival*. National Center for Clinical Infant Programs, Washington, D.C., 1987, pp. 4–5.

51. Office of Technology Assessment: "Neonatal Intensive Care for Low Birthweight Infants: Costs & Effectiveness." Washington, D.C., December 1987.

52. *European countries with a home visiting system.**

For special indications		Always at least one
	Denmark	x
	Ireland	x
	Netherlands	x**
	Norway	x
	Switzerland	x
	United Kingdom	x
	Belgium	x
x	Federal Republic of Germany	
x	France	

*Spain is presently instituting such a system as well
**Netherlands has a maternity care worker for eight hours a day through the 10th day at home.

C. Arden Miller, *Maternal Health & Infant Survival*. National Center for Clinical Infant Programs, Washington, D.C., 1987, p. 24.

53. Sheila B. Kammerman, and Alfred J. Kahn. *The Responsive Workplace: Employers and a Changing Labor Force.* NY: Columbia University Press, 1987, p. 56.

54. Sheila B. Kammerman, Alfred J. Kahn and Paul Kingston. *Maternity Policies and Working Women.* NY: Columbia University Press, 1983.

55. Development Services. *Family Day Care in the United States: Summary of Findings.* A Final Report of the National Day Care Home Study, September, 1981, p. 45.

56. Gwen Morgan, *The National State of Child Care Regulation 1986.* Watertown, MA, Work-Family Directions Inc., 1987.

57. Food & Nutrition Service, U.S. Department of Agriculture. *Food Program Update for May 1985.* Program Information Division/PRAB August 1985. This program requires receiving centers to take part in training workshops and serves as a valuable incentive to family day care providers to become registered and trained.

58. The Alan Guttmacher Institute, *Blessed Events and the Bottom Line: Financing Maternity Care in the United States.* New York: Alan Guttmacher Institute, 1987.

59. J. William, M.D., *et al., State Surveillance of Birth Defects and Other Adverse Reproductive Effects,* U.S. Dept. of Health & Human Services, April 1987.

60. *Ibid.*

61. *Ninth Annual Report,* 1987, p. E-5, p. 4.

62. U.S. House of Representatives, 100th Congress, 1st Session, *Child Abuse and Neglect in America: The Problem and the Response,* "Hearing before the Select Committee on Children, Youth, and Families," U.S. Government Printing Office, March 1987, p. 3.

63. Analysis by Child Trends, Inc. of public use data from the Child Health Supplement to the 1981 National Health Interview Survey and Cycle III of the Health Examination Survey, 1966–70. Data collected by the National Center for Health Statistics, Divisions of Health Interview Statistics and Health Examination Statistics. Reported in *U.S. Children and Their Families: Current Conditions and Recent Trends, 1987,* "A Report Together with Additional Views of the Select Committee on Children, Youth, and Families," U.S. House of Representatives, 100th Congress, 1st Session, Washington, D.C.: U.S. Government Printing Office, March 1987, p. 66.

RECENT DEVELOPMENTS IN INFANT AND CHILD HEALTH: HEALTH STATUS, INSURANCE COVERAGE AND TRENDS IN PUBLIC HEALTH POLICY

Sara Rosenbaum

MOST AMERICAN CHILDREN are born healthy and grow into thriving and productive young adults. But a significant, disproportionately low-income percentage suffer from serious health problems. Furthermore, given the strong association between poverty and ill health among children, the steep and sustained rise in childhood poverty during the 1980s has placed increasing numbers of children at medical risk. Additionally, because minority children are far more likely to be poor, their health status measurements are particularly troubling.[1] While Congress and the states have taken notable steps in recent years to address the health needs of poor children, the reforms represent only the first modest steps in a long-term effort.

The health problems associated with poverty and deprivation are well documented. Indeed, while there is some ambiguity about whether poverty causes, or is merely associated with, reduced health status among adults, its causal link to children's reduced health status is far clearer.[2] Poor children are twice as likely as non-poor children to be born at low birth weight (less than 5.5 pounds), a condition which increases by 20 times the likelihood of death during infancy.[3] Low birth weight also increases the risk of lifelong disabilities such as cerebral palsy, retardation, blindness, or vision, learning and hearing impairments.[4]

Poor children suffer higher rates of mortality from all causes, including low birth weight, neoplasms, respiratory impairments, congenital anomalies, accidents, poisonings and violence.[5] Poor children are far more likely than non-poor children to be limited in major life activities because of chronic illnesses or disabilities.[6] Furthermore, when illness and disability do strike, childhood poverty significantly increases their severity.[7]

CHILD HEALTH TRENDS, 1965–1980

The advent of the Great Society health programs for the poor—particularly, Medicaid, strengthened public health efforts, and community health centers—coupled with major advances in the technology of newborn intensive care, had a dramatic impact on poor children's access to medical care and their health status.[8] In 1963, 63% of pregnant women began prenatal care in the first trimester of pregnancy; by 1980 that figure had risen to 79%.[9] Between 1965 and 1980, infant mortality rates dropped by nearly 50%.[10] The percentage of infants born at low birth weight declined 13% between 1970 to 1979.[11] Access to newborn care technology not only improved the likelihood of survival for premature, low birth weight and sick infants, but also reduced the likelihood of severe disability among those who do survive.[12]

Other indicators of children's health status and access to care also improved dramatically. After 1965, disparities in pediatric health care utilization rates based solely on economic status significantly abated.[13] The percentage of poor children receiving immunizations and comprehensive primary medical care rose dramatically as a result of the 1967 enactment of the Medicaid Early and Periodic Screening, Diagnosis and Treatment (EPSDT) program, the most comprehensive public pediatric program ever enacted by Congress.[14]

CHILD HEALTH TRENDS, 1981–PRESENT

Beginning in the late 1970s in the case of white infants, and in 1981 in the case of black infants, the rapid pace of improvement in infant mortality rates began to slow perceptibly (Figure 1). This slowing rate of decline in U.S. infant mortality came to a virtual halt in 1985, when no statistically significant decline in infant mortality occurred.[15]

The slowing decline in infant mortality resulted from several causes, including pervasive poverty, a persistently high incidence of low birth weight births, the growing incidence of out-of-wedlock births to women with low income and inadequate family supports, and the lack of universally available maternity and infant health services.[16] Even during periods of more rapid improvement the rate of infant mortality decline in the U.S. generally was slower than in many other Western nations. By 1985, the United States ranked only 19th worldwide. In the 1950–55 period, the United States infant mortality rate placed it sixth among 20 industrialized nations. By the

FIGURE 1

Infant Mortality, by Race, 1950–1984

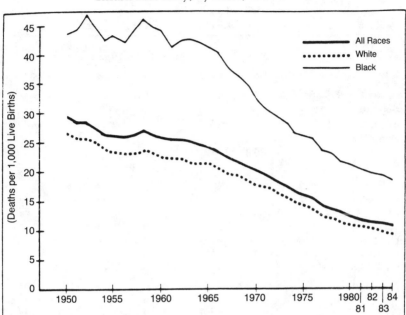

Source: Dana Hughes, *et al.*, *The Health of America's Children*, 1987.

1980–85 period the United States ranked last, behind such nations as the German Democratic Republic, Hong Kong, Belgium, France, Japan and Finland, whose 1950–55 infant mortality rates had been 1.5 to 2.5 times higher than the U.S. rate (Table 1; Figure 2).

This slowing, and finally stalled, rate of decline in overall U.S. infant mortality rates conceals even more serious problems for key sub-populations. Black infants continue to die at rates twice as high as white infants (Figure 3). Additionally, the overall infant mortality rate, which reflects all infant deaths from birth to 12 months, does not adequately reflect severe mortality problems among sub-categories of infants. Between 1982 and 1983, postneonatal mortality rates (deaths between 28 days and one year) rose nationally by three percent, and black postneonatal mortality rates rose by five percent (Figure 3). Between 1984 and 1985, black neonatal mortality (deaths in the first 28 days of life) rose by three percent—the first such increase in 20 years.[17]

TABLE 1
INFANT MORTALITY RATES
1950–1985
SELECTED COUNTRIES

Country	1950–1955		1980–1985		% Change 1950–55 to 1980–85
	Rate	Rank	Rate	Rank	
Australia	24	(4)	10	(12)	−58
Belgium	45	(14)	11	(17)	−76
Canada	36	(11)	9	(9)	−75
Denmark	28	(8)	8	(5)	−71
Finland	34	(10)	6	(1)	−82
France	45	(14)	9	(9)	−80
German Dem. Rep.	58	(16)	11	(17)	−81
Germany, Fed. Rep.	48	(18)	11	(17)	−77
Hong Kong	79	(20)	10	(12)	−87
Iceland	21	(2)	6	(1)	−71
Ireland	41	(12)	10	(12)	−76
Japan	51	(17)	6	(1)	−88
Luxembourg	43	(13)	9	(9)	−79
Netherlands	24	(4)	8	(5)	−67
Norway	23	(3)	8	(5)	−65
Spain	62	(19)	10	(12)	−84
Sweden	20	(1)	7	(4)	−65
Switzerland	29	(9)	8	(5)	−72
United Kingdom	28	(6)	10	(12)	−64
United States	28	(6)	11	(17)	−61

(Rates are rounded to the nearest whole number)
Source: United Nation's Children Fund
Source: Dana Hughes, *et al.*, *The Health of America's Children*, 1987.

While neonatal mortality (deaths in the first 28 days of life) generally reflect the incidence of low birth weight and the limits of newborn care technology, post-neonatal mortality is an especially sensitive indicator of infants' access to basic health services.[18] Three-quarters of deaths in the first 28 days of life are caused by low birth weight,[19] but the great majority of post-neonatal deaths involve infants born at normal weights.[20] Thus, elevated post-neonatal mortality rates provide a particularly grim reminder of the poverty and deprivation into which nearly one in four infants was born in 1984. Indeed, America's infant mortality problem generally is an indictment of the absence of primary health care for the poor.[21] Lack of access to primary medical care during pregnancy results in a significantly higher incidence of low birth weight births.[22] And the lack of primary health care contributes to death rates among older infants.[23]

These recent disturbing infant mortality trends have been accompanied by other signs of stagnation and erosion in maternal and infant health. Between 1980 and 1984, the percentage of infants born at low birth weight remained essentially unchanged, and between 1984 and 1985 the percentage actually increased.[24] Between 1980 and 1984 the percentage of infants born at very low birth weight (less than 3.5 pounds) increased by 3.5% for all races, 2.2% for white infants, and 8.2% for black infants (Tables 2A and B). After nearly two decades of progress, there was essentially no improvement between 1980 and 1985 in the percentage of infants born to women receiving prenatal care early in pregnancy. Moreover, between 1982 and 1984 there was a 3.8% increase in the percentage of infants born to women who received either no prenatal care at all or none until

FIGURE 2
Infant Mortality Rates, Selected Countries, 1950–1985

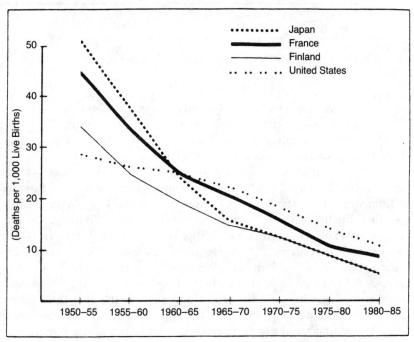

Source: Dana Hughes, *et al.*, *The Health of America's Children*, 1987.

FIGURE 3
Neonatal and Postneonatal Mortality, 1950–1984

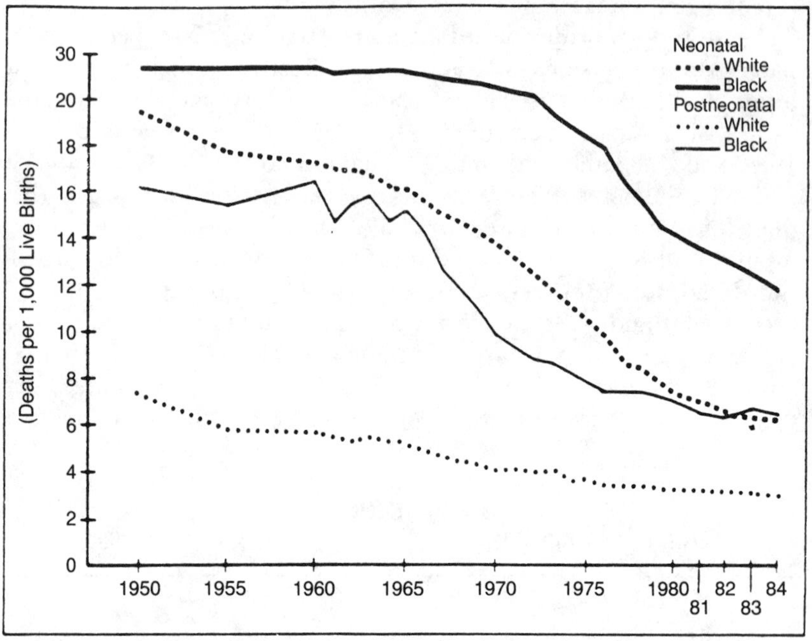

Source: Dana Hughes, *et al.*, *The Health of America's Children*, 1987.

the end of pregnancy (Tables 3A and B). Finally, between 1984 and 1985, nonwhite maternal mortality rose ten percent nationally.[25]

This stagnation and erosion in maternal and infant health indicators means that the nation will not meet even the modest infant health objectives for 1990 that were established by the Surgeon General of the United States in 1979 and reaffirmed in 1984 by the Reagan administration. A 1985 report to Congress by the U.S. Public Health Service concluded that even the modest objective of reducing overall infant mortality rates to nine deaths per 1000 live births by 1990 would not be achieved.[26] Other equally modest 1990 objectives, including reducing black infant mortality and post-neonatal mortality rates, and improving birth weight and prenatal care utilization, will not be reached (Table 4). Indeed, with respect to the Surgeon General's 1990 objective that 90% of all pregnant women begin prenatal care in the first trimester of pregnancy, not only will the nation as a whole fail to meet the goal, but neither will a single state.

While there is no comparable body of vital health statistics from which to derive health status trends among children over age one, eroding infant health indicators portend serious problems during childhood. For example, the percentage of children ages 0–2 adequately immunized against childhood disease declined between 1980 and 1985 (Table 5). This means diminished protection against communicable diseases. Since immunizations are administered as part of a comprehensive health exam, declining immunization rates may also signal eroding access to a range of primary health services.

TABLE 2A
PERCENTAGE OF INFANTS BORN AT LOW BIRTH WEIGHT BY RACE, U.S., SELECTED YEARS, 1950–1984

Year	All Races	White	Nonwhite Black	Nonwhite Total	Ratio of Black to White
1950	7.5	7.1	—	10.2	—
1955	7.6	6.8	—	11.7	—
1960	7.7	6.8	—	12.8	—
1961	7.8	6.9	—	13.0	—
1962	8.0	7.0	—	13.1	—
1963	8.2	7.1	—	13.6	—
1964	8.2	7.1	—	13.9	—
1965	8.3	7.2	—	13.8	—
1966	8.3	7.2	—	13.9	—
1967	8.2	7.1	—	13.6	—
1968	8.2	7.1	—	13.7	—
1969	8.1	7.0	14.1	13.5	2.01
1970	7.9	6.8	13.9	13.3	2.04
1971	7.7	6.6	13.4	12.7	2.03
1972	7.7	6.5	13.6	12.9	2.09
1973	7.6	6.4	13.3	12.5	2.08
1974	7.4	6.3	13.1	12.4	2.08
1975	7.4	6.3	13.1	12.2	2.08
1976	7.3	6.1	13.0	12.1	2.13
1977	7.1	5.9	12.8	11.9	2.17
1978	7.1	5.9	12.8	11.9	2.17
1979	6.9	5.8	12.6	11.6	2.17
1980	6.8	5.7	12.5	11.5	2.19
1981	6.8	5.7	12.5	11.4	2.19
1982	6.8	5.6	12.4	11.2	2.21
1983	6.8	5.6	12.6	11.2	2.25
1984	6.7	5.6	12.4	11.1	2.21

Source: National Center for Health Statistics
Source: Dana Hughes, *et al., The Health of America's Children,* 1987

TABLE 2B

PERCENTAGE OF INFANTS BORN AT VERY LOW BIRTH
WEIGHT, BY RACE, U.S., 1979–1987

Year	All Races	White	Black
1979	1.15	0.90	2.35
1980	1.15	0.90	2.43
1981	1.16	0.90	2.47
1982	1.17	0.91	2.51
1983	1.18	0.93	2.54
1984	1.19	0.92	2.56

Source: National Center for Health Statistics.
Source: Dana Hughes, *et al.*, *The Health of America's Children*, 1987.

TABLE 3A

PERCENTAGE OF BABIES BORN TO WOMEN RECEIVING
FIRST TRIMESTER CARE, BY RACE, U.S., 1969–1984

Year	All Races	White	Nonwhite	
			Black	Total
1969	68.0	72.4	42.7	44.5
1970	67.9	72.4	44.3	46.0
1971	68.6	73.0	46.6	48.1
1972	69.4	73.6	49.0	50.6
1973	70.8	74.9	51.4	52.9
1974	72.1	75.9	53.9	55.3
1975	72.3	75.9	55.8	57.0
1976	73.5	76.8	57.7	58.8
1977	74.1	77.3	59.0	60.1
1978	74.9	78.2	60.2	61.4
1979	75.9	79.1	61.6	62.9
1980	76.3	79.3	62.7	63.8
1981	76.3	79.4	62.4	63.8
1982	76.1	79.3	61.5	63.2
1983	76.2	79.4	61.5	63.4
1984	76.5	79.6	62.2	64.1

Source: National Center for Health Statistics.
Source: Dana Hughes, *et al.*, *The Health of America's Children*, 1987.

There are also indications that the incidence of childhood disability may be on the rise. Between 1960 and 1980, the percentage of children reporting a disability that limited normal childhood activities doubled, from just under two percent to nearly four percent of all children (Figure 4). Poor children are more likely than non-poor children to report disabilities of this severity.[27] Improved reporting of childhood disability may account for some of this increase,[28] but the increased incidence of very low birth weight infants, and the far greater rate of survival among these infants, may also be contributing to the greater prevalence of childhood disabilities. While newborn technology has reduced the risk of disability, it cannot eliminate it. As more low birth weight infants survive into childhood, the number of children with chronic medical conditions of varying degrees of severity will most likely increase.

About 3.7% of all children, and 5.2% of all low-income children, are seriously disabled. More than ten percent of all children (and a greater percentage of all low-income children) would be considered disabled if the standards utilized under special education programs were applied.[29] This group includes children with learning disabilities (4.5%), speech impairments (3.0%), mental retardation (2.0%), emotional disturbance (1.0%), sensory impairments (0.3%) and physical disabilities (0.4%). If children with milder functional impairments, such as uncomplicated asthma, correctable vision or hearing impair-

TABLE 3B

PERCENTAGE OF BABIES BORN TO WOMEN RECEIVING LATE OR NO PRENATAL CARE, BY RACE, U.S., 1969–1984

Year	All Races	White	Nonwhite Black	Total
1969	8.1	6.3	18.2	17.7
1970	7.9	6.2	16.6	16.2
1971	7.2	5.8	14.6	14.1
1972	7.0	5.5	13.2	13.1
1973	6.7	5.4	12.4	12.3
1974	6.2	5.0	11.4	11.2
1975	6.0	5.0	10.5	10.4
1976	5.7	4.8	9.9	9.8
1977	5.6	4.7	9.6	9.5
1978	5.4	4.5	9.3	9.1
1979	5.1	4.3	8.9	8.8
1980	5.1	4.3	8.8	8.8
1981	5.2	4.3	9.1	8.9
1982	5.5	4.5	9.6	9.3
1983	5.6	4.6	9.7	9.4
1984	5.6	4.7	9.6	9.3

Note: Late care is defined as starting in the third trimester.
Source: National Center for Health Statistics.
Source: Dana Hughes *et al.*, *The Health of America's Children*, 1987.

TABLE 4
SURGEON GENERAL'S 1990 GOALS
FACT SHEET FOR THE NATION

Infant Mortality	1984 Rate	Average rate change per year 1978–84	Average rate change needed per year to reach the 1990 goal
Total	10.8	−0.50	−0.30
White	9.4	−0.43	−0.07
Nonwhite	16.1	−0.85	−0.68
Black	18.4	−0.78	−1.07
Neonatal Mortality			
Total	7.0	−0.42	−0.08
Postneonatal Mortality			
Total	3.8	−0.08	−0.22
Low Birth weight			
Total	6.7	−0.07	−0.28
White	5.6	−0.05	−0.10
Nonwhite	11.1	−0.13	−0.35
Black	12.4	−0.08	−0.57
Prenatal Care			
Total	76.5	0.27	2.25
White	79.6	0.23	1.73
Nonwhite	64.1	0.45	4.32
Black	62.2	0.33	4.63

Source: Public Health Service, *The 1990 Health Objectives For the Nation: A Midcourse Review,* 1986.

ments and moderate emotional disturbance are included in calculating childhood disability rates, then 20% of the child population, and an even greater percentage of low-income children, would be considered disabled.[30]

Evidence suggests that the growth in activity—limiting conditions among children is occurring within selected condition classifications. For example, large reported increases between 1969 and 1981 occurred for respiratory diseases, mental and nervous disorders, orthopedic impairments, endocrine, nutritional, metabolic and blood disorders, and certain congenital anomalies (Table 6). To the extent that

TABLE 5
PROGRESS TOWARD THE SURGEON GENERAL'S OBJECTIVE FOR FULL IMMUNIZATION FOR CHILDREN AGE TWO

Year	Polio*	Measles	Rubella	Mumps	DTP*
1980	80.7	83.0	83.2	80.2	87.0
1981	80.9	81.5	83.9	79.1	87.6
1982	78.6	84.3	81.1	79.0	88.4
1983	78.6	83.9	81.9	78.1	88.4
1984	74.2	81.7	76.7	78.4	85.8
1985	76.7	81.7	77.3	78.9	85.8
1990 Objective	90.0	90.0	90.0	90.0	90.0

*Full immunization at this age is defined as three or more vaccinations.
Source: Unpublished data from Centers for Disease Control, U.S. Immunization Survey. In Kay Johnson, *Who Is Watching Our Children?* Children's Defense Fund, 1987.

FIGURE 4

ACTIVITY LIMITATIONS AMONG CHILDREN

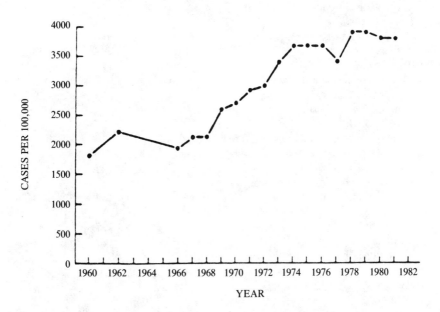

Source: Paul Newacheck, Peter Budetti, Neal Halfon, "Trends in Activity Limiting Chronic Conditions Among Children," *American Journal of Public Health,* February 1986.

TABLE 6
PREVALENCE OF CHRONIC CONDITIONS CAUSING ACTIVITY LIMITATIONS AMONG CHILDREN UNDER 17 YEARS OF AGE

Condition Groups	Prevalence per 100,000		
	1969–70	1974–75	1979–80
Impairments:			
Blindness, Impairment of Vision	71	93	75
Deafness, Impairment of Hearing	113	186	171
Impairment of Speech, Special Sense, Intelligence	385	417	567
Absence, Loss, Extremities, Certain Other Sites	23	36	28
Paralysis, Complete or Partial	128	115	115
Specified Deformity of Limbs, Trunk, Back	190	187	205
Non-Paralytic Orthopedic Impairment	130	227	209
Defect, Abnormality, Special Impairment	83	90	66
Disease and Injuries:			
Infective, Parasitic Diseases	26	20	18
Neoplasms	33	40	23
Endocrine, Nutritional, Metabolic, Blood Disorders	79	109	142
Mental, Nervous System Disorders	178	320	382
Diseases of Eye, Ear	92	202	235
Diseases of Circulatory System	150	126	112
Diseases of Respiratory System	641	945	979
Diseases of Digestive System	39	54	49
Genito-Urinary Disorders, Pregnancy, Childbirth	47	47	47
Diseases of Skin, Subcutaneous Tissue	33	76	72
Diseases of Musculoskeletal System, Connective Tissue	59	124	121
Certain Congenital Anomalies, Causes of Prenatal Morbidity	82	154	123
Certain Symptoms, Ill-Defined Conditions	72	77	83
Injuries	26	27	24
All Activity-Limiting Conditions	2680	3672	3847

Source: Paul Newacheck, *et al.*, "Trends in Activity Limiting Chronic Condition Among Children," *American Journal of Public Health*, February 1986.

any of these conditions are more prevalent among low birth weight infants, their incidence may increase as more of these infants survive.

A small percentage of children with chronic illnesses and disabilities suffer such a degree of disability that they can be considered technology-dependent. Between 17,000 and 23,000 children have conditions that require either breathing or digestion related life support systems.[31] An additional 40,000 to 75,000 children may be dependent on a somewhat less continual, but nonetheless high cost, form of care.[32] About two percent of all children suffer from one of eleven major childhood diseases, including cystic fibrosis, spina bifida, leukemia, juvenile diabetes, chronic kidney disease, muscular dystrophy, hemophilia, cleft palate, sickle cell anemia, asthma and cancer.[33]

In sum, health data indicate that the nation's modest rate of progress in improving infant health first slowed and then halted altogether during the 1980s. Moreover, a growing body of evidence indicates that fewer children are receiving primary health services and that a greater percentage of children are disabled today, perhaps in part because of the greater survival rate of low birth weight babies and the greater incidence of very low birth weight births. A significant proportion of these infants, particularly poor infants, will be left with a disability or impairment serious enough to limit normal childhood activity. Given the higher incidence of death and disability among poor children, these eroding health trends undoubtedly will continue as long as childhood poverty rates remain severely elevated.

HEALTH INSURANCE COVERAGE AMONG CHILDREN

In the United States, health insurance and direct payments constitute the two major sources of health care financing.[34] Low-income families, who by definition do not have adequate resources to pay for health care directly, have a particularly pressing need for health insurance. Moreover, these families need comprehensive coverage, since even routine preventive and pediatric care can incur a "catastrophic" health expenditure when cost is considered in relation to family income.

A disproportionate percentage of uninsured families with catastrophic expenditures have incomes below the federal poverty level. This is particularly true if the term "catastrophic" is measured in relation to family income rather than in absolute dollar terms (Table 7). Indeed, as a share of family income, direct expenditures for impoverished children are six times greater than for children living in the highest income families.[35]

Lack of insurance has a profound impact on children's use of

TABLE 7
PERCENT OF FAMILIES WITH UNINSURED CATASTROPHIC
HEALTH CARE EXPENSES BY VARIOUS THRESHOLDS OF
CATASTROPHIC EXPENSE, AND PERCENT IN POVERTY, 1977

Thresholds of Catastrophic Expense	Percent of all Families with Uninsured Catastrophic Expenses	Percent of Families with These Uninsured Catastrophic Expenses That are in Poverty
$2,200 or more	4.9%	15.2%
5 percent of family income	19.9	31.5
10 percent of family income	9.6	47.5
20 percent of family income	4.3	66.1

Source: Employee Benefits Research Institute, *Issue Brief*, 1987.

health services, particularly children with disabilities.[36] Uninsured low-income children receive 40% less medical care than their insured counterparts. Uninsured low-income children with disabilities are significantly less likely than insured poor children to have a regular source of care and only about half as likely to receive medical services.

Despite their greater need for coverage, low-income families are far more likely to be uninsured, and low-income children are even more likely to be uninsured than low-income adults.[37] Furthermore, the number of uninsured children is increasing. The chief causes of decline in health coverage are the erosion of the private insurance system and the failure of residual public financing programs to fill the growing gap left by private coverage. These two trends resulted in a 16% increase between 1982 and 1985 in the number of uninsured children, from 9.6 to 11.1 million. This increase occurred despite the most sustained peacetime economic recovery in this century.

Private Insurance. Of the $440 billion that Americans spent on personal health services in 1987, $136 billion—about one-third—was paid through private insurance.[38] Private health insurance constitutes the single largest source of financing for personal health services.[39] Thus, individuals without private health insurance, particularly those from lower-income families, lack the critical economic means of gaining health care access.

Most private insurance is provided as an employment-related fringe benefit. Seventy-five percent of all privately insured Americans are covered by employer-provided plans.[40] Employer-provided coverage is an extremely important component of employee compensation for two reasons. First, insurance costs are held down because coverage is furnished on a group basis. Second, most employers who do provide coverage underwrite all or most of its cost (that is, they pay all or part of the annual premium) for employees and their families. These employer-paid premiums constitute non-taxable income.

Even a decade ago, prior to the major recession of the early 1980s and the ensuing efforts by employers to reduce their labor costs, 26 million Americans were uninsured. During the past several years the number of uninsured Americans has grown significantly. In 1982, 17% of the non-agricultural, non-military U.S. population under age 65 was uninsured; by 1985 these numbers had increased by nearly 15%.[41] Within this overall increase, the number of workers without coverage grew by 22%, and the number of children under 18 without private coverage increased by 16%.[42] By 1985, one child in six had no private insurance.[43]

Persons without private health insurance by and large are members of the most economically pressed American families. Sixty-two percent of the uninsured, and three-quarters of all uninsured children, live in families with incomes that are less than two times the federal poverty level.[44] One-third live in families with poverty-level incomes.[45]

Because private insurance is an employment-related benefit, upper-income wage earners are far more likely to be privately insured than moderate or low-wage workers.[46] Moreover, the nation finances private insurance through tax losses (as a business-related expense for the employer and as non-taxable income for the employee). Thus, it is the highest income workers who receive the most valuable insurance subsidy, given the higher degree of compensation and the higher margin at which their incomes are taxed.

Ironically, although private insurance for the under-65 population is overwhelmingly furnished as an employment benefit, the majority of uninsured are workers. In 1985, 70% of the uninsured either were full-time, full-year workers, or lived in families headed by a full-time, full-year worker.[47] Of the more than 12 million uninsured children, almost three-quarters lived with a family head who worked.[48]

There are numerous reasons for the increase in the number of children who are not covered by private health insurance. Most of the reasons reflect long-term trends, and therefore the number of uninsured children may well continue to increase.

First, the relationship between employment and health insurance obviously means that almost all families with no currently employed members are likely to be excluded. Second, the employer-based system also excludes poorly paid workers, since insurance is a key aspect of employee compensation. For example, 30% of all employers who pay only the minimum wage to more than half their work force offer no health insurance.[49]

Third, the system excludes children of workers whose employers either do not offer coverage to employees' dependents or offer it only at an unaffordable cost (without subsidizing the family portion of the annual premium). 20% of children who are not insured nonetheless live in a household in which the family head has employer-provided insurance.[50]

Subsidization of employees' annual premium costs—particularly the cost of family coverage—is most prevalent in the case of large firms, manufacturing firms, and firms that pay higher wages. Moreover, employer subsidies for family coverage appear to be particularly vulnerable to reduction as the pressure to contain labor costs increases. One-third of the respondents in a recent nationwide employer survey reported that they had reduced contributions to their workers' (or their workers' dependents') annual insurance premiums, thereby increasing their workers' share of premiums.[51] The failure to provide subsidized insurance among firms employing poor workers means that children living in low income working families are only half as likely as those living in non-poor working families to be privately insured.

Two other factors contribute to the long-term nature of the trend toward less private insurance coverage of children. First, as children increasingly live in families headed by single parents, the likelihood that they will not be privately insured grows (Figure 5). This is true in part because female workers tend to be employed in lower-paying jobs which are less likely to offer insurance,[52] and in part because the lack of two workers means that there is no second wage earner to compensate in the event that the first wage earner is uninsured.

Second, the United States is witnessing a major shift in the type of jobs the economy provides, away from employment in the manufacturing industries and toward gowth in the service sector.[53] Manufacturing jobs generally have included greater levels of employer-paid fringe benefits, particularly health insurance. Service jobs, by contrast, are often part-time and lower-paying; and even if full-time, these jobs are significantly less likely to provide health insurance. To the extent that the American economy continues this shift, the nation may be witnessing the inexorable collapse of a large segment of the employer-based insurance system and the resulting dis-insurance of a sizeable proportion even of middle class families over the long term.

Beyond the threshold issue of eligibility for benefits are problems involving the scope and depth of private coverage. While the Pregnancy Discrimination Act[54] prohibits exclusion of routine maternity

FIGURE 5

Percentage of Children in Family Types Who Are Uninsured

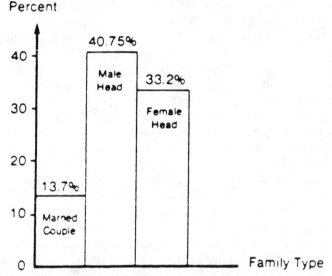

Source: Margaret Sulvetta and Katherine Swartz, *The Uninsured and Uncompensated Care: A Chartbook*, 1986.

benefits from private plan coverage, it exempts firms of fewer than 20 employees.[55] More than five million privately insured women are uncovered for routine maternity care.[56]

Moreover, despite the growing emphasis on plan coverage of health maintenance and preventive services, many plans still do not cover routine screening and preventive pediatric care, and others subject coverage of even preventive care to deductible requirements that effectively negate the value of preventive benefits for poorer families. Prepaid health plans that emphasize "first-dollar" preventive health coverage are an increasingly popular insurance option among larger firms that provide higher levels of compensation. But a prepaid plan option is less prevalent among firms employing primarily low-income workers. Indeed, health maintenance organizations traditionally have avoided marketing their services to less affluent (and therefore, potentially sicker) populations. So serious is the lack of comprehensive coverage for preventive care among lower-income children that in 1980, a publicly insured poor child eligible for Medicaid was 1.5 times more likely than a privately insured poor child to have received preventive health care during the year.[57]

Families with marginal incomes are in no position to purchase medical care unless it is absolutely necessary. Thus, low-income children with inadequate private coverage frequently have medical needs that go unmet, just as if they were completely uninsured.[58]

At the other end of the medical cost scale, many insurance plans place restrictive lifetime limits on covered expenses and contain no feature to protect families facing high-cost catastrophic illnesses from huge out-of-pocket expenses. It is not uncommon for families with gravely sick infants or children to find that within a matter of a few years, or even months, their children have used up their lifetime or annual plan coverage. Moreover, if these families attempt to change jobs they may find that their children continue to be uncovered under the new benefit plan's pre-existing condition exclusion clause.

As with eligibility for coverage, the depth of benefits in an employer plan is a direct reflection of the degree of compensation an employer wishes to provide. The broader and deeper a plan's coverage is, the more expensive it becomes. Poorer workers on average are less likely to have comprehensive coverage, even though they are in greater need of it. While the Tax Reform Act of 1986 curtails firms' flexibility to discriminate against poor workers by providing more comprehensive fringe benefits to their highly compensated employees,[59] it is unclear whether firms will respond by enriching benefits for all employees or by reducing coverage and simply rewarding more highly compensated workers in other ways.

At least one economist has estimated that the cost alone to the U.S. Treasury of the employer-based health insurance system in 1986 alone was over $50 billion.[60] This makes the employer-based insurance system second in size only to Medicare. Yet the private insurance system has not produced equitable coverage and benefit results; and if anything, the inequities appear to be growing. Moreover, states are preempted by federal law from regulating the structure or content of employer insurance unless it is purchased through a private insurance company.[61] Since nearly half of all employers now self-insure and thus are protected from state regulation under the Employee Retirement Income Security Act (ERISA), it is virtually impossible to remedy these problems at the state level, although many states have attempted to do so.[62]

Public Insurance. The inequities of the private insurance system demand some type of residual public health financing system for the millions of uncovered families. Even if Congress were to enact federal laws to expand and strengthen the employer-based system, as legislation introduced by Senator Edward Kennedy during the 100th Congress would do,[63] millions of persons with limited or no connection to the work place would still be uncovered. Unfortunately, however, there is no uniform public health insurance program for families with children similar to Medicare for the elderly and disabled.

The only federal, non-military program offering insurance-like benefits to families with children is Medicaid, the nation's largest grant-in-aid program for the poor. Enacted in 1965 as an adjunct to Medicare, Medicaid was intended to "piggyback" onto public cash assistance programs for persons receiving benefits under the Aid to the Aged, Blind, or Disabled (AABD)* programs, or Aid to Families with Dependent Children (AFDC) programs.[64] As a result of its linkage to public cash assistance programs, Medicaid by and large requires coverage only of those persons whose family characteristics and deep poverty qualify them for financial aid. Therefore, children who are not "dependent" as defined under the AFDC program (i.e. children who do not live in families in which one parent is absent, dead, incapacitated or unemployed), historically have been excluded from mandatory coverage.

Since 1965 states have had the option of covering poor children living in two-parent working families. But until 1984, when this coverage was mandated for children under age five, nearly half chose not to do so.[65] Similarly, since 1967 states have had the option to extend Medicaid to pregnant women ineligible for AFDC benefits either because they either had no children yet or had husbands at home.[66] But, until 1986, when such coverage was mandated, 18 states failed to do so.[67] Since 1965, states have had the option of covering "medically needy" persons (certain individuals, including children, whose family incomes slightly exceed AFDC eligibility levels). Yet in 1987, 14 jurisdictions still did not cover these families.[68] Finally, as states have allowed their AFDC eligibility levels to fall far below the federal poverty level,[69] a declining percentage of even categorically eligible poor families have qualified for coverage (Figure 6).

Thus, because of these fundamental barriers to Medicaid coverage of children—restrictive "categorical" eligibility standards, extremely restrictive financial eligibility criteria and states' failure to exercise coverage options available to them—the percentage of poor children covered by Medicaid has fallen dramatically over the past decade.[70] This declining coverage of poor children was further exacerbated by the Omnibus Budget Reconciliation Act of 1981, which eliminated previously required coverage of children ages 18 to 21 who had

---

*Later consolidated and expanded into the Supplemental Security Income (SSI) program.

FIGURE 6

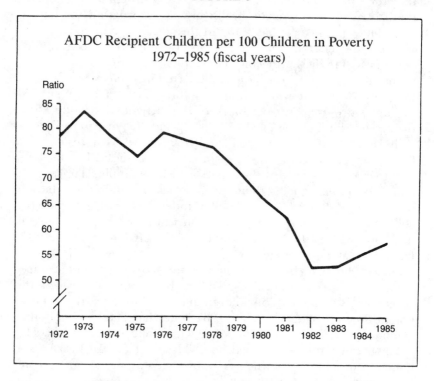

AFDC Recipient Children per 100 Children in Poverty
1972–1985 (fiscal years)

Source: Children's Defense Fund, *A Children's Defense Budget,* 1988.

formerly received AFDC benefits. The Act also severely curtailed
AFDC (and thus Medicaid) benefits for adults and children living in
poor working families.[71] As a result of this latter action, nearly
500,000 children lost Medicaid coverage immediately,[72] and hundreds
of thousands of others were permanently barred from coverage.[73]

For those children who do qualify for Medicaid, the scope of
benefits furnished, and the cost-sharing protections provided, are far
more extensive than those found in most private insurance plans.
This is particularly true in the case of primary services, because of
the comprehensive preventive medical and dental benefits available
through the Medicaid preventive screening program (known as the
Early and Periodic Screening Diagnosis and Treatment Program).
However, many states nonetheless fail to provide adequate levels of
benefits, especially in the case of extremely sick children in need of
intensive care. For example, 17 state Medicaid programs currently
place arbitrary limits on the number of inpatient hospital days they

will cover.[74] Moreover, many states maintain such low levels of reimbursement that in many communities virtually no provider (especially obstetricians) will accept Medicaid patients.[75]

Medicaid's eligibility, benefit and provider participation problems are compounded by the severe lack of publicly-funded health providers to serve the uninsured or inadequately insured poor. By 1986 only 13 states maintained publicly subsidized prenatal clinics on a statewide basis, and only 23 states provide inpatient delivery services for even a portion of their medically indigent pregnant women (of the 9 million uninsured women of childbearing age in 1984, two-thirds had family incomes below 200% of the federal poverty level— approximately $18,000 annually for a family of three in 1987). Moreover, no state offered a statewide system of comprehensive primary care services for medically indigent children.[76] In 1986, some 600 federally funded community and migrant health centers served over five million medically underserved Americans (65% of whom were children or women of childbearing age), but another 20 million persons remained unserved.[77]

Finally, the federal Supplemental Food Program For Women, Infants and Children (WIC) provides basic health care and vital nutritional supplementation to over three million pregnant women, nursing mothers, infants and children annually. Given the positive association between nutritional supplementation and birth weight, on the one hand, and the negative consequences of nutritional deficiency on the other, WIC benefits constitute a key health service.[78] Yet in 1987, WIC served only 40% of all eligible women and children.[79]

FUTURE DIRECTIONS IN CHILD HEALTH POLICY

The grave shortcomings of the public and private health care financing systems for pregnant women and young children have taken a terrible toll in both human and financial terms. Infants born to women who receive either no care or inadequate care are at far greater risk of death and preventable, lifelong disabilities. It has been estimated that between 1978 and 1990, the nation will experience an "excess" of more than 330,000 low birth weight births, at a cost of $2.5 billion, a cost which might have been averted had their mothers received adequate maternity care.[80]

This human tragedy also carries major financial consequences. Repeated studies have shown that preventive investment in maternity and pediatric care, including prenatal care, risk-appropriate deliveries and care during infancy and childhood which includes regular exams, immunizations, and treatment of acute and chronic health conditions, can save anywhere from two to fourteen dollars for every dollar invested.[81] Yet, other than South Africa, the United States is the only Western industrialized country that does not have a national maternal and child health policy.[82]

If public health goals in infant and child health are to be achieved, and if all children, regardless of family structure or economic status, are to have access to a reasonable level of medical care, then the following reforms must take place:

- All pregnant women and children must be insured, either publicly or privately. All poor children and their families should have access to Medicaid, and all near-poor families should be able to enroll in Medicaid for an income-adjusted monthly premium, if they do not otherwise have adequate private coverage.
- There must be sufficient and appropriate health providers to meet the needs of underserved communities and populations. This means that funding for the community and migrant health centers should be sufficiently increased so that all underserved communities and providers have access to primary medical care.
- Additionally, funding for the Title V Maternal and Child Health programs should be increased so that every underserved community can have specialized maternity and pediatric services for medically and socially at-risk families with children.
- Eligibility standards governing federal public health programs must be simplified and unified, so that women and children can more quickly obtain both medical and nutritional services. Moreover, the benefits available under Medicaid must be made more uniform, so that geographic location no longer determines whether a child has insurance or whether his or her insurance covers an adequate range of benefits. Provider reimbursement standards must be set in accordance with reasonable criteria and public health agencies and health centers should be reimbursed on the basis of their reasonable costs.
- The WIC program should be expanded to serve all financially needy women, infants and children at nutritional risk.
- Funding increases for immunizations must be sufficient to ensure that every child is immunized against preventable disease.

These fundamental improvements are needed in order to ensure that children receive necessary medical care prior to birth and throughout childhood. There are indications that the nation is slowly heading in the right direction. Despite major deficits and budget constraints which in recent years have stymied many vital social policy reforms for families and children, modest but notable progress has been made in reformulating national maternal and child health policies. Legislation recently passed or currently pending in both Congress and the states holds the promise of long-term reform over the next decade.

Medicaid. During the 1980s, there has been no better example of fundamental, positive changes in public policy than in the area of public insurance coverage for low-income children. These advances have begun to compensate for the reductions of the early 1980s. Since the 1981 state and federal retrenchment in Medicaid coverage of children, there has emerged a new consensus at all levels of government that the traditional rules governing Medicaid eligibility for families with children—namely, the same criteria used to detemine eligibility for AFDC—are simply inappropriate standards to gauge the need for publicly-subsidized insurance. This is particularly true at a time when so many millions of low-income persons, including millions of workers and families, are falling outside the private insurance system.

Ironically, the 1981 Medicaid cutbacks themselves helped fuel this reversal in thinking, in part because of their documented adverse effects on coverage of the poor and in part because the 1981 legislation also included new state options to expand coverage for pregnant women and children without also having to provide Medicaid coverage for more expensive populations such as the aged and disabled.[83] These developments coincided with the economic recovery, (which led to the availability of additional state revenues), and a growing awareness of child health problems, the Medicaid coverage options available, and the cost-effectiveness of child health care.

Together, these events encouraged a number of states to expand Medicaid coverage of children. By 1986, between 12 and 15 states had broadened their coverage of pregnant women and children. During 1987 and 1988 more than 40 states adopted major new Medicaid maternal and child health expansions.[84] Others supplemented these Medicaid expansions with additional public health funding to develop maternity and pediatric clinics. A series of federal reforms encouraged and accompanied these state activities. These federal reforms, taken together, comprise the basis for a significant modification and restructuring of Medicaid from what has been essentially an adjunct to welfare into a basic public health program for persons without access to the private insurance system. The most important Medicaid reforms enacted to date include the following laws:

- legislation passed in 1984 and 1986 which requires states to extend Medicaid to any pregnant woman or child under age five with family income below AFDC eligibility standards, regardless of family composition;[85]
- legislation enacted in 1986 (strongly supported by both the Southern and National Governors' Associations), which for the first time permits states to provide Medicaid to pregnant women and children under age five with family incomes above AFDC financial eligibility levels but below the federal poverty level, considerably simplify Medicaid financial eligibility standards, and dramatically revise Medicaid enrollment procedures to more quickly enroll pregnant women;[86] by December 1987, over half the states had taken advantage of this new flexibility;
- legislation passed in 1987 which permits states to provide Medicaid to pregnant women and infants with family incomes below 185% of the federal poverty level and to extend benefits to all low income children under age eight; and[87]
- legislation enacted in 1988 mandating coverage of all pregnant women and infants with family incomes below 100% of the federal poverty level and pending a broad new set of benefits for families making the welfare-to-work transition.[88]

Other pending Medicaid legislation would permit states to extend coverage to many near-poor families for an income-adjusted premium. Those assisted would include families making the transition from AFDC to work,[89] families with disabled children,[90] and other poor or uninsured families.[91] Such a structural change would provide for these families an insurance subsidy analogous to the one provided to upper-income, privately-insured families through the tax system. These bills, if enacted and implemented, along with legislation to strengthen the private health insurance system, would dramatically reduce the lack of insurance coverage among American families with children.

Other Health Reforms. In addition to the Medicaid reforms, other key structural reforms include: the Education for Handicapped Children's Amendments of 1986 which for the first time provide federal funding for the development of early intervention programs for infants and toddlers suffering, or at risk of, developmental delay;[92] additional revenues for the Title V Maternal Child Health Block

Grant Program and expansion of the Community Health Centers and Immunization programs.[93]

CONCLUSION

The issue confronting policymakers is not whether the nation can afford health reforms for children but whether it can afford *not* to enact long-term improvements. Young people between the ages of 16 and 24 comprised 23% of the U.S. population in 1978, but will constitute only 16% by 1995.[94] One in three of our new workers will be members of a minority group. As the number of young workers steadily declines, therefore, business and industry will be forced to rely upon workers and potential workers in whom we traditionally have failed to invest. Our future prosperity now depends in large part on our ability to enhance the prospects and productivity of a new generation of employees that is disproportionately poor, minority, unhealthy, undereducated and untrained. Good health can make the difference between a thriving, productive and competitive workforce and one hampered by preventable illnesses and disabling conditions. Our national well-being depends on the future of child health policy.

NOTES

1. United States Census Bureau, *Current Population Survey,* Washington, D.C., 1987.

2. Lisa Egbuonu and Barbara Starfield, "Child Health and Social Status," *Pediatrics,* Vol. 69(550), May, 1982.

3. Surgeon General, *Healthy People,* Washington, D.C., U.S. Department of Health and Human Services, 1979.

4. *Ibid.*

5. Egbuonu and Starfield, *op. cit.*

6. Paul Newacheck and Neal Halfon, "Access to Ambulatory Care Services for Economically Disadvantaged Children," *Pediatrics,* Vol. 78(5), November, 1986, pp. 813–819.

7. Egbuonu and Starfield, *op. cit.*

8. Karen Davis and Cathy Schoen, *Health and The War on Poverty.* Washington, D.C.: Brookings Institution Press, 1987.

9. Peter Budetti, John Butler and Peggy McManus, "Federal Health Program Reforms: Implications for Child Health," *Milbank Memorial Fund Quarterly,* Vol. 60(1), 1982, pp. 155–181.

David Rogers, Robert Blendon and Thomas Rodney, "Who Needs Medicaid," *New England Journal of Medicine,* Vol. 307(1), July 1, 1982, pp. 13–18.

Congressional Research Service, *Infant Mortality.* Washington, D.C.: Government Printing Office, 1985.

10. Dana Hughes, *et al., The Health of America's Children.* Washington, D.C.: Children's Defense Fund, 1987.

11. *Ibid.*

12. Office of Technology Assessment, *Neonatal Intensive Care for Low Birthweight Infants: Costs and Effectiveness.* U.S. Congress. Case study No. 38, December, 1987.

13. Davis and Schoen, *op. cit.*

Joel Kleinman, "Access to Ambulatory Care: Another Look at Equity," *Medical Care,* Vol. XIX:10, May 1981, pp. 1011–1029.

14. Sara Rosenbaum and Kay Johnson, "Providing Health Care for Low Income Children: Reconciling Child Health Goals with Child Health Financing Realities," *Milbank Memorial Fund Quarterly,* Vol. 64(3), 1986, pp. 442–478.

15. National Center for Health Statistics, *Advance Report of Final Mortality Statistics,* 1985 No. 21, Public Health Service, Washington, D.C., 1987.

16. Dana Hughes, *et al., The Health of America's Children.* Washington, D.C., Children's Defense Fund, 1987.

Institute of Medicine, *Preventing Low Birthweight.* Washington, D.C.: National Academy Press, 1986.

C. Arden Miller, "Infant Mortality in the U.S.," *Scientific American,* Vol. 253(1), July, 1985, pp. 33–37.

17. Dana Hughes, *et al., The Health of America's Children.* Washington, D.C.: Children's Defense Fund, 1988.

18. Barbara Starfield, "Motherhood and Apple Pie: The Effectiveness of Medical Care for Children," *Milbank Memorial Fund Quarterly,* Vol. 63(3), 1985, pp. 523–46.

19. Dana Hughes, *et al., The Health of America's Children* Washington, D.C.: Children's Defense Fund, 1987.

20. Starfield, *op. cit.*

21. Miller, *op. cit.*

22. Dana Hughes, *et al., The Health of America's Children.* Washington, D.C.: Children's Defense Fund, 1987.

23. Starfield, *op. cit.*

24. Dana Hughes, *et al., The Health of America's Children.* Washington, D.C.: Children's Defense Fund, 1988.

25. *Ibid.*

26. Public Health Service, *Midcourse Review,* Washington, D.C.: U.S. Department of Health and Human Services, 1986.

27. Newacheck and Halfon, *op. cit.*

28. Paul Newacheck, Peter Budetti and Neal Halfon, "Trends in Activity Limiting Chronic Conditions Among Children", *American Journal of Public Health,* Vol. 76(2), February, 1986, pp. 178–184.

29. John Butler, Sara Rosenbaum and Judith Palfrey, "Ensuring Access to Health Care for Children with Disabilities," *Sounding Board, New England Journal of Medicine,* Vol. 317, July 16, 1987, p. 162.

30. Newacheck, Budetti and Halfon, *op. cit.*

31. Office of Technology Assessment, *Healthy Children: Investing in the Future.* Washington, D.C.: Government Printing Office, February, 1988.

32. *Ibid.*

33. Butler, Rosenbaum and Palfrey, *op. cit.*

34. Data from the Health Care Finance Administration (HCFA).

35. Newacheck and Halfon, *op. cit.*

36. *Ibid.*

Judith Singer, John Butler and Judith Palfry, "Health Care Access and Use Among Handicapped Students in Five Public School Systems," *Medical Care,* Vol. 24(1), January, 1986, pp. 1–5.

Robert Blendon, Linda Aiken, Howard Freeman, Bradford Kirkman-Liff and John Murphy, "Uncompensated Care By Hospitals or Public Insurance for the Poor: Does it Make a Difference?" *New England Journal of Medicine,* Vol. 314(18), May 1, 1986, pp. 1160–1163.

37. Margaret Sulvetta and Katherine Swartz, *The Uninsured and Uncompensated Care: A Chartbook.* Washington, D.C.: National Health Policy Forum, 1986.

38. Unpublished data from the Health Care Finance Administration (HCFA).

39. *Ibid.*

40. Employee Benefit Research Institute (EBRI), *Issue Brief.* Washington, D.C., 1987.

41. *Ibid.*

42. *Ibid.*

43. *Ibid.*

44. *Ibid.*

Sulvetta and Swartz, *op. cit.*

45. *Ibid.*

46. Employee Benefit Research Institute (EBRI), *Issue Brief.* Washington, D.C., 1987.

47. *Ibid.*

48. Sulvetta and Swartz, *op. cit.;* Newacheck, Budetti and Halfon, *op. cit.*

49. Alan Monheit, "Health Insurance for the Unemployed: Is Federal Legislation Needed?" *Health Affairs,* Vol. 3(1), Spring 1984, pp. 117–132.

50. Employee Benefit Research Institute (EBRI), *Issue Brief.* Washington, D.C., 1987.

51. A. S. Hansen, Inc., Health Care Survey, January 20, 1986. (Reported in *Medical Benefits,* Kelly Communications, Charlottesville, VA., February, 1986).

52. Rachael Gold and Asta-Maria Kenny, "Paying for Maternity Care," *Family Planning Perspectives,* Vol. 17(3), May/June, 1985, pp. 103–111.

53. Bureau of Labor Statistics, *Employment Projections for 1995* Bulletin No. 2197, U.S. Department of Labor, March, 1984.

54. PL 95-555 (1978).

55. Sara Rosenbaum and Dana Hughes, "Financing Maternity Care" (Un-

published paper presented at the Bush Institute Conference on Maternity Care, May, 1986.) (Available from the Children's Defense Fund, Washington, D.C.).

56. Alan Guttmacher Institute, *Blessed Events and the Bottom Line*, New York, 1987.

57. Margo Rosenbach, "Insurance Coverage and Ambulatory Medical Care of Low Income Children: United States, 1980," *National Medical Care Utilization and Expenditure Survey*, Series C, Analytic Report No. 1, Washington, D.C.: Department of Health and Human Services, Ps. No. 85-20401, September, 1986.

58. *Ibid.*

59. PL 99-514.

60. Alain Enthoven, "Health Tax Policy Mismatch," *Health Affairs* Vol. 4, Winter 1985, pp. 5–14.

61. Sara Rosenbaum, "Children and Private Health Insurance," Kennedy School of Government, Harvard University, 1986.

62. *Ibid.*

63. S.1625.

64. Rosemary and Roger Stevens, *Welfare Medicine*, Free Press, 1974.

65. U.S. House of Representatives, Report No. 98-442, to Accompany H.R. 4136, 1983.

66. *Ibid.*

67. *Ibid.*

68. Dana Hughes, *et al.*, *The Health of America's Children*. Washington, D.C.: Children's Defense Fund, 1988.

69. Congressional Research Service, *Children in Poverty*. Washington, D.C., 1985.

70. John Holahan and Barbara Cohen, *Medicaid: The Trade-Off Between Cost Containment and Access to Care*. Washington, D.C.: Urban Institute Press, 1987.

71. General Accounting Office, *An Evaluation of the 1981 AFDC Changes: Final Report*, No. 85-4, Washington, D.C.: Government Printing Office, 1985.

72. *Ibid.*

73. Rosenbaum and Johnson, *op. cit.*

74. Employee Benefit Research Institute (EBRI), *Issue Brief* Washington, D.C., 1987.

75. Janet Mitchell, "Medicaid Mills: Fact or Fiction?" *Health Care Financing Review*, Vol. 2(1), Summer, 1980, pp. 37–51.

76. Sara Rosenbaum, Dana Hughes and Kay Johnson, "Results of a 1986 Survey of State Title V and Child Health Agencies' Programs for Medically Indigent Pregnant Women and Children" *Medical Care*, Vol. 26(4), 1987, pp. 354–378.

77. National Association of Community Health Centers, *Two Decades of Achievement*. Washington, D.C., 1986.

78. Ellice Lieberman, Kenneth Ryan, Richard Manson and Stephen Schoenbaum, "Risk Factors Accounting for Racial Differences in the Rate of Premature Births," *New England Journal of Medicine*, Vol. 317(12), September 17, 1987, pp. 743–748.

Joel Kleinman and Samuel Kessel, "Racial Differences in Low Birthweight," *New England Journal of Medicine*, Vol. 317(12), September 17, 1987, pp. 749–753.

79. Dana Hughes, *et al.*, *The Health of America's Children*. Washington, D.C.: Children's Defense Fund, 1988.

80. *Ibid.*

81. Institute of Medicine, *Preventing Low Birthweight*. Washington, D.C.: National Academy Press, 1986.

Southern Governors' Association, "Task Force to Reduce Infant Mortality: Final Report," Washington, D.C., 1985.

Select Committee for Children, Youth, and Families, "Opportunities for Success: Cost Effective Programs for Children," U.S. House of Representatives, 1985.

82. Miller, *op. cit.*

83. Sara Rosenbaum, "Reducing Infant Mortality: The Unfulfilled Promised of Federal Health Programs for the Poor," *Clearinghouse Review*, Vol. 13(11), November, 1983, pp. 1–33.

84. Dana Hughes, *et al. The Health of America's Children*. Washington, D.C.: Children's Defense Fund, 1988.

85. PL 98-369 (the Deficit Reduction Act of 1984) and PL 99-272 (the Consolidated Omnibus Budget Reconciliation Act of 1986).

86. PL 99-509.

87. PL 100-203.

88. PL 100-360.

89. H.R. 2627.

90. S.1760.

91. S.1139.

92. PL 99-157.

93. PL 99-509.

94. Children's Defense Fund, Memorandums form Health Division Prenatal Care Campaign.

POVERTY, FAMILY AND THE BLACK EXPERIENCE

James P. Comer

THERE ARE AT LEAST three major causes of economic poverty among individuals. The first is structural—the absence of either self-employment or other employment opportunities. The second is socio-environmental—the presence of factors which lead to attitudes, values or ways which inhibit employment, employment seeking and job retention. The third is personal—limited individual development and functioning in areas needed for success in the modern job market—including social and interpersonal patterns of behavior, psycho-emotional and moral attitudes, speech and language skills, thinking and school learning abilities and others. All three causes are interrelated and can be more or less at play at the same time.

Policy-makers can develop approaches which diminish the structural causes of poverty, and which promote attitudes and behaviors that help communities and families support adequate individual functioning among most people. To accomplish these tasks with respect to children, policy-makers need an understanding of the processes of child development and the kinds of experiences and support children need to function well. However, they also need to understand the way institutions and conditions external to the developing child and family are operating, or have operated in the past, to either promote or prevent poverty.

As a nation of former immigrants, current immigrants, former slaves, former prisoners and other persons who once lived under difficult conditions and who overcame, we revel in and glorify the spirit of independence and individual effort that has made great national and individual success possible. But we also overstate the case, underestimating the cost and the role of structural factors which influenced such success in the past, and failing to recognize the changes that have occurred for over one hundred and fifty years that make the individual and family escape from poverty more difficult today than it was in earlier times. These misperceptions are particularly pervasive with regard to poverty among minority groups in the United States, especially blacks.

THE EFFECTS OF ECONOMIC AND SOCIAL CHANGE

When enough families are able to earn a living, meet basic needs and function reasonably well, then social networks and communities usually constitute wholesome environments in which adequate child growth and development are the norm. Good functioning is most likely when authority figures within such networks are able to influence most people to live by socially desirable standards. This is possible because constructive belief systems—often grounded in religion, but sometimes based on a family, community or national ethos—positively influence the behavior of the families involved. But, although minimal income is not an absolute deterrent, desirable family functioning is nonetheless more difficult to sustain without a reasonable threshold level of economic opportunity.

Prior to 1900, most heads of households in this country could gain employment or engage in self-employment in a largely agricultural economy without education or any special skills. In rural areas it was possible to produce the goods and services needed for survival. Families often worked together to do so even into what was the early industrial era after 1865. And many could live off the excess of agricultural products even when they were unemployed. Transportation was slow and mass communication was limited; thus, information and influences from outside a community were minimal. These economic and social conditions together gave great power to belief systems generated by authority figures—religious, political, economic and parental—within a community.

Children grew up in families that were enmeshed in social networks of selected and more or less accepting friends, kin, organizations and institutions. Each social network had political, economic, social and emotional ties to, and a particular status in, the larger but local society. Through local and regional institutions, groups were tied to institutions of the still larger national society. Despite significant exceptions and variations, a highly dominant mainstream culture evolved nationwide. The degree to which heads of households could provide for themselves and their families largely determined their sense of adequacy, well-being and belonging. But these features of self-esteem were also determined by the family's and social network's ability to identify with, believe in and, in turn, experience well-being in the local culture and beyond. The sense of well-being and belonging encouraged families and their social networks to live by standards and belief systems established and reinforced by authority figures and leaders at every level of the society. And in this period in American history the standards and expectations were more or less the same at every level.

These conditions created a sense of community and relatedness. School was a natural part of the community. As a result there was an automatic transfer of authority from home to school. This transfer permitted neighbors, friends, school staffs and others to promote a kind of functioning and development of children in and out of school that was generally accepted as desirable. Moreover, the level of development needed to carry out adult tasks was not very high. One could leave school with only modest education, obtain a job, provide for self and family, experience a sense of adequacy for being able to do so, and in turn be motivated to perform well as a family member and citizen.

But by 1900 about half our population was in urban areas. And between 1900 and 1945 the nation's economy became based on heavy industry. Employment and self-employment more often required a moderate level of education or special training, although there were still many economic opportunities for uneducated people. After 1900 it became increasingly difficult for families to produce their basic human needs themselves or to live on agricultural abundance. They became increasingly vulnerable to economic downturns. And the level of personal development necessary to earn a living was creeping upward. Children from the families who functioned best in the pre-1900 period received social and developmental experiences that prepared them to function adequately as adults after 1900 more often than children from families who were not functioning well in the prior generation.

Although the economy changed significantly during the 1900–1945 period, the nature of community changed only modestly. Right into World War II, America remained a nation of small towns and rural areas. The cities were, in many respects, actually collections of small towns. Transportation development occurred fairly gradually, as the horse and buggy age of the turn of the century really gave way fully to the automobile age by 1945. Compared to today, mass communication was also limited and affected the day-to-day lives of families much less than it does now. With limited transportation, heads of households often walked to work and to recreational and other activities. And recreation was still usually communal—among friends, through social and religious groups and organizations. Under these circumstances, authority figures still interacted with each other a great deal and the powerful among them were able to influence greatly the way most people lived. And parents, teachers, neighbors and friends were still the major sources of information, guidance, direction and control for children.

After World War II, the economy moved rapidly into the last stage of the industrial era, or the science-based, early technological period.[1] Most importantly, education and/or training became the ticket of admission to primary job market opportunities, whether the job actually required it or not. Children from families that functioned reasonably well in the previous economic era were able to give their children a developmental experience that would allow them to acquire the high level of education and training needed to be successful in the job market of this era; and the same scenario is applicable to the post-industrial age that has emerged in the 1980s.[2]

The science and technology age spawned conditions that decreased the sense of community which existed prior to the 1950s. Improved transportation began to make it possible for adults to work long distances from where they lived. Recreation became less often communal and more often took place outside the local community. This decreased the interaction among important authority figures in the lives of children. Public policy encouraged suburban sprawl, mostly without any provisions being made to create community in the new settings, or to maintain a sense of community in the urban places being abandoned. Health, education and other public policies were made with little attention to how they would affect community and family life, and child development. Racial and class biases in housing contributed to the isolation of minorities and different income groups.[3]

Television emerged as a powerful and pervasive force in the lives of children and adults alike. It brought attitudes, values and ways from around the world to children directly, not through the important authority figures who in all the previous history of the world had provided children with knowledge about and interpretation of their environment and experiences. Sometimes the information was different from and in conflict with what parents were trying to teach their children. And most of all, young people simply received much more information, and more models for behavior, than ever before.

In some ways all of this was liberating because powerful authority figures could not impose unfair attitudes and conditions on vulnerable groups as easily as in the past. But behavioral expectations were no longer as clearcut, the environment was not as predictable as in the past, and the sense of relatedness and belonging could not exist to the same extent. Constructive role models—teachers, doctors, policemen, others—became more distant to many. While the school usually remained a part of the neighborhood, it was often not a part of the social network or community of many families.

As social and class differentiation increased, distrust and eventually alienation developed between a variety of service givers and the poor. Identification and internalization of the attitudes, values and ways of middle-class America and its institutions took place less often. And the transfer of authority between home and school was no longer automatic. Many families were alienated to the point that they had attitudes, values and ways that were sharply different from those of the mainstream society—the value of education being one. Such conditions permitted much more acting up and acting out on the part of children than was possible when the sense of community and relatedness was greater. The organization and management of schools was not adjusted in a way that would enable them to help non-mainstream children or their families manage the complexities of the new age.[4]

Nonetheless, children are no more mature in the post 1950s world than children ever were. Given the complexity of today's society and economy and the high level of development needed to function in it, they need more adult support for development than ever before, yet they probably have less than ever before. In addition to a loss of support for development from the existence of a community, there are fewer extended families. There are more families in which both adults are working. There are more families in which no adults are working. There are more families headed by young single parents.

CHILD DEVELOPMENT, EDUCATION AND POVERTY

Even families with adequate income and education feel stressed by the complexities of this age and need help in supporting the development of their children. Despite the need, we have an education system in which a large number of professionals, if not a majority, have not had adequate training in applied child development, and cannot establish and manage schools that support the development of students.

The purpose of child rearing and development remains the same—to enable children to function adequately as children and adults in a competitive, democratic, open society. Children are born totally dependent for growth and development on the interest and skills of their parents or caretakers, and the public policies and practices which promote the ability of families, schools and other institutions to influence it.

Newborns have biological potentials which must be developed before they can care for themselves. They have aggressive drives which must be channeled into the energy required for work and play, or life; otherwise, such drives can be expressed in ways that are harmful to the child and to others. Children have the capacity for relationships, but this capacity, too must be developed in a constructive way. Without adequate adult care the newborn will be underdeveloped overall, intellectually retarded, psychologically disturbed or can die.

In the process of providing the child with basic needs, emotional attachments are established between the parents and child. These attachments give parents or adults the leverage or power to aid the growth of children along developmental pathways. Children first learn to behave in a particular fashion by imitating, identifying with and internalizing the attitudes, values and ways of their parents. These early relationships are far more powerful than is frequently realized. They are the template, or prototype, for all future relationships. This is not to say that significant growth, development and change cannot take place after the first couple of years of life, but the great importance of these early experiences must be appreciated.

Growth takes place along many developmental pathways simultaneously. There are several in which growth and development are critical for adequate school or academic learning—social-interactive; psycho-emotional-affective; moral; speech and language; intellectual-cognitive-academic.[5] School or academic learning is facilitated by adequate development in all of these other areas. Development along these pathways takes place through ordinary interactions between child and caretaker.

In the process, children develop control over harmful impulses and learn how to wait, sit still, take in information and concentrate on activities and tasks that will permit them to learn, first at concrete and then at abstract and higher levels. At the same time, with adequate care, children remain capable of spontaneous thought, exploration and imagination. They are responsive to the instruction of "important others." Early interactions provide the child with the beginnings of inner control, direction, motivation and a sense of personal responsibility, because exhibiting such behavior brings positive feedback from those who matter. This enables the young child to experience a sense of adequacy and confidence. It permits him or her to experience a sense of belonging and security. Such children can approach school at five years of age with a reasonable chance for success.

The degree to which adequate preschool development takes place depends greatly on the skill, sense of well-being, and motivation of the primary caretaker or parent. The presence or absence of these conditions depends a great deal on the experiences and level of success of the caregiver. Also, the attitudes, values, childrearing patterns and other ways of parents are greatly influenced by the social network of friends and kin to which they belong. And, while there are multiple social networks, all subscribe to attitudes, values and behaviors that are either mainstream, marginal or antisocial. This greatly affects the kind of experiences, attitudes, values and habits a child receives and adopts prior to school.

Children from mainstream social networks more often receive the kind of experiences, and are expected to develop the kind of capabilities and performance outcomes, that are desirable for functioning in modern society. This increases the likelihood that they will make a positive impression on and receive a positive response from school staff. This, in turn, facilitates a positive attachment, or "bonding," between the child and school staff, enabling the child to imitate, identify with and internalize the attitudes, values and ways of the school, including academic learning. When the experiences, expectations and tasks of the home and school are similar, parents and staff are able to reinforce each other. And throughout the first three or four years of school, positive interactions between a child, school and parents enables him or her to internalize academic learning as a value as well as to gain the discipline and skills to succeed. By the time a child is in the developmental phase in which he or she is attempting to diminish emotional ties to adults, around nine or ten years of age, academic learning and desirable social behavior have already become their own values and habits.

Children from social networks that are marginal to the mainstream of the society have different preschool experiences even when their parents are caring and have reasonably good childrearing skills. Many such parents are alienated from social norms—they may not be able to read or write well themselves, may not be employed, do not vote and cannot teach their children the social-interactive, problem solving or other skills needed in school. Such children often gain skills that are useful on the playground, in the housing project or on the street, but they are skills that are not useful in school; in fact, they often create problems. A child who comes home and complains about being beaten by other children and is told that if he or she does not fight back there will be another beating at home is learning behavior that may be functional for survival. But such responses will get children into difficulty in school, where they are expected to negotiate and work out disagreements, or involve school personnel in doing so.

Similar patterns of behavior may not be wrong, bad or even undesirable at some times or in some places. Thus, when families are living under economic and social stress—more often the case for non-mainstream families—parents are less often able to promote the level and kind of development needed for school success.

Underdevelopment in the social-interactive area is often viewed as bad behavior. Inadequate psycho-emotional development is often seen as immaturity. Children who manipulate, take the possessions of others, distort the facts and more are usually viewed as troublemakers with low morality levels—liars, thieves, irresponsible. And children with poor self-expression, limited curiosity about things of importance in school and with little apparent drive for knowledge are viewed as having limited ability. All of these perceived shortcomings may represent underdevelopment that could be modified by appropriate school and home responses. But more often than not the response on the part of the school is to punish such children or to have low academic and behavioral expectations for them. This leads to a struggle between school staff and child and often to a downhill behavioral and academic course for the child.

Because most children are easily influenced by adult caretakers before the age of eight or nine years, even the most underdeveloped children can respond positively to reasonably caring and effective school staff. And as a result, there can be growth and development in all of the critical areas through the early school years. But around eight or nine years of age, about third grade or so, at least two developments begin to limit the school achievement of underdeveloped children. First, they develop the cognitive capacity to understand that they are different in style from the mainstream children and from school staff, and the significance of this. If they have not developed a positive relationship to academic expectations by this period, they are also not likely to be prepared for the higher level of learning that is now required. Simultaneously, they are entering a developmental phase in which they begin to pull away from their emotional and social dependence on adults. These factors combine to decrease the importance of academic learning to them. Academic learning is not internalized as a value of its own; the discipline and motivation to learn is not adequately developed. This often leads to inadequate academic performance and early school leaving.

The experience of children from anti-social networks is similar to that of children from social networks marginal to the mainstream. They have learned troublesome attitudes, values and habits that most often lead to school failure. But there is even less chance that they can form positive attachments and bonding with school people. And failure in school is even more likely.

In this post-industrial age, most children who fail in school—children who do not gain academic skills or credentials or adequate social or interpersonal skills—are likely to fail in life after school. They are able to hold only marginal jobs, if they are able to hold a job at all. They experience personal mental anguish, even illness, to a disproportionate degree. They are overinvolved in all of the social problem areas. And it is highly likely that their children will have a similar experience in the next generation, perpetuating poverty, personal anguish and social problems.

Blacks have had a more traumatic social history and have been more adversely affected by changes in the economy, educational requirements, racial bias and antagonisms than other groups of Americans. As a result, there is a disproportionate number of marginal and anti-social black families. And the troublesome relationships between black families under the greatest stress and mainstream institutions make it difficult for many black parents to prepare their children for school, and make it difficult for schools to respond to the needs of their children. Guilt and denial relative to the experience of blacks permits rationalization and scapegoating, and makes it difficult to appreciate the role of structural forces in creating poverty among many. And yet, we must be able to understand the economic, social, environmental and individual problems the black experience has created, in order to develop effective public policies and practices needed to promote success in school and to prevent and reduce poverty.

THE BLACK EXPERIENCE AND POVERTY

Most groups who came to America were able to experience a reasonable degree of cultural continuity in the process and were able to undergo several generations of development that paralleled economic change in this country. Most groups were able to maintain either a language, religion and/or other aspect of the culture of their old country. Some moved in large numbers from one place in the old country to one place in the new country. This permitted a degree of social comfort and cultural cohesion.

Opportunities in the mainstream of the society facilitated family functioning and stability and served to motivate families to prepare their children to achieve. This set up a push-pull phenomenon—a pull for development from outside of the family and a push for development from inside the family and social network. And, again, the economy permitted people to achieve with low levels of education and training prior to 1900, but required moderate levels between 1900 and 1945, and high levels after 1945, particularly after the 1960s.

The initial black experience in America, unlike that of any other ethnic group, was characterized by the involuntary imposition of cultural discontinuity and by strictly enforced exclusion from the mainstream of American society. The conditions of slavery destroyed the fundamental infrastructure of the Africans' cultural and social institutions. Formal segregation, and active and passive discrimination, continued into the post-World War II period to maintain economic and social isolation for black families. And effective political power—both cause and effect of cultural cohesion—has only been won in the 1970s and 1980s.

The political, economic and social institutions of Africa had provided guidance, direction and motivation for participation in the societies of Africa in a way that people experienced a sense of adequacy and well-being. In the movement to this country, however, Africans lost not only their language and religion, but also were denied all of their other guiding institutions of community and society. Only aesthetic remnants of their culture that did not interfere with slavery were permitted. The conditions of slavery did not promote cultural cohesion.

Indeed, a slave culture was imposed. Slavery was a system of forced dependency. The slaves had no way to experience adequacy other than through the acquisition of an adopted religion, or by performing as a "good slave"—an adequacy determined by the master—in effect, an inherent statement of *inadequacy.* For most slaves there was no way to work toward a better life condition.

Knowledge from the social and behavioral sciences tells us that these conditions are all severe obstacles to good mental health. In consequence, troublesome attitudes, values and habits were created among a significant number of the slaves—general acting-up and acting-out behavior, working as slowly as possible, leaving tools in the field to rust and other forms of passive aggressive rebellion, functional as a defense of the psyche against the self-abasement of slavery, but irresponsible and self-harmful as personal habits after slavery. Hopelessness, depression, low self-esteem and a variety of other troublesome conditions were created by slavery. And among many blacks, these troublesome conditions, attitudes, values and habits were transmitted from parent to child for generation after generation, as slavery was replaced by segregation and discrimination.

Some blacks took the Protestant religion prominent in the South and fused it with the remnants of African culture and created the Black Church. The Black Church provided a belief system and a culture that enabled many to experience a sense of adequacy, worth and hope for a better future in Heaven. And since some lived under less oppressive conditions in slavery, together the Black Church and less oppressive conditions were protective factors for some slaves and enabled them to function as reasonably stable and adequate people and families during and after slavery. In a 1969 study of black students from the Southeast selected for their academic potential, 98% were the children of Black Church ministers, officers, and usher board members.[6] It is no accident that the Civil Rights leadership and now the political leadership of the black community is disproportionately made up of religious leaders compared to other groups.

Opportunities in the mainstream of the society after slavery could have intersected the pattern of defeat experienced by most black individuals and families. But the vote was denied to blacks through violence and subterfuge. This was the case for many right into the middle of the last stage of the industrial era, the 1960s. And without either the vote, or the numbers necessary to exploit it effectively where it did exist, blacks could not gain through politics the means to significant economic or social power. For the most part, blacks continued to be closed out of the economic mainstream. And without either political or economic power it was possible for blacks to be closed out of educational opportunities throughout the period during which the rest of America was preparing for the age of science and technology.

As late as the 1930s, four to eight times as much money was spent per person on the education of white children as on the education of black children in the eight states that had 80% of the black population. The disparity was as great as 25 times in areas that were disproportionately black. Such higher education as was permitted and financed was mainly in the professional areas—teaching, nursing, religion, medicine and law—for the purpose of preparing young people to serve other blacks, and thus the ends of segregation as well. In the middle of the 1960s, one-half of Harvard University's endowment was more than the endowments of the more than 100 black colleges combined. The absence of political, economic and social opportunity for blacks within the mainstream of American society sharply limited the norm in the community. And the high level of racial antagonism that existed because blacks did not have political, economic or social power prevented even those who were well educated from receiving significant opportunities in the mainstream.

Despite these difficult conditions, most black families functioned reasonably as families well into the 1950s. The rural, small town and church culture, and income from work at marginal jobs, permitted many heads of households to meet their adult responsibilities—to care for themselves and their families as responsible citizens of their communities and the society. And as a result, as late as the 1950s, only about 22% of black households were female-headed—close to the 14% for white households which were female-headed.[7] Most black communities were reasonably safe.

But just as racial barriers began to weaken in the 1940s, education was becoming the ticket of admission to primary job market opportunities. Blacks, greatly undereducated before the 1950s, were most adversely affected by this development. The country was at that point entering the last stage of the industrial era, with an increasingly science and technology-based economy, but a disproportionate number of blacks were greatly undereducated and unskilled. And, in addition, the positive impact of the Black Church and rural culture—generators of functional attitudes, values and habits—were lost for many in the dislocation caused by migration from the rural South to urban centers of the North and South. Many families that once functioned quite well began to function less well.

With the emergence of a late industrial economy in the 1940s, families functioning best limited their size in order to gain greater economic opportunity. This was the case for the most successful black families as well as whites. But many black families not functioning well, indeed those functioning least well, did not limit their size to the same degree. Thus, since the 1940s those black families most marginal to the mainstream of the society have been having the greatest number of children. These are the families least able to take advantage of the opportunities that have opened up as a result of the Civil Rights movement. Thus at this point, parts of the black community appear to be going in opposite directions—some are functioning well and preparing their children for opportunities never available before; some are locked into social network attitudes, values and habits that limit opportunity, and maintain and promote poverty.

When large segments of neighborhoods are poor and isolated from the mainstream of society, other negative conditions emerge and a vicious cycle sets in. Heads of households who cannot get primary job market work opportunities lose respect for and confidence in themselves. Marriages more often do not occur, or fall apart. On the other hand, many seek a sense of personal adequacy and self-fulfillment through having children, although they cannot provide for them. These conditions promote negative attitudes about self and others, anti-social and self-destructive behavior and low expectations.

Economic development is less likely to occur in such areas. And, as a result, an underground economy of drugs, trading in stolen property and the like often emerges. Teenage pregnancy, gang membership, welfare dependency and a number of other troublesome behaviors are much more likely under these circumstances than efforts to participate successfully in the mainstream of the society. Families living under these conditions are not prepared to give their children the kind of preschool experiences that will allow them to present themselves in school as socially and academically competent young people with a reasonable opportunity for success in the classroom and in the society.

Over time, the existence of this pattern, and its effect on several generations of children, have led a subset of the black population to extreme differentiation from the attitudes, values and habits of the mainstream of the society. Alienation and anger towards the mainstream have developed among large numbers of people trapped in social networks different from it. Non-mainstream attitudes, values and habits have been transmitted to succeeding generations to the point that the so-called "underclass"—different from both blacks and whites in the social mainstream—has been created. It must be emphasized that *an underclass has been created*, in the first instance by destructive social and economic circumstances reinforced by inappropriate public policies and practices, not by inherent cultural norms. It can and must be diminished or eliminated by changes in mainstream public policies and practices; it cannot be effectively reduced by black community efforts alone.

Social, economic and political forces from the beginning of this country through the present—from slavery to the age of science and technology—in one way or another led to poverty or inadequate income among a disproportionate number of black families. Socio-environmental factors which sustained exclusion, and antagonistic attitudes towards blacks, added psychological and social stress, resulting in behavior problems and attitudes among a segment of the population that has been less protected by the kind of institutions that generate organizing and constructive belief systems and conditions. Families that functioned reasonably well despite difficult conditions under an agricultural and industrial society function less well under a science and technology-based economy. As a result, a disproportionate number of black children do not experience the kind of individual development that permits them to prepare for the modern job market as children, and to participate in it as adults, creating poverty for themselves and setting the stage for poverty among their children in a subsequent generation. Without successful intervention the problem will be worse in succeeding generations, in that those families under the greatest social stress, in all groups, have the largest number of children.

POVERTY REDUCTION

The kind of successful early childhood development that increases the likelihood of early and later school success must be at the heart of any effort to address poverty among the black poor. The War on Poverty contained this focus in Head Start, as well as in other programs needed to reduce the level of poverty—child care, job training, community development and others. The major shortcoming of the War on Poverty was that it did not serve the vast majority of those in need, and it was not sustained long enough for implementors to learn from early efforts and to develop more effective approaches in subsequent years.

But, in addition to not being inclusive enough, programs directed specifically at minorities, blacks in particular, did not address a critical issue—relationships. Because of our national need to understand ourselves as a nation of successful individuals, without a class of victims—or to see the wounds of victims as self-inflicted—desirable public policies and practices, from school integration to public housing and health provision, have been carried out without consideration of the relationship of much of the black poor to the mainstream social system throughout our history, and its impact on behavior. Because these programs were not responsive to relationship ties—both positive and negative—they have been less successful than they might have been. This and other national developments have led to a backlash against the poor and minorities. Both the backlash and intervention shortcomings must be addressed.

EDUCATION, FAMILIES AND SOCIAL NETWORKS

The education of most poor children will not be improved by most of the reforms suggested by scholars and public policymakers over the past five to ten years. These reforms address personnel and curriculum standards primarily. Even when school reorganization is mentioned, the concern appears to be about school size and staff control more than staff-family-student relationships. Most poor children fail in school because their home experiences and relationships do not prepare them for the school experiences which, in turn, leads to difficult staff-family-student relationships, and student underdevelopment and underachievement. School success will be more possible for low-income children, and more minority group children, when schools systematically decrease the real and potential alienation between school and families and their social networks, and make it possible for the children to experience the positive attachment and bonding, imitation, identification and internalization of the attitudes, values and ways of school personnel and programs, that leads to adequate development and learning. The Yale Child Study Center team has developed a model designed to achieve these ends.

The School Development Program model was established in 1968 in two elementary schools in New Haven, Connecticut as a collaborative effort between the Yale Child Study Center and the school system. The two schools involved were the lowest-achieving in the city, had poor attendance and had serious relationship problems among and between students, staff and parents. 99% of the students were black and almost all were poor. Parents were angry and distrustful of the school. There was hopelessness and despair among the staff.

The Yale Child Study Center staff—social worker, psychologist, special education teacher, child psychiatrist—provided traditional support services from these disciplines. But they were focused more on trying to understand the underlying problems and how to correct them, or prevent their manifestations wherever possible, than on treatment of individual children, or on finding deficiencies among staff and parents. Three program components were established in response to the apparent needs—a governance and management group, representative of parents, teachers, administrators and support staff; a mental health or support staff team; and a parents' group.

The make-up of the governance and management group permitted the kind of agreement or consensus about expected child behavior and performance, and staff behavior and performance, that existed nationally in a natural way prior to the 1940s, when the school was a natural part of the community. The mental health team worked in a way that provided the staff with knowledge of child development and behavior and the skills to use it in the classroom, and throughout the school, to help the students grow and to compensate for the children's underdevelopment in critical areas—social-interative, psycho-emotional, moral, speech and language and intellectual-cognitive-academic. The parents' program was designed to support the overall work of the school.

As parents worked with staff—in a climate of mutual respect and general agreement—a message was sent to the students that the expectations of home and school were basically the same. As the governance and management group addressed problems and opportunities in the school, utilizing knowledge of child development and behavior, the functioning of students, staff and parents improved, and the hope and energy levels of the staff increased. They eventually developed a comprehensive school plan that focused on improving the social climate, which, in turn, permitted an adequate focus on the academic program.

Increased time for planning led to an improved academic program. Eventually the curriculum—and, indeed the entire school experience—was designed to compensate for student underdevelopment. An active staff development progam helped teachers, administrators and parents alike gain the skills necessary to promote student growth. Highly significant academic and social gains followed.[8] This model is now being used in a number of schools in New Haven and in other school districts.

This model recognizes that historical conditions have created family and social network functioning problems for many, and have resulted in the underdevelopment of children entering school. At the same time, schools have not been organized in a way that addresses the potential and actual relationship problems that interfere with student growth and development. This model puts in place mechanisms and operations that permit the necessary groups to come together—despite suspicion and distrust created by differences in race, class, education, etc.—in a way that allows all of the adults involved to support the development of students.

There are many other successful school progams serving low-income families across this country. The research of the late Ron Edmonds identified corollaries of school success in low-income communities[9] and a number of schools have created these conditions. Westside Preparatory School in Chicago, directed by Marva Collins, and a number of other private schools have been able to meet the needs of poor children who have been unsuccessful in public schools. But to address significantly the problem of poverty through education, programs to serve such children must be successful on a large scale. This requires success in *public* schools. Generally, most school intervention projects have focused on improving the academic achievement of poor children and not on overall development throughout their years in school. The mission of the school is to prepare children for life success, with school success and work readiness being secondary outcomes. A focus on development at every level, through adult maturation, is needed to prepare young people to cope successfully in the complex world of today.

In families locked in social networks that are reactive to their exclusion from the mainstream, there are often negative attitudes about work and achievement. Many young people grow up in homes where parents do not work, work infrequently, have difficult work experiences and respond negatively to them, and so on. Many simply do not receive information about what it takes to work successfully.

Many live in neighborhoods in which the underground economy—composed of marginal or criminal work activities—is financially more rewarding than the mainstream economy. In many neighborhoods the pimp, the prostitute, the drug dealer and other, similar "professionals" have the highest incomes. Without knowledge of or access to mainstream social interactive and work skills and employment opportunities, the motivation for academic learning declines as young people assess their ability to succeed in the mainstream workforce and society. Intervention efforts, then, must go beyond improving school performance and must provide the necessary skills and contacts in the mainstream world of work. Students must be connected—through programs involving home and school—from kindergarten through high school.

The Yale Child Study Center School Development Program has developed a Social Skills Curriculum for Inner City Children. It integrates the teaching of social skills and basic skills, and appreciation of the arts, in four areas of activities in which young people will need experience in order to succeed in the mainstream world of work and society—business and economics, health and nutrition, politics and government, spiritual/leisure time. Through a number of simulated and real activities in these four areas the youngsters experience the relevance of basic skills to mainstream work and societal expectations. This increases their interest in basic academic work. It also improves their social interactive skills, more needed in today's workforce than in the past. The project is now developing similar programs for the middle school and the high school. At the high school level, in particular, there is an effort to create a network of exposure, experiences and jobs—in the real world where possible—that will make students aware of opportunities as well as demonstrate the kind of skills and behaviors necessary to capitalize on them. Again, just as with school staff, careful attention must be paid to the relationship between students from low-income backgrounds on the one hand, and employers on the other. Mutual respect and responsibility must be promoted—they cannot be assumed.

Making it possible for students to participate in the mainstream workforce would appear to be an obvious benefit, and thus no reinforcement or support for this effort would seem to be necessary.

But such participation, for many, requires a change in social network ties and relationships—even a break. Sometimes the break is with longtime friends and relatives, even parents—who are, among other things, a greater source of positive self-affirmation than members of the societal mainstream. It is for this reason that acceptable mainstream attitudes, values and ways must be supported and reinforced by groups who are relevant and important to the children and young adults among the poor. Appreciation of this need led to the creation of a Black Family Roundtable in New Haven.

The stimulus for the development of the Black Family Roundtable was the National Conference on the Black Family sponsored by the National Association for the Advancement of Colored People (NAACP) and the National Urban League in 1984. In 1985 the NAACP and the Urban League in the New Haven area created an Ad Hoc Committee on the Black Family made up of 14 black leaders drawn from all segments of community life—education, business, religion, politics, housing, labor, social welfare and so on. The work of this group eventually led to the establishment of the Black Family Roundtable in 1986. The Roundtable works in two major areas— traditional advocacy on behalf of the black community and support for healthy youth development. Approximately 30 black community organizations, including a significant number of Black Churches, have been asked to support the work of the Roundtable.

The focus of the Roundtable on traditional advocacy issues should result in more efficient and effective action in this area, but, at least as important, it gives the organization credibility within all segments of the black community. Because the Black Church has been the major adaptive institution within the black community, its presence in all areas of Roundtable work is critical. Credibility throughout the black community will, it is hoped, enable the organization to sponsor youth development activities such as scout troops, youth clubs, etc. Through these activities, the black community that is most a part of the mainstream society will have the opportunities to develop meaningful relationships with black youth, and will be in a position to transmit the kind of attitudes, values and behavior that will lead to success in school and in life. This program is new and still evolving, but its importance is its recognition of the relationship problem between the mainstream of the larger society and the black community, the black poor and alienated in particular.

Black community effort, however, will be successful *only* in conjunction with changes in mainstream public and private policy and practice in housing, jobs, economic development, crime reduction and other areas. It is *extremely* difficult to promote and sustain desirable family functioning in crime-ridden communities, where there is little economic opportunity, and where there is little sense of relatedness and acceptance in the mainstream of the society. Under such conditions, constructive belief systems and desirable behaviors cannot survive and thrive among enough families and individuals to create adequate preschool experiences for children in general.

PUBLIC POLICIES AND PRACTICES

Public and private policy-makers must understand the coping problems of many among the poor as issues of relationship, development and reactive behavior rather than as a lack of ability or desire, and willful anti-social behavior. Policy-makers must understand how changes in the economy since the 1940s have made it more difficult for many families to cope, how scientific and technological developments have decreased local community support for child development and socialization for adult life, while simultaneously increasing the level of development needed to succeed—the highest level ever required in the history of the world. Public and private leadership—particulary the media, but schools as well—must take responsibility for attacking the myths that undergird attitudes responsible for growing hostility towards the poor, the minority poor in particular. Without such understanding among the general population it will be difficult to impossible to establish the kind and levels of projects and programs necessary to significantly reduce poverty.

In addition, institutions training professional and other service personnel need to strengthen their focus on child development and relationship issues. This is particularly true of schools of education. Even today it is possible for the majority of educators to receive credentials in their profession without taking a single applied child development or social and human behavior course. As mentioned above, this often leads to punitive responses to and low expectations of children who are underdeveloped or developed in ways that do not prepare them for school. And, obviously, there needs to be some way to "retool" those who are already working in schools without the needed understanding and perspectives. But the need goes beyond the school.

Over the course of our history we have made a number of public policy errors, in part because policy-makers have limited understanding of child development and social and human behavior. For example, housing policies which forced the most successful families out of public housing projects often left former sharecroppers and tenant farmers, least socialized and prepared for functioning in the main-stream of the society, without the role models and social organization around them needed to promote conditions that would lead to successful mainstream functioning. And even as the country moves toward tenant ownership and management in an effort to promote self direction and desirable functioning, policy-makers must take into account that many such tenants have not had leadership experiences prior to this time, and probably will not have adequate leadership skills without training and support. Similarly, businesses and other agencies attempting to work with schools serving the poor must recognize the causes of school management failure and the resultant student-staff-parent underachievement in them. Without such under-standing, efforts to help often simply complicate and overwhelm the school—or, at best, lead to limited success. With adequate under-standing of schools and the problems of the poor, it is possible to design work exposure and experiences for young people and their parents—through the school—that will better prepare students for mainstream functioning in the world of work.

Again, early childhood programs must be at the heart of any effort to reduce poverty in this country. It is through adequate socialization here that children can be prepared for school success. It is also here that families can be involved in ways that allow them to better support the development of their children. In the process, many parents gain the motivation to improve their own level of functioning; and, in programs properly designed, parents often gain the skills needed to function in the mainstream of society. These efforts in school, com-bined with housing programs that are sensitive to the needs of the poor and job training programs similarly designed, can significantly increase the potential of poor families to function.

The Bible says, "Ye have the poor with you always." That may indeed prove to be true; but, it is also true that in the United States we have the capacity to limit significantly the number of people who live in poverty, and to reduce the severity of their condition. We must do so, for not only does poverty stunt the growth and development of children and limit the fulfillment of their lives as children and as adults, it also limits the quality of life of the overall society. Poverty today—more than in the past—can destabilize a nation when the forces generating it are allowed to go unchecked. Thus, both for altruistic reasons and for reasons of concern about the welfare of our nation, we must attempt to find ways to prevent and reduce the ravages of poverty.

NOTES

1. Peter F. Drucker, *The Age of Discontinuity*. New York: Harper & Row, 1968; and Gerald D. Nash (Ed.) *Issues in American Economic History*. Boston: Heath & Company, 1964.

2. Charles E. Silberman, *Crisis in the Classroom: The Remaking of American Education*. New York: Vintage Books (Random House), 1970.

3. James P. Comer, *Beyond Black and White*. New York: Quadrangle/New York Times Book Co., 1972.

4. James P. Comer, *School Power: Implications of an Intervention Project*. New York: Free Press, 1980.

5. Alison Clarke-Stewart and Joanne Koch, *Children: Development Through Adolescence*. New York: Wiley, 1983.

6. James P. Comer, Martin Harrow and Samuel Johnson, "Summer Study-Skills Program: A Case for Structure," *Journal of Negro Education*, Vol. 37(1), Winter 1969, pp. 38–45.

7. U.S. Department of Commerce, Bureau of the Census. *Statistical Abstract of the United States*. Washington, D.C.: Government Printing Office, 1958 and 1978 volumes.

8. James P. Comer, *School Power: Implications of an Intervention Project*. New York: Free Press, 1980.

9. Ronald Edmonds, "Making Public Schools Effective," *Social Policy*, Vol. 12(2), 1981, pp. 56–60.

EQUAL OPPORTUNITY FOR INFANTS AND YOUNG CHILDREN: PREVENTIVE SERVICES FOR CHILDREN IN A MULTI-RISK ENVIRONMENT

Stanley I. Greenspan

DURING THE 1980s, a number of studies have been conducted aimed at describing accurately the factors present in a child's life that contribute to the existence of serious and damaging developmental problems. The results of these studies now provide the basis for identifying and dealing with some of the major causes of educational and social failure that arise in infancy. New approaches are being developed for multi-problem families that rely on an evolving understanding of the way children's minds grow in response to the conditions of their environment, and particularly in response to the kind of interactions they have with those who are their primary caretakers.

THE EXPERIENCES OF EARLY CHILDHOOD AND THE ABILITY TO LEARN*

Equal opportunity for our citizens is one of American society's most fundamental ideals. Historically, this has meant, among other things, providing children with a good education, through laws requiring that they attend schools. Indeed, mandating that each child have an education is, in many respects, a cornerstone of the "equal opportunity" ethic.

But physical access to education starting with kindergarten is no longer believed to guarantee access to opportunity to learn. It has become clear that many children with fine potential are already educational failures by age four because the critical establishment of

---

*An earlier version of this section appeared in the Outlook section of the *Washington Post*, March 14, 1988.

learning capacity that occurs in the first three to four years of life has been defective, or its development has been ignored.

Until relatively recently in our history, many infants didn't survive, and those who did were considered basically only bundles of reflexes. Young children were not given, even informally, the status and rights of persons until they were old enough to talk and follow rules. Adults assumed that real learning only began with the onset of a fully developed capacity for reasoning. In this context, beginning children's formal education when they had developed to the point that they were ready to read, write and use numbers seemed to make sense.

But now we know otherwise. The very abilities needed to learn, reason, talk, follow rules and comprehend shapes and symbols are themselves the product of preceding years of active learning. Such basic behavior as paying attention and concentrating, trusting and relating to others, controling impulses and actions, being imaginative and creative, distinguishing fantasy from reality and having positive self-esteem is either learned or not learned for the first time during the first three or four years of life. If children have not learned to act and to interact in these specific ways before formal schooling begins, they will be impulsive, without hope, distractable and irrational.

In spite of the evidence, many people remain skeptical that vital learning occurs in the first years of life. Even though it has been known for a while that by five years of age the brain has grown to three-quarters of its full size, it is only relatively recently that we have been able to figure out when and how specific different emotions and intellectual capacities develop.

We now know that a newborn can tell the difference between his or her mother's voice and someone else's. He or she can (and will, if encouraged) copy physical behavior of head and face. If the newborn's world is chaotic and/or inattentive in the extreme a child will exhibit distraction and confusion, or withdrawal. The evolving mind and personality are learning to react negatively rather than positively to the world around it. A mother who fails to touch, look at, or talk to her infant, or who shakes the infant too aggressively is likely to have a baby who either seems to look inward or who stares at distant objects, showing no recognition of or interest in other people.

By four months, the infant being raised in a generally positive and interactive environment feels secure, and is ready to relate to others, to feel close and trusting. Four-month-olds can already take a special interest in their parents or other caretaking adults. If the world is aloof or overly intrusive, however, instead of smiling happily and forming positive expectations, an infant learns to withdraw from others, to be distant and fearful. A few angry sounds and some frantic gestures might be followed by gradual listlessness and eventually an indifferent solemn look.

By ten months, "cause and effect" learning is well established. The infant whose parents "read" his other communications has already learned how to have an impact on the world and to communicate with his or her own brand of logic—if I cry or reach out, I will be picked up. Babies at this age can learn an impersonal type of "cause and effect" by banging a block on the floor and hearing the sound. They can only learn that each of their own feelings and intentions can have an impact on other persons, however, if they receive clear, logical, empathetic feedback from their caregivers. And if different inclinations and associated gestures lead to different responses, babies also learn to separate out the "meaning" of their own different feelings and intentions.

Between 18 months and two years, children can begin to see how parts fit into a whole, to communicate across space with gestures, sounds and a few words and to control impulses and behavior. Wish and intentionality are now part of a pattern.

At this age, an environment that is significantly undermining, abusive or overly permissive will teach a child to be fragmented, passive or antisocial and destructive.

By age two, the child is encountering a large and complex world. What we call play or pretending is important behavior in the testing of concepts and ideas that structure this complexity, both in terms of outside reality and in terms of the child's feelings. By three, children are learning to form an image of who they are and to separate what is real from what is not real. They also are ready to feel positive self-esteem and optimism or they are beginning to be trapped in negativism and despondency. Before age four, children need opportunities to reason about their needs and frustrations, to explore their imaginations, to articulate their thoughts and feelings and to develop the ability to see limits. They are beginning to use ideas as a basis for logical thinking and problem-solving and to use language for communicating thoughts and for labeling and understanding feelings.

In an arbitrary environment where ideas are misunderstood, ignored or not encouraged, young children tend to become overly concrete, devoid of basic literacy skills such as the ability to see abstractions, and are at the mercy of immature coping strategies. In such situations, four-year-olds learn to deal with frustrations either by hurting others, by exhibiting disorganized behavior, or by becoming helpless and self-destructive. These patterns of nonconstructive but functional acts, including avoidance, withdrawal and the direct discharge of behavior, are the same patterns found in older children and adolescents who are delinquents, drug users, and/or the chronically helpless.

The early environmental determinants of success and failure are all too clear. At one extreme, there are warm, consistent, loving relationships which provide physical safety, pleasurable emotions and special experiences geared to the child's changing needs. At the other extreme, there are inconsistent early relationship patterns, a lack of physical safety, emotions of anger and rejection and a failure to adjust to meet the child's changing developmental needs. Yet, there is evidence that even with factors present that create great stress, such as a mentally ill parent, families that provide elements of the former can teach their children to cope effectively. There is also mounting evidence that when the latter conditions prevail, children can fail to experience each of the necessary early learning opportunities, coming into early childhood devoid of the most basic social and intellectual competencies.

Clearly, in the first four years of life, children are experiencing their most fundamental lessons—learning to focus, to be intimate, to control their behavior, to be imaginative, to separate reality from fantasy and to have positive self-esteem. Well-mastered, positive lessons afford them real intellectual access to the educational system and, therefore, to a reasonable degree, equal opportunity. Without these early lessons, however, access to subsequent education and opportunities can hardly be truly equal. The child who cannot focus his attention, who can't decode simple sounds, much less read letters, who is suspicious rather than trusting, sad rather than optimistic, destructive rather than respectful, and one who is lost in a sea of frightening fantasy rather than grounded on a foundation of reality—such a child has little opportunity at all, let alone "equal" opportunity.

Whatever abilities children might be born with, as they mature they do not experience biological development separate from environmental needs nor, for that matter, from physical, intellectual or emotional experiences. Poor nutrition, lack of consistent loving care and lack of appropriate emotional interactive and cognitive opportunities can all, either separately or together, seriously compromise development. In the extreme, even proper brain growth will be compromised by severe lacks in any one of these areas.

THE CONCEPT OF THE MULTI-RISK FAMILY

As converging findings from both human and animal studies have indicated strongly that the vast majority of developmental problems in infancy are influenced by both biological and experiential environmental factors, it has become more apparent that the optimal time for prevention and treatment is early in the course of the disorder. Yet a large gap still exists in the development of clinical techniques and tools to assess, diagnose and intervene in a comprehensive manner.

We have, however, made major advances in identifying the capacities that are key to developmental progress, and in associating these capacities, or their lack, with specific conditions present in patterns of family interaction. Further, we have been able to associate the probability of negative patterns with certain social conditions and other family characteristics, so that we can now identify families likely to be at risk of multiple problems, and, hence, likely to have children with significant disabilities. This progress has permitted the creation of new intervention models which, while not yet in widespread use, nonetheless show promise.

Our present ability to monitor developmental progress using rather explicit guidelines, facilitates early identification of those infants and young children who are progressing unsatisfactorily. For example, it is now possible to evaluate infants who have difficulty developing a capacity for focused interest in their immediate environments, or who fail to develop a positive emotional interest in their caregivers. It is also possible to assess an infant's inability to learn "cause and effect" interactions and complex emotional and social patterns, or by age two to three, to create symbols to guide emotions and behavior. In exploring the factors that may be contributing to less than optimal patterns of development, focusing on multiple aspects of development in the context of clearly delineated developmental and emotional landmarks opens the door to comprehensive assessment, diagnosis and preventive intervention strategies.

IDENTIFYING AT-RISK POPULATIONS

In multi-risk-factor families, the parents are often psychologically impaired, social and economic stress is usually high and the parents are generally deficient in a variety of coping functions (including self-care, planning for the future and judgment). Children in these families are at risk not only of infant mortality but of illness, injury and serious disability as well, particularly in the areas of psychological and social functioning during the first years of life.

In the classic descriptive work on multi-risk-factor families by Pavenstaedt,[1] only 13 families (which had 40 to 50 children between the ages of 2½ and 6 years) were studied. Nevertheless, clinical impressions from the study are striking. Almost all the children showed social and psychological characteristics more consistent with 1½ to 2-year-olds in their egocentricity and need-orientation. Their ability to use a symbolic (or representational) mode to plan for filling their own needs and to consider the needs and actions of others was limited, and they had variable self-esteem. They tended to think in fragmented, isolated units, rather than in cohesive patterns. They were not capable of goal-directed, organized action and were limited in their ability to socialize and interact appropriately for their age. The children already had an ingrained defeatist attitude and the core of an aimless (either asocial or antisocial) personality.

To find out how children learned such negative patterns we conducted an in-depth prospective clinical study of multi-risk-factor families.[2] A clinical approach, which studies infants, children and families from multiple perspectives and assesses the degree to which developmental milestones are being met, allows extraction of the clinical characteristics of vulnerable infants and families. It has been known for some time that certain populations are clearly at greater risk than others for poor cognitive, social or emotional development (e.g., teenage mothers, low-income families, infants with low birth weight, and/or chronic physical illness). The cumulative impact of multiple risk factors, including psychological as well as social characteristics, however, until recent years has not been clearly identified.

This study focused on cumulative risk and involved 47 families referred by prenatal clinics or other agencies with doubts about their child rearing capacities (65% by medical facilities, 11% by social service facilities and only 17% by mental health facilities). Many of the multi-risk families, often thought of as "social" and/or "economic" challenges, had a high degree of psychiatric illness, including some whose backgrounds included severe developmental interferences and disturbances in psychosocial functioning. In addition, early difficulties in interaction abilities with their infants were observed. 64% came from families with a history of psychiatric distrubance, 34% had experienced psychiatric hospitalization themselves and an additional 15% had some type of outpatient contact with a mental health provider.

Of these mothers, 44% had experienced physical abuse and 32% sexual abuse prior to age 18, while 45% reported current physical abuse and a tendency to abuse or neglect their own children. (There were significant correlations between past and present abusive patterns.) Over two-thirds (69%) had experienced significant disruptions of a parental relationship or parent surrogate relationship prior to adolescence. Over 75% had impaired psychosocial functioning in either the family, school, peer or work setting in childhood, adolescence and now in early adulthood.

Some 18 items were considered to be unfavorable and put into an "Index of Misfortune." Fifty percent of the mothers had nine or more "misfortunes" compared to a low-risk comparison group which generally had none of these events.

In addition, a series of reliable psychiatric ratings of various ego functions dealing with impulses and regulation of emotion, self-other boundaries and maternal/relationship capacities predicted high-risk group membership correctly about 98% of the time and low-risk group membership about 85% of the time. Overall, close to 95% of these cases were correctly classified.[3]

In general, the babies in the program, most of whom had been at risk before birth, but had apparently normal patterns of development at birth (prenatal intervention having assured adequate nutrition and other supports, including appropriate medical care), showed significantly less than optimal development as early as the first months of life. Pediatric, neurological and neonatal examinations at one month of age, for example, showed developmental progression, but not the increased capacity for orientation that is the norm. The study's high-risk group tended to be less developed in orientation, habituation and motor organization than average children at one month, even after a few families with the greatest risk had left the program.[4]

By three months of age, instead of a capacity for self-regulation, organization and an interest in the world, a number of babies showed increased tendencies toward muscle rigidity, gaze aversion, and an absence of organized sleep-awake, alert, and feeding patterns. Their caregivers, rather than offering the babies comfort, protection and an interest in the world, tended to withdraw from them or overstimulate them in a chaotic and intermittent fashion. At about the ages of two to four months, we expect to find in an infant the beginnings of a deep, rich emotional investment in the human world, especially in primary caregivers. We also expect a human environment that will "fall in love" with the child and, in turn, will "woo" that child to return the feeling in an effective, multi-modal, pleasurable manner. Instead, a significant number of these children exhibited a total lack of involvement in the human world or an involvement that was noneffective, shallow and impersonal, and we saw caregivers who were emotionally distant, aloof, impersonal and highly ambivalent about their children.

Between three and nine months of age, one expects an infant's capacity for interacting with the world in a reciprocal, causal, or purposeful manner to further develop and form a foundation for later organized causal behavior or thinking (reality orientation and testing). Instead, in the multi-problem families, the child's behavior and feelings remained under the control of his internal states in random and chaotic or narrow, rigid and stereotyped patterns of interaction. The child's environment, instead of offering the expected optimal contingent responsiveness to the child's varied signals, tended to ignore or misread them. The child's caregivers were overly preoccupied, depressed or chaotic.

Toward the end of the first year of life and the beginning of the second, the child in the multiple-risk-factor family, instead of showing an increase in organized, complex, assertive and innovative emotional and behavioral patterns (for example, taking his mother's hand and leading her to the refrigerator to show her the kind of food he wants), tended to exhibit fragmented, stereotyped and polarized patterns. These toddlers were withdrawn and compliant or highly aggressive, impulsive, and disorganized. Their human environment tended to be intrusive, controlling, and fragmented. The toddler may have been prematurely separated from his caregivers, or the caregivers may have exhibited patterns of withdrawal instead of admiringly supporting the toddler's initiative and autonomy and helping him to organize what were at that point more complex capacities for communicating, interacting and behaving.

As the toddler's potential capacities continued to develop in the latter half of the second year and in the third (18 to 36 months), profound deficits could be more clearly observed. The child, instead of developing capacities for internal representations (imagery) around which to organize his behavior and feelings, and for differentiating ideas, feelings and thoughts pertaining to the self and the non-self, either developed no representational or symbolic capacity, or if the capacity did develop, it was not elaborated beyond the most elementary descriptive form so that the child's behavior remained shallow and polarized. His sense of the emerging self, as distinguished from the sense of other people, remained fragmented and undifferentiated. The child's potentially emerging capacities for reality testing, impulse regulation and mood stabilization were either compromised or became extremely vulnerable to regression. In other words, we saw patterns consistent with a later borderline and psychotic personality organization, or with severe asocial or anti-social, impulse-ridden character disorders.

At this stage, the underlying impairment manifested itself in the child's inability to use a representational or symbolic mode to organize behavior. In essence, the distinctly human capacity of operating beyond the survival level, of using internal imagery to elaborate and organize complex feelings and wishes and to construct trial actions in the emotional sphere, and of anticipating and planning ahead were compromised. In many of our families, the parents simply did not have these capacities. Even when they were not under emotional distress or in states of crisis or panic, they did not demonstrate a symbolic mode, as evidenced in the lack of verbal emotional communication (only one aspect of symbolic communication) and in the lack of symbolic play. Such families tended to be fearful and to deny and fail to meet needs in their children that were appropriate for their ages. They engaged the child only in non-symbolic modes of communication, such as holding, feeding and administering physical punishment, and at times they misread or responded unrealistically to the child's emerging communication, thus undermining the development in the child of a sense of self and a flexible orientation to reality.

Needless to say, the mastery by the children in these families of higher level developmental tasks was even more difficult. At each new level of development, the infants and toddlers who, for a variety of reasons, had survived earlier developmental phases intact, invariably challenged the multi-risk-factor environment with their new capacities; for example, with their capacity for symbolic communication. The healthier the toddler, the more challenging and overwhelming he was likely to be to the people around him. In a pattern that we have frequently observed since this original study, the child moved ahead of the parent (engaging, for example, in symbolic play around themes of dependency or sexuality), and thus the parent became confused and either withdrew from, or behaved intrusively toward the child. The youngster who experiences developmental failures, including the failure to develop a full representational or symbolic capacity (the basis for formal school experience later on), will be handicapped in subsequent opportunities for learning.

APPLICATION OF MULTI-RISK CLINICAL CRITERIA TO A NON-INTERVENTION, HIGH-RISK POPULATION

The findings from a related study of a population of multi-risk families demonstrates that family, psychological and infant interactional patterns—independent of socio-economic status (SES)—correlate with poor outcomes at the age of four. They further show that cumulative risk patterns during infancy can be used to predict as much as a 25-fold increase in the probability of poor cognitive outcomes at the age of four.[5] The results of this study suggest that cumulative risk factors place infants and families at greatest risk.

Participants in this study were recruited only with the aim of looking at the effects of different types of parental emotional disturbances on IQ development in children. As a group, however, the individuals involved exhibited patterns consistent with those found in multi-problem or multi-risk families described above. Of the approximately 200 families followed from pregnancy, a broad range of socioeconomic categories was represented: white, black and Puerto Rican, with family sizes ranging from one to ten children. Approximately one quarter of the women were either single, separated or divorced. Their education ranged from completion of the third grade to the acquisition of advanced college degrees.

Ten variables that appeared to be clinically relevant from prior studies were selected to categorize the families into high and low-risk families. Multi-risk status was defined operationally in this study according to the number of high-risk variables in any family.

Multi-risk patterns had far greater impact than any one risk factor alone. For verbal IQ outcomes at the age of four, two standard deviation differences emerged between the lowest and the highest risk groups, i.e., between families with only one or two risk factors compared with families having six or more. Perhaps the most important finding of this study, however, is the fact that interactive, familial and psychological variables, as measured by multiple-risk criteria, have an impact on later developmental outcomes even within single socio-economic groups. It is often thought that poverty, or socio-economic status more generally, accounts in its own right for poor developmental outcomes. This study demonstrated that, quite to the contrary, interactive, psychological and familial patterns account for poor developmental outcomes even when socio-economic status is held constant.

To highlight these findings, in another analysis, families were divided into low, moderate and high-risk groups, depending on the number of risk factors in the family. A most striking result of this analysis was to indicate that if a family falls into the high-risk group, characterized by four or more factors, the children have a 25 times greater probability of falling into the low IQ category.

It should also be pointed out that the same relationships described here for intellectual performance were also found for aspects of emotional and social functioning at the age of four.[6] The latter relationships, though, while significant, were not as dramatic. This is most likely due to the types of measures used rather than a lesser degree of impairment in emotional functioning.

The implications of being able to identify high-risk patterns in infancy and early childhood for potential preventive programs is enormous. Further research could establish probabilities of poor developmental outcomes associated with specific familial, interactive and constitutional patterns in infancy. Such research has the promise of bringing a degree of specificity to developmental diagnosis and preventive intervention which has only been possible for a limited number of disorders in general medicine.

A MODEL PROGRAM

In order to address the issue of how the negative effects of multiple risks in the infant and family might be reversed, a pilot program was implemented to develop the technology for a larger-scale demonstration of preventive interventions.

Called the Clinical Infant Development Program (CIDP), the pilot was able to study performance in depth of 47 multi-risk-factor families.[7] The approach developed a regular pattern of services; the CIDP organized service systems on behalf of the family's survival needs, such as food, housing and medical care. It also provided a constant emotional relationship with the family and, most important, offered highly technical patterns of care, including approaches to deal with the infant's and family's individual vulnerabilities and strengths.

In addition, the program had a special support structure to provide partial or full therapeutic daycare for the child, innovative outreach to the family, and ongoing training and supervision of the program staff at one site. To respond to the full range of the family's concrete needs, various community agencies would need to be involved; however, many of these families, for a variety of reasons, were adept at circumventing offers of traditional supports. The component of a comprehensive effort that was absolutely necessary, was a close relationship of participants with one or more program staff. Such relationships were not easy to establish, since distrust was often ingrained in each parent, as well as in the family unit. Further, once established, relationships needed to grow to parallel the infant's development and needs in order to help the parents facilitate that development. The relationship pattern needed to render growing regularity, emotional attachment, and a therapeutic process which facilitated describing and examining interpersonal patterns. To provide this human relationship, the study used both a team and a single primary clinician. In order to give it appropriate significance, the CIDP developed a therapeutic relationship scale which could be rated reliably, differentiated high and low-risk groups, and correlated with other measures of caregiver functioning (Table 1).

When the program began, agencies were alerted to send their "most difficult and challenging" cases, leading the CIDP to become known as the group that would "go anywhere to see anyone." Calls were received from prenatal clinics regarding mothers who had missed appointments, who appeared confused and who were not adequately following medical guidance. Calls were also received from protective service case workers. The calls usually involved a family in which the mother was pregnant, displayed a lack of interest in her yet unborn new baby, and had a history of neglecting older children.

The key to recruiting and forming an alliance with these families lay in the staff's ability to deal with patterns of avoidance, rejection, anger, illogical and anti-social behavior and substance abuse. Experi-

TABLE 1

DIMENSIONS OF THE THERAPEUTIC RELATIONSHIP

Steps in the Therapeutic Process

Regularity and Stability	Attachment	Process
1. Willingness to meet with an interviewer or therapist to convey concrete concerns or hear about services.	1. Interest in having concrete needs met that can be provided by anyone (e.g., food, transportation, etc.)	1. Preliminary communication, including verbal support and information gathering.
2. Willingness to schedule meeting again.	2. Emotional interest in the person of the therapist (e.g., conveys pleasure or anger when they meet).	2. Ability to observe and report single behaviors or action patterns.
3. Meeting according to some predictable pattern.	3. Communicates purposefully in attempts to deal with problems.	3. Focuses on relationships involved in the behavior-action pattern.
4. Meeting regularly with occasional disruptions.	4. Tolerates discomfort or scary emotions.	4. Self-observing function in relationship to feelings.

Steps in the Therapeutic Process		
Regularity and Stability	Attachment	Process
5. Meeting regularly with no disruptions.	5. Feels "known" or accepted in positive and negative aspects.	5. Self-observing function for thematic and affective elaboration.
		7. Makes connections between the key relationships in life including the theraputic relationship.
		8. Identification of patterns in current, theraputic, and historical relationships to work through problems and facilitate new growth.
		9. Consolidation of new patterns and levels of satisfaction and preparing to separate from the theraputic relationship.
		10. Full consolidation of gains in the context of separating and experiencing a full sense of loss and mourning.

Source: S. I. Greenspan; Psychopathology and Adaptation in Infancy and Early Childhood: Principles of Clinical Diagnosis and Preventive Intervention.

enced clinicians were selected because of their ability to deal with such behavior. In the early phases of the work it might be necessary for the "primary clinician" to make five or six home visits. These visits would include knocking on the door, hearing a very suspicious participant behind the door walking around, making a few comments through the door, not getting an answer, but returning three days later. This pattern would continue until the individual on the other side of the door would feel comfortable enough to open the door to let in the primary clinician. This pattern might repeat itself intermittently for a number of months.

Even more difficult challenges were posed by participants who eagerly embraced the offering of services and who then would "flee" by missing three or four appointments, including not calling or returning telephone calls. The continual offering of an interested ear would, in most cases, eventually meet with success. Occasionally, it would take a year before a constant pattern of relatedness would evolve. Overcoming a tendency to say, "they're not interested in help," "they told us they don't want us," "they're not motivated," "we're being a burden to them," "we're making them upset" and so forth, was a key challenge for the CIDP staff.

Organizing responses to a family's concrete needs and offering the family a close human relationship, however, are not enough. This human relationship must be able to help the parents understand some of these maladaptive coping strategies and teach them how to deal with their own needs, as well as those of their infant. In addition, special clinical techniques and patterns of care to reverse maladaptive developmental patterns in the areas of emotion and social interaction, sensory-motor development and cognition must be available at the appropriate time. For example, a mother who is suspicious, hyperactive, and tends to deal with stress by hyperstimulating her already over-reactive baby, requires an approach that shows her how to not only sooth her baby but also help her baby deal with his own over-reactivity.

Such interventions must occur over a sufficiently long period to allow the family's own strengths to take over and be sustained; they cannot be successful if they are crisis interventions lasting only a few months. A mother's capacity to nurture and facilitate the development of a new baby was significantly more advanced after two years with the program than when she entered the program pregnant with an earlier child.[8] In other words, when the helping relationship was offered over an extended period of time, the frequently observed tendency of multi-problem families to deteriorate further upon the birth of each subsequent child began to be reversed.

Many parents in the program began their childrearing as teenagers and commonly experienced progressive deterioration in their own functioning and that of their infants with each subsequent birth. In most instances, even when a woman had had four or more children, this pattern of deterioration reversed itself by means of appropriate clinical techniques and services. A number of multi-risk families, after entering the program, experienced a gradual improvement in the mother and a modest but positive change in the first baby born thereafter. If the family remained in the program and a second baby was born, the change in the family was more dramatic, reflected in the new baby's more optimal development from birth.

Infants in the intensive intervention group also showed a capacity to recover from early perinatal stress or developmental deviations.[9] Even when an infant's development had deteriorated during the first three months of life (as evidenced by lack of human attachment, chronic gaze aversion, muscle rigidity, and emotional instability), appropriate interventions often resulted in better self-regulation and attachment capacities within one to four months.[10] The process of therapeutic work first called for determining the types of experiences that were either unpleasant or satisfying for the infant. Also identified were those underlying feelings in the parent that might be interfering with the latter's ability to provide comforting and pleasurable inter-actions. In most cases, families could then be helped to deal with their unique problems. These problems appeared either in the infants, as auditory and tactile sensitivities, or extreme unstableness of mood, or in the parents, in the form of severe psychopathology, patterns of rejection or overstimulation. The clinical work was extremely chal-lenging but the staff often found the most challenging cases the most rewarding.[11]

FUTURE CHALLENGES

While a great deal of progress has been made, an enormous amount of work on this approach remains to be done. Additional models are needed which demonstrate how to work with the physical, cognitive, emotional, social and familial aspects of development. The application of such models to a range of common challenges in primary care settings for infants, children and their families, includ-ing motor and language delays, high-risk parenting situations and emotional-social disorders, should be implemented and evaluated.

In addition, while the normative developmental landmarks have been well delineated, more studies documenting disturbed patterns in development are required. Such basic questions as the relative contribution of fine and gross motor delays to emotional problems, or the contributions of difficulties in sensory processing to emotional, social and intellectual difficulties need to be addressed. The demar-cation of a developmental timetable involving cognitive, emotional, and social functioning now permits both short and long-term detailed studies of the factors that determine both optimal and poor develop-mental outcomes. In addition, the ability to follow development through each phase will permit short-term studies to be applied to longer-term ones.

It is time to undertake new programs of research to examine the efficacy of comprehensive approaches to preventive intervention and further our understanding of the pathogenesis of psychomotor, cognitive and emotional difficulties. While it may be thought that one should fully understand pathogenesis before embarking on intervention, medical care has always attempted to offer the best care available, and through clinical programs of research, to refine diagnostic and intervention strategies.

Therefore, an important goal will be to evaluate various groups of at-risk or developmentally disordered infants and families, especially those seen in primary health care settings. These would include infants with motor, sensory, sensory-motor, cognitive, emotional and social delays, infants in at-risk families or environmental settings and infants experiencing combinations of the above. In addition, infants with chronic physical illness, low birthweight and/or those presumed at genetic risk for emotional or cognitive disorders (such as offspring of schizophrenics, manic-depressives, learning-disordered parents and parents with unique sensitivities to environmental stress) should be examined.

The assessments of these populations will further our understanding of the origins of disturbed development. Of particular interest is the relationship among biological, constitutional, maturational and experiential-environmental factors. Studies might include:

- the role of irregularities in sensory processing on cognitive and psychosocial delays;
- the role of the infant's emotional status on interactive patterns with caregivers on overall developmental progress;
- the role of parental personality functioning and family patterns in the infant's developmental progress;
- the role of cumulative risk in developmental outcome; and
- the developmental role of specific genetic-biological risks, in the context of different interactive and family patterns (including sensory and motor lags or irregularities, parental schizophrenics and multi-risk families, parents with manic-depressive illness, families with histories of learning difficulties and families especially sensitive to environmental stresses).

Another major challenge involves the further development of clinical tools and training approaches. While a number of research instruments have been developed to assess various aspects of cognition and emotion, relatively few clinical tools can be used in primary care settings to assess psychosocial as well as intellectual development and disturbance.

The types of studies suggested will permit exploration of specific hypotheses. However, they also will facilitate, within each study, the exploratory hypothesis-generating investigations necessary to define the individual differences in patterns of sensory processing, fine and gross motor capacities, social interaction, and family functioning that contribute to various types of difficulties. These studies are essential for improving the specificity of diagnostic and preventive intervention strategies.

NOTES

1. E. Pavenstaedt, *The Drifters*. Boston: Little Brown & Co., 1967.
2. S. I. Greenspan, S. Weider, R. A. Nove, P. F. Lieberman, R. Laurie, M. E. Robinson (Eds.) *Infants in Multi-Risk Families; Case Studies in Preventive Intervention*. New York: International University Press, Clinical Infant Reports No. 3.
3. S. Wieder, M. Jasnow, S. I. Greenspan and M. Strauss, "Identifying the Multi-Risk Family Perinatally: Antecedent Psychosocial Factors and Infants' Developmental Trends," Infants' Developmental Trends," *Infant Mental Health Journal*, Vol. 4(3), 1984.
4. J. A. Hofheimer, A. F. Lieberman, M. E. Strauss and S. I. Greenspan, *Short-Term Temporal Stability of Mother-Infant Interactions in the First Year of Life*. Adelphi, MD: Clinical Infant Development Research Center, 1983.
5. A. J. Sameroff, R. Seifer, R. Barocas and S. I. Greenspan, "I.Q. Scores of Four-Year-Old Children and Social-Environmental Risk Factors," *Pediatrics*, Vol. 79(3), March 1987.
6. A. J. Sameroff and R. Seifer. Paper presented at Society for Research in Child Development meeting, April 1983.
7. S. Wieder and S. I. Greenspan, "Effects of Interventions with Multi-Risk Families." In S. I. Greenspan, S. Wieder, A. F. Lieberman, R. A. Nover & M. E. Robinson (Eds.), *Infants in Multi-Risk Families: Case Studies of Preventive Intervention*. International Universities Press, 1987. (*Clinical Infants Reports*, No. 3).

Except for a few brief comments, details of recruitment efforts and clinical service approaches and assessments used are described elsewhere (Greenspan, 1981; Greenspan, *et al.*, 1987; Wieder, Jasnow, Greenspan, and Strauss, 1984).

8. S. Wieder and S. I. Greenspan, *op. cit.*
9. J. A. Hofheimer, S. S. Poisson, M. E. Strauss, F. D. Eyler, and S. I. Greenspan, "Perinatal and Behavior Characteristics of Neonates Born to Multi-Risk Families," *Developmental and Behavioral Pediatrics*, Vol. 4(3), 1983.

10. S. I. Greenspan, S. Wieder, *et al., op. cit.*

S. Wieder and S. I. Greenspan, *op. cit.*

S. I. Greenspan, *Psychopathology and Adaptation in Infancy and Early Childhood: Principles of Clinical Diagnosis and Preventive Intervention.* New York: International Universities Press. (*Clinical Infants Reports*, No. 1).

11. S. I. Greenspan, S. Wieder, *et al., op. cit.*

BREAKING THE CYCLE OF DISADVANTAGE: NEW KNOWLEDGE, NEW TOOLS, NEW URGENCY

Lisbeth Bamberger Schorr

INCREASING NUMBERS of young people are coming into adulthood unemployable, bearing babies they are unable to support and rear, and becoming part of a continuing cycle of misery and dependency. While these threats to American dreams of continuing prosperity and expanded opportunity are now widely recognized, new tools that could help reverse the growth of an American underclass go unutilized.

It is now possible to identify a series of early interventions that can help prevent such damaging outcomes as adolescent pregnancy, school failure, and juvenile crime. These outcomes, whose long-term consequences are destructive to the individuals involved as well as to society as a whole, make their appearance at the transition from childhood to adulthood, but almost always have their roots earlier in life. Twenty years of findings from both research and experience shed new light not only on the antecedents and consequences of damaging outcomes, but also on the interventions that can reduce their incidence.

The good news that emerges from these findings is the extraordinary convergence in the elements of what works: the basic attributes of successful programs—whether they offer health care, social support, child care, early education or some combination of all of these—are strikingly similar. The disturbing news is the evidence that the programs that are successful in preventing adverse outcomes among those growing up in the most damaging environments are often quite

The study on which this chapter is based was done under the auspices of the Harvard University Working Group on Early Life, with support from the Carnegie Corporation of New York. This chapter is adapted from the book, *Within Our Reach: Breaking the Cycle of Disadvantage*, by Lisbeth B. Schorr with Daniel Schorr, published in the spring of 1988 by Doubleday/Anchor Books.

different from prevailing programs, and from programs that work for populations at less serious risk. The discontinuity between what works for the majority and what works for the families that face the greatest risks challenges many long-standing beliefs and raises difficult political questions. Before turning to these, it is important to consider the role of human services in the broad attack on social and economic disadvantage, and to review what is now known about the nature of effective interventions.

THE RELATIONSHIP BETWEEN ECONOMIC STRATEGIES, WELFARE REFORM, AND HUMAN SERVICES

More jobs, jobs that pay better, expanded job training, more sensible housing policies, and a welfare system that provides effective income support while helping more recipients to become productively employed would obviously reduce substantially the incidence of poverty and social pathology in American communities. The frequent accompaniments of inadequate income—homelessness, hunger, family stress and despair—would not continue, in such large measure, to add to the destructive legacy of the next generation.

But non-economic strategies are as essential as economic strategies if the future is to change for American children at highest risk of damaging outcomes. Just as high school graduates who are competent and willing to work can't support a family if there are no jobs at a decent wage, so expanded economic opportunities cannot be seized by young people whose health has been neglected, whose education has failed to equip them with the skills they need, and whose early lives have left them without the capacity to persevere and without hope.

Economic strategies, even when coupled with a far more rational welfare system, will not eliminate the need for more effective services for disadvantaged children and their families. This nation is unlikely to redistribute its wealth so equitably in the foreseeable future that services to deal with the consequences of poverty will become unnecessary. Children and families have needs that cannot be met by economic measure alone, and that cannot be met by individual families alone. And, although a services strategy will accomplish little in the absence of employment opportunities, the essential first footholds for the climb out of disadvantage for many living in persistent and concentrated poverty are most likely to come in the form of more effective services and institutions.

INTERVENTION IS MORE EFFECTIVE EARLIER THAN LATER, AND CAN COME FROM OUTSIDE THE FAMILY

By the time adolescents actually drop out of school, become pregnant too soon, or are in serious trouble with the law, helping them to change course is a daunting task. It is possible to help adolescents in trouble to make a successful transition to adulthood, but earlier help is better help. The more long-standing the neglect, deprivation and failure, the more difficult and costly the remedies. Help early in the life cycle is more effective—failure and despair don't have as firm a grip, and life trajectories are more readily altered.

Of course, early interventions present the problem of all real investment—the cost comes sooner, the dividends later. And, not only does a long time elapse between intervention and payoff, which makes prompt demonstration of effectiveness impossible, but the "profits" are likely to end up on a different ledger than the expenditure. (There may be a three-fold return on every dollar spent in the preschool period to prevent elementary school failure, but the prevention dollar comes from a budget that is rarely, if ever, part of the budget that realizes the later savings.) Benefits to the individual, and to society, may never be attributable to any one agency's budget.

Many thoughtful Americans remain skeptical about the idea of expanding social programs to help young children, not only because the payoff is delayed, but also because they see childhood as a time when character and values should be formed within the family.

In pastoral, bygone days, children's characters may have developed without significant benefit or harm deriving from influences outside the family. But no longer—not in an era of economic uncertainty, working mothers, shrinking families, protective services and foster care, high teenage unemployment and ubiquitous street drugs. In today's world, social policy can significantly strengthen or weaken a family's ability to instill virtue in its children.

Liberals and conservatives used to talk about values and character in very different ways. Conservatives would extol their singular importance, and liberals would worry that rhetoric about values and character was being used as a cop-out by those who would not acknowledge the need for government programs. Today, people with widely divergent ideologies can meet on the common ground that the family is central, but that children are most likely to grow into sturdy adults when the family is buttressed by social institutions, including churches, schools, community agencies—and government.

All families need help from beyond the family. But for the families whose children are growing up in the most destructive environments, effective services are essential protectors against adverse outcomes. The children at highest risk of long-term damage, whose families most need help to provide them with a minimal environment for healthy growth, include:

- children growing up in neighborhoods of concentrated poverty and social dislocation;
- children growing up in persistent poverty;
- children growing up in families that are homeless;
- children growing up with a mentally ill, alcoholic or drug addicted parent;
- children growing up with an isolated parent; and
- children at risk of neglect, abuse or removal from home.

PROGRAMS THAT WORK

Programs that have changed outcomes for such children, and offer clear documentation of success, come from the domains of family planning, prenatal and child health care, family support, social services, preschool care and education and elementary education.[1] A brief description of two such programs will illustrate some of the common characteristics of effective early interventions.

Homebuilders, a program of intensive family services,[2] began in 1974, when the staff of the Tacoma, Washington, Catholic Children's Services took stock of the dismal state of organized help to families threatened with removal of a child. Reports of neglect or abuse would trigger the agency's intervention, but the family's tangle of troubles (which might consist of not enough food or clothing, no income, a depressed mother, an alcoholic or abusive father, a sick relative, dilapidated housing, disconnected utilities) almost always exceeded by far the capacity of the fragmentary services that were available. The alternative was to remove the child from its family, possibly to set it adrift in a foster care limbo for years to come.[3] Having determined that existing services aimed at helping families to function were woefully inadequate and frequently resulted in unnecessary removals of children from home, the Tacoma agency, with the help of a federal grant, came up with a plan that ultimately created a social service version of the medical intensive care unit.

The new program assembled a team of professionals, all with graduate degrees in social work, psychology or counseling, whose services were made available to any family which, in the judgment of a child welfare, juvenile justice or mental health agency, stood in imminent peril of the removal of a child.

Today, Homebuilders staff—as they have now done for more than a decade—meet with the family on its own turf, always within 24 hours of referral. They listen to all family members and take as much time as necessary to resolve the immediate crisis. They then help the family learn new ways of coping, so they will not fall back into crisis after the intensive intervention ends. Each staff member is responsible for no more than three families at once, and the agency is prepared to help for a pre-defined period—usually lasting six weeks. In ten years of the program's operation in Tacoma and Seattle, out-of-home placement was averted for 90% of the many hundreds of families served.

It is true that home visits—which, especially in the initial days of working with a family, often last many hours—are more demanding of staff than seeing clients at conveniently scheduled times from behind one's desk in the comfort of one's own office. Staff who go into clients' homes must be able to function well in unstructured, unpredictable, and sometimes dangerous situations. On call 24 hours a day and seven days a week, workers must be able to juggle personal schedules to meet the sometimes overwhelming needs of their clients. But staff members agree that a case load small enough to enable them to do justice to their clients' needs, and the sense they are succeeding, more than compensate for the personal convenience they sacrifice.

The cost of the Homebuilders program, which averaged about $2,600 per family in 1985, is modest when compared to the projected cost of out-of-home care that is saved. Homebuilders calculated that funding agencies realize a five- to six-fold return on every dollar invested.

By mid-1987, at least eight states were experimenting with large-scale implementation of Homebuilders intensive family services, and seem to be achieving similarly impressive results, preventing both unnecessary placements and unnecessary public expenditures. In addition, a large number of local agencies are employing some or all of the principles developed in Washington State—often with training and consultation from the rapidly growing Homebuilders organization itself.

In what may be its most daring venture in replication, the Homebuilders group accepted an invitation from a consortium of five public and private agencies in New York City to adapt its program for use in the Bronx. As yet, no one knows for sure whether a program that clearly works in the predominantly white, comparatively uncomplicated State of Washington, can be made to work in the Bronx, an area of concentrated poverty, largely black and Hispanic, and dependent on the services of the bureaucratically most complicated city in America.

After a period of extensive planning and training in both Seattle and New York, the first Seattle-trained Homebuilders called on a family in the Bronx on May 4, 1987. In the first few months of operation staff found, as they had expected, that poverty is much more intrusive and determining of people's lives in New York than in Washington State, and that the task of obtaining additional services for their clients is infinitely more difficult in the Bronx than in Seattle. The staff were less prepared for the larger and more destructive role that drugs, especially crack, play in the world of the Bronx, and are currently trying to adapt their intensive care model to the more devastating circumstances their Bronx clients face.

But Homebuilders, the Edna McConnell Clark Foundation which is providing support, and the New York City Consortium are optimistic about the ability of Homebuilders to function successfully in the Bronx. They are also impressed with accumulating evidence that the very process of importing the Homebuilders model to New York is shifting the focus of some of the city's public and private agencies toward a greater emphasis on preserving families, preventing out-of-home placement, and rendering intensive, round-the-clock services.

A second example of an intervention that has changed outcomes in a high-risk population is a program of intensive nurse home visiting to pregnant women, new mothers and their infants, launched in 1974 in Elmira, New York.[4]

Elmira is an Appalachian industrial town, with a population that is 95% white. Described by *The New York Times* as a community of "lost jobs, broken families and fading hope," Elmira is a vivid example of the decline of American heavy industry. Its rates of confirmed cases of child abuse and neglect are the highest recorded in New York State—exceeding those of some of the nation's worst urban slums.

Despite the inauspicious setting, the nurse visitors succeeded in reducing the incidence of child abuse, neglect and accidents and improving the health of participating mothers and babies. They also succeeded in increasing the number of teenage mothers returning to school and employment, and in decreasing the number who became pregnant again and were dependent on welfare support.

The program was the product of a year of joint planning by the local health and human services community and the University of Rochester Departments of Pediatrics and Obstetrics/Gynecology. Registered nurses who were themselves mothers and were considered compassionate, sensitive and mature enough to provide emotional support along with education and nursing care, were given special training to work with high-risk families.

400 families participated in the program's experimental phase. Any woman in Chemung County pregnant with her first child was welcome, but special efforts were made to enroll teenagers and women who were unmarried, unemployed or on welfare—the population at greatest risk of pregnancy complications and difficulties with parenting, yet least likely to be reached by traditional health and human services.

During the prenatal period, the nurses usually made about nine home visits, each more than an hour long, during which they tried to help mothers see how their behavior could affect their health and that of their unborn child; helped to prepare the mothers for labor, delivery and the early care of their newborn; and discussed the mother's, or parents', plans for employment, schooling, contraceptive use and spacing of future children.

After the baby was born, the same nurse, now having a solid relationship, continued helping the mother or parents to understand—and act on their understanding of—the unique characteristics and abilities of their infant, and the infant's nutrition and health needs. Nurse and mother would discuss the importance of responding to the baby's cues, and of encouraging the baby to enjoy progressively more complex motor, social and intellectual experiences.

The nurses knew they had to be especially alert to the parents' preoccupation with survival problems—what Dr. David Olds, the program's founder, calls the "unending chain of stressful events" experienced by so many socially disadvantaged women during pregnancy and the first years of their baby's life. Unemployment, marital conflicts and difficulties with finances and housing can make it impossible to convert knowledge about good health practices and child care into action.

The nurses worked explicitly on strengthening the women's supports, helping them to establish links both with other family members and friends, and with community services. The nurses tailored the content of visits to individual circumstances, listened carefully, provided emotional support, and always tried to be available in times of stress, while encouraging the young parents to develop their own problem-solving skills. The nurses often acted as a bridge between the women and their obstetricians and pediatricians, many of whom were unaware of how the multiple problems of the environments in which these women lived could interfere with desirable health habits during pregnancy and with good care of the child.

The Elmira program based its evaluation on a four-year study of participants, randomly assigned to control and treatment groups. The results were dramatic:

• Among the women at highest risk, those in the home visiting program had one-fifth the verified cases of child abuse and neglect of the "unvisited" during the first two years of their children's lives.
• Among the poor unmarried women, participants returned to school more rapidly after delivery, were employed a greater part of the time, obtained more help with child care and had fewer subsequent pregnancies over the next four years.
• Among pregnant girls under 17 and those who smoked, program participants had heavier babies and fewer premature babies than their unvisited counterparts.
• Mothers in the program restricted and punished their infants less frequently and provided more appropriate play materials. Their babies were seen less frequently in the hospital emergency room, and had fewer accidents and fewer incidents of swallowing foreign substances, probably as a result of bettr supervision of the children's immediate environments.

The Elmira experiment is significant not only because it was able to change outcomes for a population at high risk of later damage, but also because it serves as a warning of what can happen when the consequences of diluting a program in the process of replicating it are not recognized. Like many other successful model programs, the Elmira program was watered down as it emerged from the protection of foundations, federal grants and an academic base, and entered the cold world of budget-pinched local services.

Home visiting in Elmira is now run by the local health department and funded by Medicaid. On the day it took over the program, the health department—besieged by funding cuts and demands that seemed more urgent—doubled the nurses' case loads. The original nurses were immediately pressed to shorten their visits and to drop families when the babies were four months old. They found themselves in an environment in which their work suddenly seemed less valued. They felt they couldn't give their clients the kind of attention and support they required. They could instruct the young mothers on when to phone the doctor, but there was not enough time to puzzle out how to manage when there was no other adult around, no telephone in the building and the baby seemed really sick. They could advocate a return to school, but were unable to stay long enough to explore with the young mothers the obstacles that had to be overcome. More leisurely conversations became casualties of the doubled case load and brisker climate in which the nurses now worked.

Within months of the program's conversion from demonstration project to mainstream operation all the original nurses had resigned. Their replacements are competent and committed nurses, but are aware that they are no longer able to provide the same intensive care their predecessors did.

There is no way to know for sure (there being no money in the current budget for evaluation), whether the exchanges that no longer take place are indeed luxuries that can be dispensed with without affecting outcomes. The nurses that worked in the original program believe, on the basis of their own experience and much research, that the parts of the program that have been eliminated are in fact the subtle but essential stuff of which effective support to vulnerable families is made.

ATTRIBUTES OF INTERVENTIONS THAT WORK

We now know that at every stage of a child's early development, interventions exist that can improve the odds for a favorable long-term outcome. But the programs that have succeeded in changing outcomes for children at highest risk of later damage differ, in fundamental ways, from prevailing services. We cannot build on successful programs unless we understand the differences.

Programs that are successful in helping children and families who live in concentrated poverty and disadvantage typically offer a *broad spectrum of services*. They know that social and emotional support and concrete help (with food, housing, income, employment—or anything else that seems to the family to be an insurmountable obstacle) may have to be provided to enable a family to make use of other services, from antibiotics to advice on parenting.

To respond to their clients' or patients' untidy array of needs, staff make sure that services are *coherent and integrated*. When necessary, staff cross traditional professional and bureaucratic boundaries. These programs rely only rarely on referrals to other agencies. They take special pains to maintain continuity in relationships, and to assume responsibility for assuring that child and family needs are in fact met, regardless of bureaucratic or professional compartmentalization. No one says, "This may be what you need, but helping you get it is not part of my job or outside our jurisdiction."

Most successful programs find that services cannot be rigidly routinized. Staff members and program structures are fundamentally *flexible.* Professionals are able to exercise discretion about meeting individual needs (which new mother needs three home visits every week and which needs only one during the first month), and families are able to decide what services to utilize (whether and when to enroll their child in the available day care program), and how they want to participate (whether to work in their child's school as a library volunteer, a paid aide or a member of the parent advisory body).

Successful programs *see the child in the context of family, and the family in the context of its surroundings.* The clinician treating an infant for recurrent diarrhea sees beyond the patient on the examining table to whether the child's health is threatened by circumstances that require a public health nurse or social worker to help the family obtain non-medical services. The successful school mobilizes parents in collaborative efforts to impart a love of reading. Successful programs in every domain offer support to parents who need help with their lives as adults before they can make good use of services for their children.

Professionals in successful programs are perceived by those they serve as people they can *trust,* people who *care* about them and *respect* them. Staffs of these programs tend to be highly skilled. Most emphasize how much training, support and time it takes to establish the kind of relationships that actually bring about change. Although many human service programs have been successful in utilizing well-supervised nonprofessionals, trained on the job, experience with families living in the most marginal and stressed circumstances suggests that these families need help that requires a level of skill and judgment that is best provided by well-trained professionals.

In successful programs, *professionals are able to redefine their roles and to find ways to escape the constraints of a professional value system* that confers highest status on those who deal with issues from which all human complexity has been removed.[5] These professionals venture outside familiar surroundings to make services available in nontraditional settings, including homes, and often at nontraditional hours. The program does not ask families to surmount formidable barriers, unassisted, before they can get what they need. It makes sure that payment arrangements and eligibility determinations do not pose insuperable obstacles. It does not set preconditions—such as keeping a series of fixed appointments in far-away places, or a display of adequate "motivation"—that may screen out those most in need. On the contrary, successful programs try to reduce the barriers of money, time, fragmentation, geographic and psychological remoteness—that make heavy demands on those with limited energy and organizational skills. Instead of waiting passively to serve only those who make it through the daunting maze, these programs persevere to reach the perplexed, discouraged and ambivalent—the hardest to reach who are likely to benefit the most.

In sum, the programs that are effective in changing outcomes for high-risk children are *comprehensive,* operate at an unusual level of *intensity* and *adapt the content of their services to the distinctive needs of the population they serve.* Health care that is adequate for monitoring the pregnancy of a healthy middle-class woman may totally bypass the most pressing needs of an undernourished, depressed, drug-using pregnant teenager. The parent support component of a preschool program, occasionally helpful to middle-class participants, is often essential for high-risk families. Intensive, comprehensive, individualized services with aggressive attention to outreach and to maintaining relationships over time may be frills for more fortunate families, but are rock-bottom necessities for high-risk populations, whose level of energy and tolerance for frustration may be low, who are likely to have more than one problem at a time and whose experiences in searching for help are likely to leave them profoundly discouraged and unable to use services as customarily offered.

NEW FOUNDATIONS FOR THE SPREAD OF EFFECTIVE PROGRAMS

The distinctiveness of the characteristics of programs that succeed in helping families surrounded by concentrated poverty and social dislocation suggests a fundamental contradiction between the needs of these children and families and the traditional requirements of professionalism and bureaucracy. This contradiction helps to explain why programs that work for these high-risk populations are so rare and why less effective programs are so much more prevalent. It is a contradiction that future attempts to build on successful programs must take carefully into account.

Just as programs that have proven successful have many common attributes, patterns can be discerned in past failures. Many failures have resulted from a mean-spirited unwillingness to help those most in need. Many have resulted from a lack of understanding of the nature of the problem, of how effective, intensive and comprehensive interventions can be, and of how much help for the seriously disadvantaged is enough. And some of our failures result from a lack of understanding of how promising programs can be widely replicated.

If interventions that work are to become widely available to those who need them most, we need a new political commitment that will endure over time, a deeper understanding of the insights that come out of the experience of the last 20 years, and a new determination to solve the problems of widespread implementation.

First, we must recognize that, for children with many strikes against them, *damage cannot be prevented by simplistic, one-pronged approaches* of any kind. Because narrowly-defined interventions aimed at precisely defined problems make for ready measurement, assessment and replication, because it is easiest to mobilize political support to fight one simple evil with one simple remedy, we are left with half-way programs which fail to ameliorate profound social problems. Effective action requires a new consensus that complex, deeply rooted tangles of troubles cannot be successfully attacked with isolated fragments of help, or with help rendered grudgingly.[6]

Second, we must come to *a more sophisticated understanding of the interplay between local action and national and state policies.* Powerful forces and institutions, far removed from valiant local efforts to establish and maintain effective programs, can threaten the survival of valuable local programs, and the chances of successful replication. Failure to recognize this will lead to repeated disappointments, as local efforts overcome formidable barriers and result in excellent programs that soon wither because local efforts alone turn out not to be enough.

Reimbursement arrangements of public and private third party payers that do not reflect the complexities of effective interventions undermine the stability of well-designed local programs. When services such as outreach, counseling and support are not paid for by Medicaid and private health insurers, then hard-pressed health programs will not provide them no matter how essential to the program's purposes. When reimbursement definitions do not reflect the higher costs of providing service to poor, multi-problem families, then programs that provide the poor with the care they need cannot survive. That is why there is no correlation between a program's survival and how successful it is in achieving improved outcomes for families at risk.[7]

Third, we must be prepared to *change the administrative and policy context in which programs for disadvantaged families and children are expected to operate.* It is no coincidence that programs with demonstrated success in changing outcomes for disadvantaged children have, for the most part, developed in unusual conditions. They have been able, for a variety of reasons, to operate free of "normal outside constraints." With some exceptions (such as WIC and Medicaid), most were funded initially with private seed money or with government grants which did not flow through ordinary channels or carry the usual encumbrances. In almost all cases, these programs originated in circumstances that were somehow idiosyncratic. Several began under the auspices of a university with a mandate to conduct service experiments; some had a specific charge from the federal government's War on Poverty; some had explicit mandates from state legislatures or governors; many began when the special circumstances of the moment allowed an effective leader to insulate the program from normal political and bureaucratic pressures.

That successful programs have come out of unusual circumstances does not negate their significance, if only because it is important to know that there *are* programs that have succeeded in solving seemingly intractable social problems. Even if they are idiosyncratic in origin, model programs provide a vision of what can be achieved. But when proven programs, performing vital functions, are available in only a few isolated places, relying on unique talents and commitments to prevail in the face of perverse incentives, that is, at the most fundamental level, poor public policy.[8]

Fourth, evaluation researchers and program administrators need to find *better ways of collecting the kind of evidence of effectiveness that will be convincing to the body politic.* At the same time, at least some of the agencies and institutions funding human services must come to recognize that judgments about what works cannot be based on numbers alone, but must rely on common sense, prudence and a thoughtful synthesis of an accumulation of wisdom and experience. Twenty years ago, when social policy was formulated in an atmosphere of boundless optimism, the combination of a little theoretical research, fragments of experience and a lot of faith and dedication were enough to justify a new social program. Today budget deficits, fears of wasting money and perpetuating dependency and a gloomy sense of social problems beyond solution result in a much greater need for tangible evidence of effectiveness as a condition for support of any social program. Yet the reasonable demand for evidence of effectiveness must be tempered by an awareness of the dangers of converting both program input and outcomes into terms that may be readily measured but are otherwise irrelevant. Many of the central components of effective interventions are elusive, and progress toward the development and implementation of effective interventions can be hampered by attempts to evaluate programs prematurely and in narrow fragments. Assessments which promise policy significance should take priority over the pursuit of findings that offer quantifiable elegance but are ultimately trivial.[9]

Fifth, more Americans need to become familiar with the *powerful evidence that already exists of the positive impact of intensive early interventions on long-term outcomes for children.* Many programs have documented substantial direct savings from effective interventions.[10] But monetary savings are not the only returns society realizes when it invests in improving outcomes for children growing up at risk. If effective early interventions were more widely available, employers, including the armed forces, would be able to draw on a larger pool of skilled, healthy and motivated young Americans. Budgets for law enforcement and prisons would reflect the economic effects of less crime. Young people better equipped for parenting would mean lower rates of dependency, school failure and school-age childbearing in the next generation.

The decision to invest in decent services and schooling for disadvantaged children cannot be made solely on the basis of how much the taxpayer saves, without taking into account values that cannot be measured in dollars. Yet, the knowledge that economic costs will be recovered is central—even if the later savings don't show up on the ledger of the same administrator who authorizes the expenditure. It is also essential to be aware of the costs of *not* making the investment. As the Committee for Economic Development found after studying the long-term effects of early and sustained intervention in the lives of disadvantaged children, "improving the prospects for disadvantaged children is not an expense but an excellent investment, one that can be postponed only at much greater cost to society." [11]

Sixth, interventions aimed at high-risk populations must be able to attract and train enough skilled and committed personnel. To this end, *the value system within which professionals learn and work must take better account of the special needs of disadvantaged children and their families.* When it comes to professional status and economic compensation, in health care, social services and education, basic services rank low, preventive services rank low and the provision of services to the least powerful ranks lowest of all.

Narrowly drawn boundaries that limit what is expected of a professional are for many the very essence of professionalism. Thus physicians apply their biomedical expertise to meet the health needs of poor and overwhelmed families, but are defeated by a combination of gaps in their own training, counterproductive reimbursement policies and the lack of support systems that could help meet these families' health-related needs. Teachers are often in the same demoralizing position. Their training has not equipped them to deal with the collection of difficulties that many pupils bring to school—but they are aware that these problems get in the way of school learning, and that nobody else is dealing with them either. Social workers and many other professionals work in settings where they see unmet needs so overwhelming that they can only continue functioning by

looking away from matters beyond the confines of their own special-
ties.

Professionals in most fields are more proficient in responding to
circumscribed problems than to a combination of problems. When
they encounter difficulties that extend beyond their expertise they
are inclined to retreat to what is more familiar; the limits of their
training set the limits of their practice. Both training and practice
reflect the low priority assigned to the special needs of the poor. Both
training and practice could, however, change rapidly in a more
encouraging climate.

In the early days of the War on Poverty, when word went out that
federal support was available to establish comprehensive health centers in forsaken rural areas and inner-city slums, health professionals
by the hundreds left narrow pursuits in laboratories and private
medical practice and rapidly acquired the skills to respond to newly
defined needs.

A similar phenomenon occurred when Head Start began. The
overwhelming response from local communities, in the summer of
1965, to the availability of funds for comprehensive services for
preschool children would have ended in chaos had there not been an
equally massive response from the nation's pediatricians, child development specialists, clergy, teachers and social workers. Many dis-
rupted their personal and professional lives and worked unbelievable
hours—"all because they believed in what was happening."[12] They
changed the climate in which a new generation of child development
and early education professionals defined the challenges of the future.

At many times in our history, gifted and committed people in all
walks of life have responded to newly articulated human needs. With
thoughtful planning, solid leadership, and serious resolve, that could
happen again.

The seventh major obstacle to broad implementation of effective
programs that must be overcome is the scarcity of skills with which to
make a good program work amid harsh bureaucratic realities. *The
development and dissemination of skills necessary for the administration of
complex and intensive new programs within large bureaucracies* require far
greater attention, and more investment, than they have received in
the past.

Obviously, the replication of any initiative on a broad scale involves
a certain amount of bureaucratization. Massive paperwork requirements suddenly appear, along with regulations that discourage the
flexibility and creativity central to the program's successful operation.
Agency boundaries develop willy-nilly. Perhaps the worst part is that

these problems ae not necessarily created because small-minded or uncaring people are in charge. Rather they often reflect a legitimate need for accountability. They are the understandable consequence of imposing some measure of standardization to prevent abuse and assure high quality.

The bureaucratization which accompanies large-scale replication is most threatening to the effective interventions here described because they have attributes that are particularly delicate and easily destroyed when they become part of heavy-handed bureaucracies. If the most effective tools we have for breaking the cycle of disadvantage are to be protected from destruction while being made more widely available, professionals, politicians, advocates and caring citizens must all make the detailed questions of how bureaucracies actually deal with people their continuing concern. As governors, county executives and mayors come to appreciate how badly agency boundaries correspond to family needs, they may provide more aggressive leadership in building bridges across agency and jurisdictional lines. At the same time, the flow of resources to high-risk populations must become sufficient to obviate the need to choose between an elegant program that works for a few, and a diluted version that serves many—inadequately.

The task of devising strategies for surmounting obstacles to widespread replication of successful programs is at least as difficult as devising a successful intervention in the first place. The development of effective strategies involves the give and take of many minds, many interests, many disciplines and many levels of practical experience. The arenas for action are far more varied than they were perceived to be twenty years ago. While the federal role remains crucial, state and local governments are increasingly competent and increasingly concerned about vulnerable populations, especially including poor children. Public-private partnerships are also pioneering flexible new approaches to achieving the common good.

No one level of government, and certainly no isolated private efforts, can bring us to nirvana. Because successful programs serving high-risk families are in many different stages of development, and because they operate in diverse contexts, the best next steps will require a number of different strategies. Converting successful local efforts into state or national policy, and formulating national policies that will support successful state and local efforts raise different issues in health, social services, day care and education. What needs to be done can't be orchestrated by any one group or body—although a President and a few other highly visible leaders who understood, cared and provided "bully pulpit" leadership on these issues would make a big difference.[13] A program of grants combined with intensive technical assistance would go far toward getting a critical mass of high quality services into areas of concentrated social dislocation.

A NEW AND SHARPER FOCUS ON THE "TRULY DISADVANTAGED"

Whether our highest priority goal for the next decade is to assure a better-educated pool of productive workers, to reduce the tax dollars that pay for welfare support and prisons, or to end pervasive alienation and achieve a national sense of community, we must focus more sharply on the most difficult and most urgent social problems— even if this requires major departures from traditional approaches.

Many Americans committed to improving the lives of those left out of the general prosperity firmly believe that the problems of the disadvantaged are best addressed by including them in a larger framework. The politics of social reform has had as its primer the Social Security Act of 1935. The popularity and success of programs of universal entitlement taught that political victories were directly dependent on the breadth and heterogeneity of the beneficiary population. Progress seemed to be contingent on a perception of need for governmental help as universal (as in Social Security and Medicare), or as resulting from bad luck (as in the birth of a handicapped child). The greatest and most lasting reductions in the numbers of the poor were made by "incorporating the poor through the political back door."[14] A broad constituency has been seen as necessary not only for initial enactment of legislation, but to maintain a quality program over the long run. Programs aimed at the most deprived, by contrast, were regarded as too hard to protect against deterioration. Programs for the poor, we were taught, became poor programs.

But the determination to avoid a specific focus on the seriously disadvantaged may by now have become counterproductive. It may be time to reassess whether the high value placed on universal coverage, still valid with respect to relatively simple income transfer programs like Social Security, should continue to hold for complex human service programs. A close examination of the long-term successes achieved by programs and institutions serving high-risk populations, clearly demonstrates that children in greatest danger of later damage need interventions that are more intensive, more comprehensive and often more costly than those needed by families living in less disadvantaged circumstances.

Justice for disadvantaged populations has traditionally been equated with equitable access to services, assuming equal need and equal efficacy of treatment. It now appears that equal access, while necessary, is not sufficient. For children who are growing up in persistent and concentrated poverty, in families that are overwhelmed and surrounded by others in similar straits, equal access does not spell equity. Effective help to severely disadvantaged populations requires that services be of the highest quality and that the range of services reflect the broad range of needs in this population.

Services for high-risk groups can be provided as part of a universal program or rendered exclusively to a high-risk population. A home visiting program for high-risk mothers, for example, could be an intensive version of a universal program, or could be focused exclusively on poor pregnant teenagers.[15] What is essential is that programs for those with the greatest needs must be clearly designed to take those distinct needs into account.

Now that we know there are interventions that can help the children who are growing up in destructive environments, now that we know how to prevent damage before it occurs, the highest priority in the next decade's efforts to break the cycle of disadvantage and dependence must go to making intensive, high-quality services available early in the life cycle to the populations living in areas where the risks to healthy development are concentrated. This will require new funds and sweeping changes—in local, state and federal legislation, in procedures for allocating resources, in bureaucracies, and among professionals.

Only a clear understanding of our common stake in effecting these changes will provide the necessary impetus. "Common stake" does not necessarily mean that only common programs, serving the middle class and disadvantaged alike, will do. A sense of common interest can also derive from a recognition of the great stake we all have in breaking the cycle of intergenerational disadvantage.

When educational failure, adolescent crime and teenage childbearing combine to create long-term social devastation, the damage becomes so massive that every American acquires a stake in its prevention. Although some of the adolescents who leave school early and have babies too soon (and even some who commit serious crimes) will ultimately become self-supporting, responsible and productive adults, more will be trapped by the interaction of men without jobs, women without husbands, children without fathers and families without money, hope, skills, opportunities—as well as without effective supports and services that might help them escape. The young people in these circumstances will become the long-term welfare dependents, the unemployed and unemployable, and the parents unable to form stable families of their own. Many will join the ranks of the hungry and homeless. Surrounded by despair, neglect and violence, these young people are likely to lack any vision of the future which would inspire present sacrifice. Disconnected from the mainstream of American society, unable to make the transition to productive adulthood, they will get stuck at the very bottom of American society and become part of a growing underclass.*

We all pay to support the unproductive and incarcerate the violent. We are all economically weakened by lost productivity. We all live with fear of crime in our homes and on the streets. We are all diminished when large numbers of parents are incapable of nurturing their dependent young. We have an enormous common stake in undoing the bonds that keep children in misery today, and threaten to keep their children even more permanently excluded from America's mainstream.

Earlier in this century, the routes up and out of poverty worked less well for blacks and other minorities than for native-born whites, but they were plentiful. Most poor and otherwise disadvantaged families lived in environments that provided day-to-day evidence that hard work, ambition and perseverance brought rewards—reflecting in large part the expanding demands for unskilled labor. Moving up from disadvantage did not require either the personal heroism or intensive help from outside it does now.

Ladders up from the bottom are fewer today; they are harder to locate and to climb. Because, as a result of macro-economic and technological developments of the last two decades, it has become so much more difficult for disadvantaged young people to *beat the odds,* the societal role in *changing the odds* has become far more critical.

Today, forces largely beyond individual control, particularly the slowdown in economic growth and the shift to service and high technology occupations, propel families into the underclass and keep them there. Between 1973 and 1984, the proportion of young men able to support their families plummeted, while—in direct conse-

---

*The term "underclass" has been shunned by many lest the label be seized on to blame the poor for their poverty, or to mark off a small minority with problems that seem so intractable that they will be dismissed as impossible to help. But I agree with William J. Wilson that the liberal reluctance to address candidly the clustering and concentration of social casualties has ceded the territory to conservatives who see both causes and remedies in exclusively individualistic terms, and who cannot imagine a successful response through societal intervention and support.[16] Especially those of us who are working with evidence that demonstrates that intensive social efforts can reach and help even those who are now stuck at the bottom, must focus attention on the distinct needs of the most disadvantaged populations that have been so seriously neglected by prevailing systems and institutions.

quence—the number of female-headed families skyrocketed, as did the number of children growing up in environments that undermine healthy development.[17]

As economic opportunity shrank for the less skilled of all races and backgrounds, the many blacks who were in a position to take advantage of expanded opportunities to obtain higher education and enter the professions, business or the skilled trades moved up and out, with devastating effects on the inner-city areas they left behind. Professor William J. Wilson calls it "one of the most important social transformations in recent U.S. history." Although there are still plenty of people in these neighborhoods who work very hard, there is no longer the critical mass of stable, achievement-oriented families that once provided neighborhood cohesion, sanctions against aberrant behavior, support for churches and other basic community institutions. Missing are the essential practical connections to mainstream society, the informal ties to the world of work that provide models of conventional roles and behavior and could alert youngsters to job openings and help them obtain employment. In America's inner cities today there are too few neighbors whose lives demonstrate that education is meaningful, that steady employment is a viable alternative to welfare and illegal pursuits, and that a stable family is an aspect of normalcy.[18] The vacuum is being filled, says Yale University psychiatrist James Comer, by drug pushers, pimps and prostitutes. "They're often the only successful people that the kids see."[19]

In depressed neighborhoods of all kinds, drugs have vastly exacerbated other social dislocations, from robbery to personal violence, adding an element of pathology that earlier generations did not have to cope with.[20]

More and more families, stressed and depleted, are surounded by others in similar straits. This concentration of the persistently poor, unskilled, alienated, unemployed and unmarried has a high probability of negatively affecting the development of children. These children are isolated from many essential socializing influences and supports. It is hard for the head of a family, male or female, black or white, who cannot support the family, to rear children to conform to cultural expectations and to contribute constructively to society.[21]

A boy being brought up by a mother alone, even a poor mother alone, need not necessarily suffer damaging effects. In fact, a British study has shown that growing up in a female-headed household is not in itself damaging.[22] But when single parenting is not only a family fact, but a community fact, the effect—especially on boys—can be highly disruptive of normal development.[23] When the whole neighborhood is made up of families without fathers or a consistent male presence, not only the income, but the discipline and role models that fathers traditionally have provided are missing. Boys are left to learn about manhood on the streets, where the temptation is strong to demonstrate one's prowess through violence, breaking the law and fathering a child.

Since the *concentration* of misery and social dislocation is so clearly implicated in its perpetuation, the growth in the population living in areas of concentrated poverty is alarming. In only ten years, between 1970 and 1980, in the nation's five largest cities, the number of poor people living in poverty areas increased by 58%, and the number living in *areas of extreme poverty* went up by a shocking 182%![24]

Despite the evidence of worsening conditions, the services which could buffer disadvantaged children against the impact of their harsh surroundings, and strengthen families in their efforts to improve the odds for these children, remain painfully inadequate. Many services have been reduced as a result of budget cuts, but their weaknesses go deeper than budgets. The kind of schools, preschools, day care, health clinics and social services that might help are, with a few stellar exceptions, simply not reaching those who need them most. So, instead of protecting against the destructive impact of the concentration of devastation, our social institutions often contribute to it.

Considering the wealth of present knowledge about the dangers of growing up in areas of concentrated poverty and about the interventions that can change outcomes for even the most disadvantaged children, it becomes indefensible not to make these interventions available. A preventive, population-based approach to targeting interventions, as opposed to an approach based on individually established pathology, has become a realistic possibility just as it has become an urgent necessity. We not only know more than ever before about the conditions that jeopardize healthy development, we also know a great deal about where the children at risk are concentrated.

In a recent attempt to define and estimate the size of the underclass, economist Isabel V. Sawhill and sociologist-demographer Erol R. Ricketts, working together at the Urban Institute in 1986, imaginatively analyzed 1980 census data to identify every census tract with unusually high proportions of high school dropouts, welfare recipients, female heads of household and working-age males not regularly attached to the labor force. They found 880 tracts, (about two percent of urban census tracts) in which *all four of these indicators of dislocation* occurred at a rate higher than one standard deviation from the mean for the nation. These areas contained a total of 2.5 million people, or about one percent of the U.S. population. Geographically, the largest concentration of the 880 census tracts is in the Northeast.

The six cities with the highest number of these areas are New York, Chicago, Detroit, Newark, Philadelphia, and Baltimore. In the 880 census tracts, 58% of the population are black, 11% are Hispanic, and 28% are white. 36% are children.[25]

Ricketts and Sawhill would be the first to warn that these are rough calculations. The children in these 880 census tracts may be only the tip of an iceberg of disadvantage, but given the tools we now have, it would be unconscionable not to use them to help—as a beginning— at least these children. That so many American children are growing up in the midst of dense concentrations of poverty and social dislocation makes inaction intolerable. At the same time their number is small enough to make concerted efforts to locate high quality services and institutions in such areas a realistic immediate objective.

Elected officials and other leaders may object that interventions effective for those at greatest risk require a large "up-front" investment. But they can no longer contend that resources should be withheld because no one knows *how* to help, or because the evidence of high returns on such an investment is lacking.

While economic policies with more sweeping effects, and programs that would assure universal entitlement to a range of human services are being developed, we cannot afford to sit by and watch as the children and families with the greatest needs and whom we know how to help are simply abandoned. A broad coalition of citizens, professionals and political leaders must begin to move the public and private sectors to bring a critical mass of successful programs into the geographical areas with the highest concentration of persistent poverty and other indicators of disadvantage and disintegration. This will be an arduous undertaking, requiring careful planning, thoughtful use of the last two decades of experience and a vigorous determination to guard against dilutions, short cuts and false economies.

The investment and the risks are justified by the prospect that fewer children will come into adulthood unschooled and unskilled, committing violent crimes and bearing children as unmarried teenagers. Fewer of the children living in concentrated poverty today will tomorrow swell the welfare rolls and the prisons. Many more will grow into responsible and productive adults, themselves able to form stable families, contributing to, rather than depleting America's prosperity and sense of community.

Utility and self-interest, as well as humanity, should move us to apply what we have learned about preventive interventions to change the futures of the children growing up in society's shadows, and thereby to break the cycle of disadvantage.

NOTES

1. The study on which this chapter is based identified and analyzed programs that (a) have documented a favorable impact on key risk factors or outcomes among children growing up in high-risk environments, and (b) employ methods shown at a theoretical level to be promising. These programs, described fully in L. B. Schorr, *Within Our Reach*, 1988, include family planning programs in St. Paul, Minn., and Baltimore, MD; prenatal care programs in California, Maryland and South Carolina; child health programs in Mississippi, Baltimore and Los Angeles; intensive family support programs in Washington State, the Bronx, New Haven and Elmira, New York; preschool education and child care programs in Tennessee, Ypsilanti and Leslie, Michigan, New York City and Fairfax County, Virginia; and elementary schools in New Haven, Maryland, and New York City. Also federal programs including Medicaid, EPSDT, WIC, Neighborhood Health Centers and Head Start.

Systematic efforts to identify preventive programs that work have also recently been undertaken by the Committee for Economic Development (CED), the National Governor's Association (NGA) and the American Psychological Association (APA). (See especially the CED's *Children in Need: Investment Strategies for the Educationally Disadvantaged*, 1987, and the NGA's *Focus on the First Sixty Months*, 1987.) There is considerable overlap in the programs selected by these three groups and those identified in the study for *Within Our Reach*, although the processes by which programs were chosen varied considerably. This should reassure skeptics that these programs do provide objective indicators of success. From the fact that each selection process also identified programs that none of the others found, it is reasonable to conclude that no one individual or organization can put between two covers all the proven and promising efforts that succeed in responding to the complex needs of families buffeted by changing family structures, increasing poverty and decreasing employment opportunities.

2. The description of the Tacoma Homebuilders program comes from J. M. Kinney, *et al.*, "Homebuilders: Keeping Families Together," *Journal of Consulting and Clinical Psychology*, Vol. 45(4), 1977, pp. 667–673; J. M. Kinney, "Homebuilders: An In-Home Crisis Intervention Program," *Children Today*, No. 1, January–February, 1978), pp. 15–35; D. A. Haapala and J. M. Kinney, "Homebuilders Approach to the Training of In-Home Therapists," in *Home-Based Services for Children and Families*, S. Maybanks and M. Bryce, (Eds.), Springfield, IL: Charles C. Thomas, 1979; materials furnished by Behavioral Sciences Institute, Federal Way, WA: E. M. Clark Foundation, *Keeping Families Together: The Case For Family Preservation*, 1985; and interviews in 1986 and 1987 with Peter Forsythe, Director, Program for Children, and Peter D. Bell, President, E. M. Clark Foundation. Information about the replication of the Homebuilders program in the Bronx is based on conversations in 1987 with officers and staff of the Clark Foundation, with David Tobis, Senior Associate, Welfare Research, Inc., with Kathleen Feely, New York City Department of Juvenile Justice, and on materials prepared and furnished by Mr. Tobis.

3. Although foster care is intended to be a temporary arrangement, extended placements are the norm. In New York City, the average length of time a child removed from the family spent in foster care in 1980 was 4.8 years; other areas of the country report similar figures. (See D. Fanshel, "Decision-Making Under Uncertainty: Foster Care for Abused and Neglected Children?" *American Journal of Public Health* Vol. 71(7), July 1981, pp. 685–686; E. M. Clark Foundation, *Keeping Families Together*, 1985; Child Welfare League of America, *Report of the National Commission on Children in Need of Parents*, 1979.)

4. The description of the Elmira nurse home visiting program is based on a visit to the program, 30 May 1985, which included interviews with the original project director, Dr. David L. Olds, of the Department of Pediatrics, University of Rochester, the original nursing staff, the staff at the time of the visit, and officials of the Chemung County Health Department. Also see the following: D. L. Olds, "Improving Formal Services for Mothers and Children," in *Protecting Children from Abuse and Neglect*, J. Garbarino and S. H. Stocking, (Eds.), San Francisco: Jossey-Bass, 1981, pp. 173–197; D. L. Olds, "The Prenatal/Early Infancy Project," in *In the Beginning*, J. Belsky, (Ed.), New York: Columbia University Press, 1982, pp. 270–85; D. L. Olds, C. R. Henderson, R. Tatelbaum and R. Chamberlin, "Improving the Delivery of Prenatal Care and Outcomes of Pregnancy," *Pediatrics*, Vol. 77(1), January, 1986, pp. 16–28; D. L. Olds, C. R. Henderson, R. Tatelbaum and R. Chamberlin, "Improving the Life-Course Development of Socially Disadvantaged Parents," unpublished report, 1986; D. L. Olds, C. R. Henderson, R. Chamberlin, and R. Tatelbaum, "Preventing Child Abuse and Neglect: A Randomized Trial of Nurse Home Visitation," *Pediatrics*, Vol. 78, July 1986, pp. 65–78. Outcome data is from the latter three reports.

5. Sociologist Andrew Abbott has written that within a given profession, the highest status professionals are those who deal with issues defined by colleagues in such a way as to remove human complexity, while "the lowest status professionals are those who deal with problems from which the human complexities are not or cannot be removed." See A. Abbott, "Status and Status Strain in the Professions," *American Journal of Sociology*, Vol. 86, 1981, pp. 819–835.

6. Those in greatest need of services—be it in health care, family support or education—tend to face the greatest barriers in the search for help. Services for those who need them most are often too fragmented and too meager to accomplish their purpose. Children's advocates succeed in expanding access to medical care, but inside the doctor's office the content of services remains unmatched to the needs of the underserved. Extreme fragmentation of services and a "consistent pattern of failed connections" were identified in a broad review by the Children's Defense Fund as the critical weaknesses in children's mental health services. Children's problems and their need for services were often identified early, and sometimes repeatedly. But the services themselves seldom materialized. Similar findings of "failed connections" emerge consistently from reviews of case records of children killed or

seriously injured as a result of child abuse. Typically the children are known to social agencies, but the services that could prevent tragedy do not materialize. Across the country, case workers with direct responsibility for vulnerable children often experience "impossibly large caseloads, excessive and meaningless paperwork, no time to get to know the children for whom they make decisions, no time to visit families, and no training to deal with complex family problems." (See J. Knitzer, "Mental Health Services to Children and Adolescents," *American Psychologist,* Vol. 39(8), August 1984, pp. 905–911; M. A. Uhlig, "Many Child-Abuse Deaths Come in Cases Where Risk Is Known," *The New York Times,* November 9, 1987; J. Knitzer, B. McGowan and M. L. Allen, *Children Without Homes,* Washington, D.C.: Children's Defense Fund, 1978.)

7. A classic study of the factors that accounted for financial survival of rural health clinics found that the more laboratory tests a clinic provided, as a proportion of total services, the more likely it was to become self-sufficient. The more outreach services it provided, the more likely it was to shut down when grant funding came to an end. (See R. Feldman, D. M. Deitz and E. F. Brooks, "The Financial Viability of Rural Primary Health Care Centers," *American Journal of Public Health,* Vol. 68(10), October, 1978, pp. 981–987.)

Social welfare researchers Sheila B. Kamerman and Alfred J. Kahn arrived at the same conclusion with regard to social services: "There is no relation between survival of agencies and either need or impact." See S. B. Kamerman and A. J. Kahn, "Social Services for Children, Youth and Families," (A proposal to the Annie E. Casey Foundation, New York, November, 1986)

8. Weatherly and colleagues came to a similar conclusion after surveying comprehensive programs for pregnant and parenting adolescents: "The development and survival of local programs during the past decade is nothing less than phenomenal considering the obstacles they face . . . They stand as a testimony to the vibrancy, resourcefulness and responsiveness of local efforts." The researchers pointed out that the exemplary programs and services they found were exceptions, and "must inevitably remain so in the absence of basic policy changes." The difficulties at the local level which must be overcome in developing and operating good programs, and the cumbersome strategies that must be devised to overcome prevailing constraints, "favor the development of services in a relatively few fortunate (resource-rich and better-served) localities." They conclude by asking whether "the encouragement of a cottage industry is an appropriate response to . . . a serious, widespread social problem." (See R. Weatherly, *et al., Patchwork Programs: Comprehensive Services for Pregnant and Parenting Adolescents,* report prepared for the U.S. Public Health Service, Office of Population Affairs, U.S. Department of Health and Human Services, 1985.)

9. For an excellent discussion of the weaknesses of prevailing approaches to evaluation research, and how they might be overcome, see D. T. Campbell, "Problems for the Experimenting Society in the Interface between Evaluation and Service Providers," in *America's Family Support Programs: Perspectives and Prospects,* S. L. Kagan, D. R. Powell, B. Weissbourd, and E. Zigler, (Eds.), New Haven: Yale University Press, 1987.

10. For data on dollar savings from early interventions with children and families in high-risk environments, see L. B. Schorr, *Within Our Reach*, 1988. In addition, for data on dollar savings from prenatal care, see Institute of Medicine, *Preventing Low Birthweight*, 1985; for data on dollar savings from family supports, see estimates of Homebuilders, the Behavioral Sciences Institute, Federal Way, Washington, 1987; also W. Showell, *Biennial Report of CSD's Intensive Family Services*, State of Oregon, 1985; for data on dollar savings from reduction in teenage parenthood, see K. A. Moore and R. F. Werthheimer, "Teenage Childbearing and Welfare," *Family Planning Perspectives*, 1984; for data on dollar savings from nurse home visits, see D. Olds, *et al.*, "Improving the Delivery of Prenatal Care and Outcomes of Pregnancy," *Pediatrics*, Vol. 77(1), January, 1986, pp. 16–28; for data on savings from Yale day care-health care-family support programs, see V. Seitz, *et al.*, "Effects of Family Support Intervention," *Child Development*, 1985; A. Naylor, "Child Day Care," *Journal of Preventive Psychiatry*, 1982; for savings from preschool interventions, see C. U. Weber, *et al.*, *An Economic Analysis of the Ypsilanti Perry Preschool Project*, 1978; also see National Coalition of Advocates for Students, *Barriers to Excellence*, 1985.

11. Committee on Economic Development, *Children in Need: Investment Strategies for the Educationally Disadvantaged*, 1987.

12. J. M. Sugarman, "Head Start, A Retrospective View, in *Project Head Start: A Legacy of the War on Poverty*, E. Zigler and J. Valentine, (Eds.), New York: The Free Press, 1979, pp. 114–20.

13. The discussion of obstacles to widespread implementation of successful programs in this section owes much to Professor Peter B. Edelman of the Georgetown University Law School, who allowed me to make use of his rich insights and observations.

14. H. Heclo, "The Political Foundations of Antipoverty Policy," in *Fighting Poverty*, S. H. Danziger and D. H. Weinberg, (Eds.), Cambridge, MA: Harvard University Press, 1986, pp. 91–103.

15. Minnesota's Early Childhood Family Education Program provides one example of how the tension between universal and targeted services can be reconciled. Under the umbrella of a state-wide, community-based effort to help parents promote healthy child development, the program provides parenting education and support for everyone, but also aims more intensive and comprehensive services specifically toward very high-risk groups.

16. W. J. Wilson, *The Truly Disadvantaged: The Inner City, the Underclass, and Public Policy*. Chicago: University of Chicago Press, 1987.

17. 60% of young American men were able to earn enough to keep a family of three out of poverty in 1973, but only 42% were in 1984. The marriage rate of the men in this age group fell by half during this period. Since the longest spells of poverty for children are those that begin with a child being born into a single-parent family, and the most frequent long-lasting way out of poverty for children is when their mother marries, the drop in the number of young men who earn enough to support a family is a crucial factor in explaining what is keeping so many children in environments that undermine healthy development.

Data on earnings and marriage rates of young men from C. Johnson and A. Sum, "Declining Earnings of Young Men: Their Relation to Poverty, Teen Pregnancy and Family Formation," Washington, D.C.: Children's Defense Fund, 1987, and from Wilson's *The Truly Disadvantaged*, 1987.

Data on the number of female-headed families from U.S. House of Representatives, Select Committee on Children, Youth, and Families, *U.S. Children and Their Families*, Washington, D.C., Government Printing Office, 1987.

Data on escaping poverty through marriage from M. J. Bane and D. T. Ellwood, "Slipping Into and Out of Poverty: The Dynamics of Spells," Cambridge, MA: National Bureau of Economic Research, 1983.

Data on children in poverty from U.S. Congress, Committee on Ways and Means, *Children in Poverty*, Washington, D.C., Government Printing Office, 1985.

18. Here I rely extensively on the penetrating analysis of the historical roots and current dimensions of inner city poverty in William J. Wilson's 1987 book, *The Truly Disadvantaged*.

19. Dr. Comer is quoted in D. Whitman and J. Thornton "A Nation Apart," *U.S. News and World Report*, 1986.

20. Illicit drug use and drug-related crime increased at an astonishing rate (about 20-fold) between the early 1960s and the late 1970s. (See A. M. Nicholi, "The Nontherapeutic Use of Psychoactive Drugs," *The New England Journal of Medicine*, Vol. 308(16), April 21, 1983, pp. 925–33.) Since then, the use of all illegal drugs has decreased, except for cocaine, and its derivative, crack. The effects of illegal commerce in drugs has had a profound influence on life in urban slums. Drug dealers seduce ever younger children to participate in their trade. For many youngsters, drug dealing seems to offer an attractive alternative to more tedious and less well-compensated work. Police in New York and Detroit report that children as young as ten are using crack, and that 13-year-olds are not only addicted to crack, but are selling it for a large profit. (Select Committee on Children, Youth and Families, U.S. House of Representatives, Joint Hearing on the Crack-Cocaine Crisis, Washington, D.C., July 15, 1986.) Almost a third of seventh-grade students in New York State said they had used illegal drugs before they entered seventh grade. (See J. Barnabel, "State Survey Shows Extensive Drug Use Before the 7th Grade," *The New York Times*, 18 October 1984.) The use of illicit drugs at increasingly younger ages is particularly alarming in view of the evidence that the age of first use of illegal drugs is a good predictor of later heavy drug involvement. (See L. N. Robins, "The Natural History of Adolescent Drug Use," *American Journal of Public Health*, vol. 74(7), July, 1984, pp. 656–657.

21. J. P. Comer, "Black Violence and Public Policy," in *American Violence and Public Policy*, L. A. Curtis, (Ed.), New Haven: Yale University Press, 1985.

22. See D. J. West and D. P. Farrington, *Who Becomes Delinquent?*, London: Heinemann Educational Books, 1973.

23. S. G. Kellam, M. E. Ensminger, and R. J. Turner, "Family Structure and the Mental Health of Children," *Archives of General Psychiatry*, Vol. 34, September, 1977, pp. 1012–1022.

24. W. J. Wilson, *The Truly Disadvantaged*, 1987.

25. In the census tracts included in the Ricketts-Sawhill definition, more than half of the men had worked less than 26 weeks the previous year, more than a third of the households received welfare assistance, more than a third of men and women aged sixteen to nineteen had dropped out of school, and 57% of the families were headed by women. If one added a fifth criterion, that at least 20% of the population of the census tract had income below the poverty line, the numbers would hardly change—one would have to eliminate only six census tracts. (See E. R. Ricketts and I. V. Sawhill, "Defining and Measuring the Underclass," Washington, D.C.: Urban Institute, 1986; also E. R. Ricketts and I. V. Sawhill, "Defining and Measuring the Underclass," *Journal of Policy Analysis and Management*, Vol. 7 (2) Winter 1988, pp. 316–25.

GIVING CHILDREN A CHANCE: WHAT ROLE COMMUNITY-BASED PARENTING INTERVENTIONS?

Judith S. Musick
Robert Halpern

EFFORTS TO strengthen poor parents' ability to protect, nurture and care for their children have long played a role in our society's attempts to address the causes and consequences of poverty. In the current context, with poverty increasingly concentrated in families with young children, early childhood parenting issues have surfaced at many points in policy debates about reducing dependency and improving the life chances of poor children. For example, much has been made of the obstacles to attentive and nuturant parenting posed by too early childbearing. But discussion of such issues has not reflected the difficulties of altering parenting capacities and styles acquired through a lifetime of experience in a particular familial and social world, nor has it been adequately informed by accumulating program experience.

In this chapter, the authors examine the potential of community-based early parenting programs to influence the forces that shape capacity for and styles of parenting. We begin with a discussion of why early parenting interventions seem a plausible strategy for enhancing child development in low-income children. We then examine why programs may not be working as effectively as they should, and

Portions of this paper are based on two recent papers by Judith Musick. The first, "Psychological and Developmental Dimensions of Adolescent Pregnancy and Parenting: An Interventionist's Perspective," was prepared for the Rockefeller Foundation, December, 1987. The second, "Paraprofessionals, Parenting and Child Development: Understanding the Problems and Seeking Solutions," was co-authored by Frances Stott, Ph.D., of the Erikson Institute. It will appear in the forthcoming *Handbook of Early Intervention*, S. Meisels and J. Shonkoff (Eds.), Cambridge University Press.

what it would take to make them work more effectively. Finally, we discuss the implications of our suggestions for child and family policy.

COMMUNITY-BASED EARLY PARENTING INTERVENTIONS

The interventions with which we are concerned are those in which neighborhood-based agencies employ community members, sometimes in concert with professionals, to provide support for disadvantaged parents during pregnancy and/or infancy. Components of that support generally include information, feedback and guidance, help with practical problems, help with securing entitlements and services, encouragement and emotional support. Support is provided with the objective of promoting attentive parenting, parents' personal involvement and healthy child development. Community-based early parenting interventions are sometimes conceptualized as a community development strategy, designed to build or renew mutual support structures and resources in low-income communities.[1]

Three basic formats are most common in community-based early parenting programs. The first is the home-based program, in which home visiting is the major direct service activity. The second is the stand-alone group-based program, in which parent education classes or support groups located in a convenient, community-based setting are the major activity. The third is the neighborhood center, created for the purpose of providing an array of child development and family support services to young families. Such services might include, in addition to parent support groups and/or home visiting, developmental child care or respite care, health and developmental screening, personal counseling on a range of family life issues, high school completion classes, transportation and so forth.

The great majority of community-based early parenting programs are initiated by local agencies, responding to perceived neighborhood needs, with very modest, relatively short-term funding. These are generally undertaken as service programs, although they may document numbers and/or characteristics of families served. A small number of state initiatives are currently in various stages of development, as well.[2] These state initiatives typically provide a common funding base, some kind of mandate with regard to targeting, program purposes and components, and some level of technical assistance. Levels and types of evaluation activity associated with state initiatives vary. There are, finally, a small number of national service demonstrations underway, with networks of programs in different parts of the country.[3]

THE RATIONALE FOR EARLY PARENTING INTERVENTIONS FOR LOW-INCOME FAMILIES

There is a great deal of consensus about what infants need in order to grow and develop to their fullest potential. They need protection from physical and psychological harm, adequate nourishment and at least one special, responsive adult, to whom they can become attached, and who will act as guide and mediator between them and the world. As infants develop, their experience of the world, as structured and mediated by that special adult and others, begins to shape in them a sense of who they are, what they can do and what the world is like.[4] The devastating effect of poverty is not only that it directly and chronically threatens infants' physical well-being from the time they are conceived; it also undermines the capacity and resources of their parents to protect, nurture and guide them.

The effects of poverty are by no means uniform: even in the poorest of communities some parents are able to rear their children in competence-enhancing ways.[5] Such parents function to mitigate or buffer negative effects of the environment for their children. They provide consistency and predictability in an unpredictable physical and social world. They exploit positive community supports like churches and self-help groups to their fullest, protecting and nurturing their children's strengths, enabling their children to make the best possible use of whatever the community and wider world has to offer. Such parents are able to do this largely because of the greater psychological resources they possess. Although these parents' actual life circumstances and material resources may be no better than those of parents who are less protective and enabling, they are much less likely to have a sense of hopelessness or powerlessness.[6]

But for growing numbers of young, low-income adults, obstacles to attentive parenting posed by pervasively stressful living conditions, and lack of adequate support from entitlements or services for basic needs, are compounded by struggles for their own personal development, lack of personal resources and informal support systems whose costs can at times outweigh their benefits.[7] Feelings of powerlessness, futility and limited life options increasingly accompany the experience of poverty, and these feelings frame the world-view that an increasing proportion of low-income parents communicate to their children from birth. A majority of parents of infants conceived and born in poverty were themselves reared in poverty, personally experiencing its physical and psychological injuries. Low-income parents are disproportionately likely to have experienced broken attachments, neglect, even abuse as children, and to bring the residue of such experiences to their own parenting. The chronic stress associated with lack of stability and margin for error in almost every area of family life can drain physical and emotional energies, leaving few resources for attending to children's development needs. Compounding all these factors, low-income parents are disproportionately likely to be extremely young and unmarried when they begin parenting, and thus unable to draw on either personal maturity or marital supports in adjusting to the new and changing demands for parenting.

The family histories and psycho-social backgrounds of the most troubled young parents served by community-based parenting programs include such variables as absence of fathers or consistent father surrogates; frequent separations and/or inadequate nurturing from their own young, distressed mothers; many siblings sharing the mother's limited resources; premature, inappropriate assumption of adult responsibilities at the cost of personal development; exposure to violence, disorganization and unpredictability; sexual and/or physical abuse; lack of education and basic skills to bolster self-confidence and provide alternatives to early parenthood; and a gnawing hunger for affection, affiliation and the meeting of unmet dependency needs.

Such formative experiences require psychological accommodations that may be adaptive in the short-run, but all too frequently have long-term costs—for oneself, and later, for one's children. Thus, for example, a mother who herself "learned" as a child that too much curiosity and assertiveness brought negative consequences from parents or public authorities, may be more sensitive to the risks than to the developmental purposes of such behavior. Or, she may be unable to tolerate her child's normal developmental need for independence, because it feels too much like the abandonment she experienced when her own mother periodically and unpredictably disappeared from her life. Personal history from childhood and adolescence forms the sub-structure which underlies later skills, attitudes and emotions about one's children, and about one's role as a caregiving partner in a reciprocal relationship.

Early parenting interventions obviously cannot provide as powerful and continuing an influence on parenting as that provided by personal history and life situation. Intervening to strengthen the early parenting that low-income children receive, without attending as well to the social, institutional and economic context shaping that early parenting, is both practically and ethically dubious. Nevertheless, within a context of the range of basic support efforts, early parenting interventions should be able to identify the environmental stresses and resource deficits impinging on childbearing in a particular family, and, over time, the personal issues (such as those around dependence and independence) shaping parenting capacities and styles. These interventions should be able to help parents become more conscious that they are relating to the world and raising their children in particular ways, for particular reasons. Such interventions should then be able to introduce, and provide the psychological support necessary to risk new ways of parenting, and new ways of coping, problem-solving and using available resources to meet family needs.

BARRIERS TO EFFECTIVE PARENTING INTERVENTIONS

Although early parenting interventions should be able to introduce and provide the support necessary for risking new ways of parenting, coping and growing, the authors' personal experience with such programs generally suggests a number of interrelated obstacles to achieving these objectives. These obstacles include:

- the difficulty of balancing attention among families' basic survivial needs, parents' personal needs, the parent-child relationship and children's development needs;
- even when parenting is addressed, a tendency to under-estimate the complexity of parenting behavior and its determinants;
- scarcity of staff with the necessary skills to identify and address parenting issues salient to particular families; and
- implementation conditions that make it difficult to build and maintain program capacities to overcome other obstacles.

DIFFICULTY OF BALANCING PROGRAM EMPHASIS

When a program enters the life of a young, low-income family, it is both ethically and practically necessary to attend to the variety of needs that present themselves. These may include lack of basic resources such as housing, medical services or food, as well as the need for personal support around family and other crises. Parents cannot attend adequately to their children's developmental needs when they must expend most of their energy simply surviving. But, while it is difficult to hold at bay the stress created by resource-scarce family and community environments that act as barriers to nurturant parenting, it is nonetheless essential to address parents' responsibilities to and relationships with their children, if the children are to thrive.

While attending to the developmental needs of all young children should be a high priority in both the public and private spheres of American life, attending to the needs of children in high-risk life situations is especially critical. For these children there are rarely compensating forces at work in the caregiving environment to buffer them against specific threats to healthy development. If programs delay addressing children's developmental needs until other dimensions of family life have been fully addressed, precious time and opportunities will have been wasted. Once wasted, they often cannot be regained. The home visitor who spends all her time attempting to resolve a parent's current personal or financial crisis may fail to observe and intervene in parent-child difficulties until they have escalated to less manageable levels, or may even fail to notice a developmental difficulty in a child that could be greatly alleviated if that child received early diagnosis and treatment.

While the challenges of balancing the needs of parent and child may be formidable, they are not insurmountable. To take a common example, if a teen mother puts her energies into getting back on track in terms of school or work, without also taking special care to spend time with her child in growth-facilitating ways, and if that child is subsequently neglected as the mother pursues her immediate goals, then the mother's growth will ultimately be at her child's expense. Further, she will be robbed of the opportunity to develop as a parent, to fulfill the tasks of a critical and valued human role. An intervention program's function, it's very purpose, must be to encourage and facilitate the development of *both* parent and child, and to help the parent balance her own needs with those of her child.

Helping parents to return to school, to understand and interact more maturely with their families, to train for, and obtain jobs are all clearly important intervention functions. All provide parents with necessary skills, improved self-esteem and relief from undue stress, thus enabling them to cope with their children better. However, a growing proportion of poor families need more than this if we expect to reduce environmental risk for their children. Such families require intervention services which are targeted *directly* at affecting parenting practices, and at identifying children in need of specialized services as early as possible. These parenting and child-focused services will also have to be more firmly rooted in knowledge of child development and parent-child relationships than is presently the case.

UNDERESTIMATING THE COMPLEXITY OF PARENTING AND ITS DETERMINANTS

A second common obstacle to supporting low-income parents effectively in their childbearing roles is lack of appreciation for the complexity of parenting and its determinates and the difficulty of changing the caregiving environment. This does not mean returning to the victim-blaming strategies of the 1960s in which educational psychologists designed programs to "teach" low-income mothers how to be better teachers to their young children, in order to prevent "retarded" cognitive and linguistic development.[8] It does mean, however, that intervention emphases and expectations must take into account the residual effects of cumulative physical, social and psychological insults that accompany poverty. It means taking account as well of current psychosocial forces which pull the young adult in developmental directions that may be immediately adaptive but ultimately destructive. Finally, it means taking seriously the notion that parents' own past and current experiences in being cared for themselves will have a profound effect on how they care for others.

Parenting is a "relationship with a history"—a way of interacting with, nurturing and guiding a young, and initially dependent, human being, that is derived to a significant degree from a history of being related to in particular ways. As such, parenting cannot be "learned" in the same way one learns an academic discipline. Nor can it be the result of the kinds of training required for vocational competence. It is not a skill learned as one learns to cook, or to drive a car. This would appear to be self-evident; yet, many early intervention programs seem to be predicated on the notion of parenting as analogous to a job: that is, as something that can be taught, or re-taught if it has not been "learned" well initially. It is important for us to design interventions that draw on what we know (which is still far from enough) about the process by which capacity for parenting develops. An example of this is illustrative.

Several years ago, staff at the Ounce of Prevention Fund in Illinois began to take a closer look at the causes and effects of childhood sexual victimization. This was in response to repeated disclosures of sexual abuse among program participants, almost all of whom are adolescent mothers of infants and young children. In order to gain a better understanding of the scope of the problem, a survey of the prevalence of sexual victimization among pregnant and parenting adolescents was conducted at about half the Fund programs across the state. The findings from this study were very sobering. Of almost 500 mothers taking part in the study, some three-fifths had experienced sexual victimization, with about two-thirds of the victims having been abused on multiple occasions and/or by multiple perpetrators. The average age at first occurrence was 11 and a half years, and while many young women had been abused early in life, abuse was most common during the middle school and early adolescent years.[9]

Most of the young women volunteered comments at various points throughout the structured questionnaire. Anyone doubting the developmental harm or psychological pain that results from such exploitation should read some of these comments—the wounds remain raw, even years later. Shame and grief extend beyond the victims themselves to sisters or other intimates who knew it was happening, yet felt helpless to stop it. These are the wounds that these young women carry with them when they become parents.

When a girl has been unprotected in her family of origin, and socialized (prematurely and inappropriately) into sexuality through coercion, we should not be surprised if later, when she herself becomes a parent, she feels helpless and unable to exert control over that aspect of the lives of her children. The capacity to protect oneself and one's children is derived from the experience of having been cared for by others, of having a body (and mind) that has been protected from violation by concerned and nurturing caregivers. The diminished sense of personal worth and efficacy that characterize many former victims is manifested in their inability to protect their own young children (boys as well as girls) from harm at the hands of the boyfriends, sitters, or other temporary surrogate fathers who pass in and out of their lives.

When asked what they thought they could do to protect their own children from such experiences, a number of respondents in the study expressed fatalism or futility in regard to their ability to prevent such occurrences. These responses afford us the opportunity to see how pathological patterns of interaction and failures of protection are passed from one generation to the next.

"I don't know of any ways to protect my children because it can happen anywhere."

. . . "but only time will tell."

. . . "ain't nothing I can do."

In other words, the "unprotected" young children of many of the adolescent mothers interviewed were a group at very high risk for abuse themselves.

In order to strengthen the capacity of young adolescent mothers to protect their very young, vulnerable children from sexual abuse, the Ounce of Prevention Fund developed Heart-to-Heart, an intensive, clinically informed program component. This ten-week intervention has been incorporated in ongoing parent support programs. It is specifically designed to help break the code of silence and secrecy that imprisons so many former victims in the pain of their past, predisposing them to pass this on to their children. In Heart-to-Heart, adolescent mothers are educated about the incidence, causes and effects of child sexual abuse within a supportive atmosphere which encourages their coming to terms with their own abusive experiences. Once provided with this opportunity, young mothers seem more open to learning and using specific strategies for protecting their children. Communities are also made aware of the problem of child sexual abuse and of the appropriate resources required to solve the problem on an individual and community-wide basis.[10]

Such an approach to the design of intervention strategies is based on a notion of childrearing as a complex process strongly affected by the psychological history and current resources a person brings to the role of parent. Thus, interventions must often be more than educative or supportive, they must be healing as well. While it may be appealing to believe that a non-deficit approach which "builds on parents' strengths," "promotes parenting skills," or "educates parents" will be sufficient to break dysfunctional parenting patterns, in truth it may not. In some, perhaps a good many instances, we must first undo damage already done before we can begin to promote skills or educate parents. Strengths must be built *in* before they can be built *on*.

Those who design, staff and evaluate these programs must begin to take this issue more seriously than has been the case until this time. This does not mean that traditional psychotherapeutic treatment must somehow automatically be provided to all high-risk parents— that is not the point. Rather, it means that programs need to make use of clinical and research knowledge about how and why a child's development can get off track, and about how and why parents can be helped to grow in regard to those areas directly related to their capacities to nurture and guide children.

STAFF QUALIFICATIONS AND TRAINING

If changing the early caregiving environment involves changing the parent, this can best be accomplished in the context of a relationship with the parent. Where issues revolve around relationships, the principal change agents are not just the methods or curricula, they are other *people* who use them. It is these people, and the quality of the relationships they are able to establish and sustain, that will be the critical elements in any intervention. These relationships provide the scaffolds for affirming, and as necessary, building or re-building parenting strengths. Most community-based early parenting interventions are staffed at the direct service level by either trained paraprofessionals from the community or by social work/counseling professionals. Although these service providers may have had experience with adults or adolescents, they sometimes have had little education, training or work experience related to infant and early childhood development and early parenting.

Many service providers, especially paraprofessionals (or, as they are often called, lay helpers) were themselves struggling young mothers in the not too distant past. They may be too closely identified with the young parents they see, and feel uncomfortable about how well they themselves managed the tasks of motherhood when their own children were little. The effort they may have exerted to pull themselves out of poverty, often with little or no support from near or extended kin, may have taken its toll on their capacity for being enabling of their own children. Or, negative self-images established during these service providers' own childhoods may remain in spite of success experiences. The internalized residue of these formative experiences often prevents family workers from "seeing" potentially serious problems, in the children themselves, in the parent-child relationship or in the patterns of child rearing. Limitations such as these pose a very real challenge for intervention programs.

How can we promote optimal development in children at risk, if we cannot meaningfully affect the childrearing environment? How can we foster positive change if service providers, the potential agents of such change, are not adquately prepared for their job? One way, perhaps the only realistic way, is to change that service provider, transforming the way she views and understands parents, children and parent-child relationships. The Ounce of Prevention Fund's Developmental Program illustrates one strategy being employed to promote such change.

In 1986 the Fund made the decision to begin providing both traditional developmental screening and on-going observation of the parent-child (and, in many cases, grandparent-child) relationship for all of the children born to adolescent parents in the programs it administers. The creation of the Developmental Program, as it has come to be called, grew out of a recognition of the need for direct service staff to have useful techniques for understanding and assessing both children's cognitive and socio-emotional development and the parent-child relationship, and to feel more comfortable entering that relationship in their work with families.

The entire training protocol has been structured to model the kinds of observant, interactive roles Fund supervisors expect staff to fulfill vis-á-vis the parents, who will then, it is hoped, come to behave in similar ways with their children. Staff training includes observation of parents and children (using a structured observation guide), modeling, and supervised hands-on experiences in both assessment and intervention. Both didactic and interactive components have been included. Each nourishes the other and brings about a synergistic experience for the provider/trainee. Such training experiences have resulted in staff gaining a better understanding of their abilities as change agents, as well as their limitations in facilitating change.

Training is designed to help service providers make empathetic connections with parents as well as children. For example, staff trainers emphasize that pointing out a parent's strengths or skills, instead of ignoring or criticizing, is a key step in building a strong relationship. In addition, measures of child temperament (albeit rudimentary ones) have been included in the parent-child observation guide because of their usefulness in helping staff become more sensitive to individual differences among children, and to stimulate them to think about what such differences may mean to parents.[11]

The training also has been designed to foster a sense of comfort even with such "touchy" topics as discipline. Thus, for example, home visitors trained in the Developmental Program appear to be better able to set limits when they observe teen parents cruelly teasing, shaking or slapping their young children for no apparent reason. Now home visitors propose and model alternatives that are more firmly grounded in their empathy as well as in their knowledge of both parent and child.

The Developmental Program seeks to create a *chain of enablement* which fosters positive growth in paraprofessional staff, so that they in turn can foster such growth in teen parents. This method of training paraprofessionals to focus on the teen as a *parent* is designed to result ultimately in more enabling and nurturing parenting through a structured, well-planned "trickle down" effect. Will these "deeper" patterns of intervention have a meaningful effect on childrearing attitudes and behaviors? Preliminary assessments indicate that they will, for a sizable number of parents. Will these shifts in parenting attitudes and behaviors then have measurable effects on developmental outcomes for the children? We will have to wait and see. One can observe however, that the nature of the interaction between parents and children begins to change as providers change.

THE CONDITIONS OF IMPLEMENTATION

Thus far we have focused on the kinds of program emphases and staff training required to have a significant influence on childrearing in multiply-stressed young families. These specific dimensions of parenting programs have to be embedded in broader "implementation conditions" that do not undermine skillful, focused parenting work. But more often than those of us in the field would like to acknowledge, the very programs purporting to prevent or remediate problems of poor children mirror the unpredictability of the lives of the families served.

This unpredictability has many causes. One is a lack of clarity about whom the program is trying to reach, and toward what ends. Too often, programs are driven by global premises about families' needs for support that do not provide adequate specification about who needs what kinds of support, and therefore do not provide adequate bases for shaping program design and monitoring implementation progress. Moreover, attention to targeting and change objectives has to be ongoing. It is in the nature of community-based parenting programs that their sense of purpose and strategy become refined with experience in the field.

A second problem is lack of adequate attention to the critical role supervision plays in supporting family worker development and performance. Too often supervision of family workers' role performance, and nurturance of their personal growth and development, are undermined by the variety of externally-focused responsibilities that many supervisors have to assume. These may include not just raising budgets, but attending to administrative details, public relations and program documentation activities. It is important for program directors and supervisors to protect the most important function of their role: providing family workers an authoritative voice to educate, guide and interpret, and a nurturant voice to affirm their value as people, and the value of what they are doing.

In a different vein, the environments of community-based parenting programs too often are adult-focused, and do not provide physical settings for or direct programmatic attention to children. A setting and program design that are child-focused as well as adult-focused can provide developmentally rich experiences for children and an opportunity for parents to observe new or different patterns of adult-child interaction; and they can generally serve to focus program attention on children's developmental needs.

Funding patterns in community-based parenting programs are a major source of the unpredictability and unevenness characterizing the conditions of implementation. Insecurity and lack of long-term funding interact with the mercurial nature of funding "fashion" to keep agency and program directors in a constant state of anxious fund-seeking. Rather than being able to attend to the organization and substance of their programs, including such critical domains as staff training and supervision, senior level staff often spend the majority of their time writing grant proposals. This they must do in order to capitalize on the latest source of funding, for the latest social problem—drug abuse or delinquency prevention, child abuse, or teen pregnancy reduction strategies.

Just as a program is getting settled with one set of goals and program components, the funding base changes and it must accommodate. Frequently these changes are slight, more of emphasis than of actual form. Nevertheless, the changes are unsettling, for staff and participants alike. They build on the ever-present state of insecurity experienced by staff, especially community-based paraprofessional staff, whose fear of losing their (often newly acquired) jobs undermines the attention they can give to their work. When upper level staff spend all their time and energy looking for financial resources, this is conveyed all too clearly to lower level staff; they, in turn, spend all their time worrying about financial resources, and once again poor parents and their children are short-changed.

A more substantial and sustained funding commitment would be a critically important first step towards strengthening these programs. To begin with, it would result in more adequately compensated and highly motivated staff, particularly at the direct service level. More secure funding would also go a long way towards helping programs to set up and institutionalize systems of training, supervision and standards of program performance. Beyond this, it would provide the basis to allocate funds for the creation of physical environments that are more child-oriented, and more conducive to fostering healthy parent-child relationships. Increased and longer-term funding could increase the ability of these programs to provide an integrated, coherent package of family support services.

Finally, the general level of implementation in this field of practice is constrained by a critical problem often called the "demonstration-dilution" effect. Although there have been a number of exemplary model programs for poor families, once the experimental or demonstration phase is over, these programs frequently experience rapid and significant declines in quality. The promise of these programs is left unfulfilled as they move from the optimal conditions of the demonstration phase—greater funding, smaller target populations, highly skilled professional level staff, at least in supervisory positions, quality health care, developmental day care, and well organized educational or vocational programs, etc.—to the replication, or everyday, business-as-usual phase. Without the media spotlight, or scientific interest, programs can thin out, and become less focused, more *laissez faire*. The program may continue to exist, but the spirit, and consequently the substance, has been eroded.

Together, these implementation problems can make a program so fragile that it collapses if it loses a key person. Or, if it does not actually close its doors, it may go through such a protracted period of chaos and disorganization that a year or more goes by before it is back on track. That time lost can be very sad and very serious for high-risk infants and their parents. Further, these limitations interact with, and exacerbate, the failures to deal actively with child development and parenting, the most critical obstacle to successful programming. Parents, especially motivated parents, may make excellent use of the resources available in these programs, especially peer support, from caring people who listen to their troubles and help them secure basic entitlements and services. It is not hard to see, however, that their children can remain virtually untouched. This is ironic, considering that the stated purpose of most of these programs is to promote the *children's* development and to improve their chances for a better life.

In sum, improved functioning of parents is clearly necessary, but it is far from sufficient to significantly alter the future and life chances of poor children. Community-based programs must be encouraged, and then assisted in their efforts to develop interventions with a cross-generational focus: those which address in an integrated fashion young parents' own psycho-social and developmental needs, their future as potentially productive adults, and their responsibilities as parents.

It may be convenient to put off, or take lightly this charge because of the presumption that parenting problems wouldn't exist if structural or societal level supports such as those related to employment were greater. Such an approach, however, is short-sighted. Self-sufficiency is intimately tied to one's psychological resources: one's mental health and internalized expectations of self and of the world. The foundation of these resources is laid within the family, and rooted in its early caregiver-child interactions. In the absence of a solid foundation today, the child will not be able to make use of increased educational or work opportunities tomorrow during his or her adolescence and adulthood, no matter how potentially beneficial these opportunities may appear from our vantage point.

EARLY PARENTING INTERVENTIONS AND BROADER SOCIAL POLICY GOALS

We have argued that parents' capacities to care for, guide and socialize their children in competence-fostering ways are linked both to adequacy of basic material resources and to a cluster of personal traits best described as psychological resources. Psychological resources shape parents' responses to chronic stress and hardship. They determine how parents interpret the world and make it meaningful to their children. A parent who feels efficacious, and who can separate her own needs from those of her children, can allow and enable her children to go beyond where she has gone before. This enabling process cannot be ignored in public policies that seek to improve the lives of poor children.

Because there is such a scarcity of structural supports to cushion disadvantaged children and augment what the parent provides, and because there are so many threats to developmental integrity, the parenting role and functions assume even greater significance. It is ironic that in order to help their children get a good start, and move out of poverty without the supports available to more advantaged parents, poor parents need to have not just average, but better than average psychological resources.

Even were there suddenly to be better schools, better health care and greater opportunities for employment, it would still take time to undo past damage: the effects of parentally mediated experiences may last for generations. When one reads about the multi-generational effects of the Great Depression,[12] for example, one sees the naivete of the expectation that interventions, even those involving changes on the societal level, can undo in one generation the pernicious effects of past deprivations. Even when conditions improve, as they did for those who lived through the Great Depression, even when children's lives are objectively better than were their parents, the negative psychological effects may still remain. They inhere now within the family and its offspring.

But the conditions are not only not improving for many children conceived and born in poverty, they are worsening.[13] If such children are to have a chance, their parents must have internal strengths as well as external supports. In families in which such strengths have been gradually undermined, there will be no shortcuts to individual work to strengthen capacities and aspirations; for personal development, parenting and healthy family formation. Most importantly, parenting cannot be treated as a secondary concern, one which is addressed only when there has been a failure to prevent it, or when the child-parent relationship has become problematic.

FINDING A PLACE FOR PARENTING ISSUES IN THE POVERTY POLICY DEBATE

Parenting issues are implicit in the most frequently articulated policy goals for young families experiencing poverty, notably those goals related to reduction of welfare dependency, and improving the educability and school success of low-income children. Improved parenting is brought into the policy debate periodically, sometimes in relation to the former of these two goals, sometimes in relation to the latter. But it is usually dealt with in a singularly simplistic manner, with only modest appreciation for the complexities of the parenting process. Moreover, to the extent that supporting and strengthening parenting in poor families is articulated at all as a policy goal, it is articulated with a sense of ambivalence about rationale and purpose that makes it difficult to pursue.

In part, our inability to develop a coherent strategy for supporting parenting in low-income families is due to our as yet unresolved ambivalence about the causes of poverty, public responsibility for children and families and the appropriate conditions for intervention into family life. This ambivalence frequently puts those who shape the mandates and approaches of parenting programs for young families, and those who actually provide services to those families, in a difficult position. Early parenting interventions cannot provide economically disadvantaged parents with critical formative experiences that their first 17, 18 or 19 years all too frequently failed to provide. Basic feelings of trust, competence and capacity to empathize with the needs of young children are acquired within the matrix of the family, and cannot easily be altered. Unfortunately, early parenting interventions too often are expected to compensate for those foundations of healthy adulthood and parenthood that are optimally acquired naturally. Further, they are expected to bring about basic changes for which there is sometimes little support in the current environment of the young parent.[14]

The fact that parenting is rarely considered as a critical element in the personal development and identify formation of the parent him or herself further constrains our ability to develop a coherent set of policies directed toward that adult role. But even when it occurs under far from optimal circumstances, having a child represents (at least for the moment) the potential for something different in one's life. This potential must be acknowledged and responded to in the larger framework of a young adult's life situation. All too often however, early childbearing is viewed unidimensionally, in relation to other adolescent or young adult tasks that are suddenly made more complicated, or to risks created for the next generation. From such a perspective, early parenting intervention is doomed to appear an unsure strategy. It must seem a very indirect strategy to those who view basic societal change—in economic structures, culture, housing patterns, prejudices—as the only approach likely to reduce poverty and dependency, and enhance poor children's life chances.

Certainly, supporting and strengthening parenting is only a piece of a much more complex puzzle that includes prevention of too early childbearing, psychological and educational preparation of young adults for decent jobs in a decent labor market, and provisions of basic family supports, including health care and child care to low and moderate-income working families. It is, however, a far more critical and integral piece of the puzzle than is reflected in most current policy debate.

NOTES

1. Robert Halpern, "Community-Based Early Intervention Programs," *Handbook of Early Intervention*, S. Meisels and J. Shonkoff (Eds.), New York: Cambridge University Press, (forthcoming).

2. Judith Musick, The Ounce of Prevention Fund, Chicago, Illinois.

3. Robert Halpern, Ford Foundations' Child Survival/Fair Start Initiative.

4. J. Musick & F. Stott, "Paraprofessionals, Parenting and Child Development: Understanding the Problems and Seeking Solutions." In S. Meisels & J. Shonkoff (Eds.), *Handbook of Early Intervention*. New York: Cambridge University Press, (forthcoming).

Also see "Early Intervention in Cognitive Development As a Strategy for Reducing Poverty" by James Garbarino, this volume, Chapter 2.

5. R. Clark, *Family Life and School Achievement: Why Poor Black Children Succeed or Fail*. Chicago: University of Chicago Press, 1983.

6. *Ibid.*

7. J. Musick, "The Psychological and Developmental Dimensions of Adolescent Pregnancy and Parenting: An Interventionist's Perspective."

H. Weiss and R. Halpern, "Community-Based Family Support and Education Programs: Something Old or Something New?" Paper commissioned by the National Resource Center for Children in Poverty, Columbia University, 1988.

8. M. Deutsch, *An Evaluation of the Effectiveness of an Enriched Curriculum in Overcoming Consequences of Environmental Deprivation.* New York: Institute for Developmental Studies, New York University, 1967.

S. Grey & R. Klaus, *The Early Training Project.* Monographs of the Society for Research in Child Development, No. 33, 1968.

E. Schaeffer, "A Home Training Program," *Children,* March–April, 1969.

9. H. Gershenon, J. Musick, H. Ruch-Ross, V. Magee, K. Rubino & D. Rosenberg, "The Prevalence of Sexual Abuse Among Teenage Mothers," *Journal of Interpersonal Violence,* Spring, 1989, in press.

10. The Fund currently is working on developing a component directed to males.

11. V. Bernstein, C. Percansky & S. Hans, "Screening for Social-Emotional Impairment in Infants Born to Teenage Mothers." Paper presented at the Society for Research in Child Development Annual Meeting, Baltimore, MD., 1987.

12. G. Elder, *Children of the Great Depression.* Chicago: University of Chicago Press, 1974.

G. Elder, T. V. Nguyen & A. Caspi, "Linking Family Hardship to Children's Lives," *Child Development,* Vol. 56, 1985, pp. 361–375.

13. W. Wilson, *The Truly Disadvantaged: The Inner City, the Underclass and Public Policy.* Chicago: University of Chicago Press, 1987.

14. J. Musick, "The Psychological and Developmental Dimensions of Adolescent Pregnancy and Parenting: An Interventionist's Perspective."

APPENDIX
INVESTING IN PREVENTION:
TOMORROW'S LEADERS AND THE
PROBLEM OF POVERTY

Report of a Study Conducted for the
Center for National Policy by
Peter D. Hart

THIS REPORT presents the results of four meetings conducted under a grant from the Primerica Foundation.

The first meeting took place in Philadelphia on December 12, 1987; the second, in Los Angeles on January 28, 1988; the third, in Atlanta on April 27, 1988; and the fourth in Chicago on June 8, 1988. At each session, ten high-level business executives (most under age 40) who are or will likely be part of America's business leadership participated in two-hour discussions moderated by Peter Hart.

This project was undertaken on the premise that the cooperation of the baby boom generation of corporate and community leadership is key to establishing a broad base of public support for any significant new efforts to reduce poverty. In particular, it was felt that the problems of poverty-stricken children, and government efforts to mitigate those problems, might be a natural area of concern for this group of individuals who are likely to have their own young children. In addition, since corporate support for, and involvement in the problems of poor children has been important in sustaining national assistance efforts, it was necessary to determine whether the next generation of corporate leaders shares the views of those who have led the cause during the past year or two.

The Center for National Policy developed a procedure for identifying target groups of respondents in Philadelphia, Los Angeles, Atlanta and Chicago. In each case, published sources were used, as well as contacts already established by the Center through its ongoing programs. Public officials of both major political parties were involved in the process, so that a range of views and attitudes might be represented.

A prestigious site was selected for each discussion, and a formal letter and printed invitation were sent to potential participants. Senator Edmund S. Muskie, chairman of the Center, signed three of the letters with local co-signers who are well-known in their communities; a fourth letter went from a single corporate leader.

Peter Hart, the leader of the discussions, is recognized as one of the leading analysts of public opinion in the United States.

Mr. Hart has represented more than 35 U.S. Senators and 30 governors, and has conducted polls in every state but one.

Though best known for his work in the political realm, Mr. Hart has undertaken important studies of the media, economic development, violence in America, non-voting and public attitudes toward early childhood health issues. In addition, Mr. Hart recently completed a landmark study of the baby-boom generation for *Rolling Stone* magazine. Mr. Hart is widely recognized for his creative and insightful approach to focus group research.

The program for the session was divided into three parts. First, there was a wide-ranging general discussion of concerns and problems that participants feel are facing the country. This part of the discussion also sought views about the general effectiveness of government programs: perceptions about what had been done well and what has been done poorly. Further, some effort was made to explore the extent to which participants intuitively see poverty as a problem, and to identify their perceptions of its causes.

The second part of the program, conducted over dinner, was a briefing by an expert. These briefings combined a presentation of statistics about poverty and a discussion of the effects of different government programs. An effort was made to focus on programs aimed at very young children, although these were not the sole focus.

Finally, the focus group participants were again asked to discuss the issue among themselves.

The report is divided into four sections: the first two present a summary and overview of the principal findings; the third elaborates on those results; and the fourth contains representative verbatim remarks of the panelists. The outline used to direct the discussion is appended.

SUMMARY OF KEY FINDINGS

I. *These highly articulate, thoughtful and successful young leaders express a deep underlying concern about the future of the country.* In particular, they tend to worry about the long-term future of the U.S. economy and its performance in relation to the economies of other nations.

They do not appear to link this concern automatically with what they see as the problems of poverty: homelessness, poor schools and inadequate job readiness.

In general, whatever their political background, the participants initially seem to view poverty as *separate from* their own lives—as a community issue, certainly, but one that is mostly set apart from business, family or personal interests.

II. When asked to discuss *government programs that have worked well in the past*, several participants mention the Apollo space program and associate it with President Kennedy. A few also speak of the Head Start project, and some cite the WIC program. By and large, though, these participants share the skepticism about the effectiveness of government programs that is prevalent among baby boom generation individuals of all income levels and backgrounds. However, they are much more likely than general poll respondents to discuss programs systematically. They rarely use anecdotes to illustrate their points, and generally seem very well-informed about the structure and details of job training and other anti-poverty programs.

There was relatively little discussion about macro-economic policy. It seems as if these participants (again, irrespective of political affiliation) assume the existence of a serious structural unemployment problem, and see it as the principal symptom of an intractable poverty problem in the U.S.—intractable because programmatic solutions are ineffective.

III. *When presented with data that detail the extent of poverty, particularly among children, and with evidence about effective programs, participants appear to shift their feelings on the issue of poverty from low gear into high.* There is a perceptible increase in the emotional content of the post-presentation discussion sessions. For some, the information heightened a sense of hopelessness—especially among participants in one session that emphasized data on the extent of the problem. For others, probably the majority, the presentations appear to provide a reason to care more about finding workable solutions. The prospect of some success seems to engender a greater motivation to try, as well as a greater sense of personal involvement in the outcome of the effort.

IV. *By the end of the sessions, these young leaders had integrated what must be done with how best to use public and private resources.* Most express support for government attention to the problem of poverty. *Government is seen as the right institution to provide leadership and financing, while non-government entities (or, in some cases, local government) are viewed as the preferred service providers.* These preferences differ somewhat according to the political views of the individual, but there is general agreement overall.

By and large, the participants were members of the private sector, although many of them express strong public values and concerns. They have much stronger faith in the *performance* of the private sector; however, they do not see the private sector contributing to *public objectives* without a push, pull or an assist from the government.

V. After working through the issue, many of the participants appear to draw a correlation between health and education programs for young children, on the one hand, and the long-term issues of job readiness, educational success and economic well-being on the other. In all of the groups, there is a strong tendency to make day care programs the logical focal point for bringing together the long-range objective of helping children do better developmentally with the short term goal of helping poor adolescents and young adults find and keep jobs.

OVERVIEW

The basic challenge is to develop a comprehensive approach that enables young business leaders to deal with issues of the underclass in the United States. Methods must be found both to inform and to involve these executives, encouraging their input on feasible solutions and their active participation in the implementation of various programs. As noted earlier, most of the focus group members seemed not to have previously thought extensively about the issues that were raised: many lacked a comprehensive view of the causes and consequences of poverty, and most were unaware of the range of possible overall solutions.

Nonetheless, these young leaders are able to provide valuable suggestions when isolated problems are raised. They discuss their opinions concerning the origins of and potential cures for poverty, and are familiar with the variety of people who make up the poverty ranks, such as single teenage mothers, mental patients prematurely released from institutions and members of the working and middle classes who have lost their jobs and fallen through holes in the safety net. Many of the leaders we spoke with demonstrate their compassion when they speak of what their companies and they as individuals do to try and make a difference in people's lives; several sponsor high school "adoption" programs and fund scholarships for needy students. Although at present providing individual charity or scholarship aid is the route these leaders have chosen, a two-fold challenge emerges from these sessions: to persuade our young business leaders to acknowledge the relationship between poverty and their businesses, and to recognize the importance of establishing a public and private partnership to work out solutions to the problems of poverty. If informed, these leaders will respond to a comprehensive strategy aimed at the underclass.

The key to communicating effectively with business leaders on issues of the poor is in understanding their perceptions about the origins of poverty. We see two conflicting perspectives. The majority contend that the underclass springs from a lack of education, practical job training or good role models; they believe that the people in the lowest economic sphere would be able to improve their standard of living if they were given the tools and training to meet the current needs of the work force. The leaders who hold this opinion are more likely to view the poor with compassion. Leaders arguing the less prevalent view believe that people are responsible for their own welfare: if they cannot support themselves, it is because of personal failure or character flaw. These leaders will be persuaded less by compassion and more by practical and fiscal considerations.

As the discussions with the business leaders progressed, and as respondents began to consider their potential role in solving the problems of the underclass, they became less apt to consider corporate answers and more likely to focus on governmental solutions. Participants do feel they can assist in implementing change, and that the business community's approval and support is *critical* to the successful implementation of any comprehensive policy of change. However, these executives acknowledge that their own corporations do not currently make a connection between their corporate health and the problems of the underclass.

The majority of our young leaders say that the business community does not see a relationship between its own bottom line and those who live below the poverty level, although a few say that some corporations are beginning to recognize that the existence of an underclass will, in the future, harm them. These business leaders worry primarily about the *growth* of the underclass, sensing that if it expands, the future could hold bad news for business. It is important, therefore, that the business community be educated about the critical nature of the situation that already exists.

After hearing the dinner speaker's statistics, most participants express alarm at what they learned and seem more inclined to act. They are also more willing, after listening to stories of public programs that have succeeded in changing peoples' lives, to acknowledge the programs' validity and even to relate success stories of their own.

If these leaders are given greater knowledge, a comprehensive picture of the policy options, and a better understanding of past successes—and then are shown that an option will work, they are willing to spend money to implement it.

EXAMINATION OF PRINCIPAL FINDINGS

(1) *The focus group participants expect the mood of the nation to become more activist over the next few years.* Some participants had great hopes for the return to conservatism of the "Reagan Revolution" and have been disappointed; others were pessimistic from the start about Reagan's term in office, and their fears have been realized. Most think that this Administration has failed to find solutions to the nation's social welfare problems. There seems to be a consensus among these leaders that programs for the underclass have truly been cut—not only the fat, but the meat as well. Participants say Ronald Reagan has gone too far and they expect a reaction. A few have perceived the changes on college campuses, as college students seem to be more involved in social issues: "They're not all trying to get the best grades to get a Harvard M.B.A. or into Harvard Medical School, and worrying about how much they'll be making when they get out, or which job pays the most money. They're worrying about riots in South Africa, the Peace Corps and things that were popular when I was on a college campus."

Several speak of this return to activism as cyclical: "We go in cycles in the U.S. . . . . A new vision comes along when we're psychologically ready . . . It's like a pendulum. There was a swing to the right. Now, I think there is going to be a correction." Several leaders seemed to resent being reminded that they were part of the selfish "me generation" of the 1970s and 1980s; it is likely that they will be responsive to a more activist time.

(2) *Although, as noted, these young executives had not previously considered all of the causes and ramifications of the existence of an American underclass, they still recognized both the heterogeneous nature of the problem and the obligation of our society to help the poor.* Whatever their ideology, participants agree that the problems of the poor are extraordinarily complex and must be addressed. As one participant observed, "It's a long-term, structural problem that's difficult to solve with Band-Aids." Indeed, participants believe that people who are better off have an obligation to try to lessen the burdens of the underclass.

Despite a firm commitment to "do something," participants are not convinced that the problems of poverty can be eradicated, whether through actions taken by individuals, corporations or the government. Running through all the sessions was an undercurrent of helplessness. Some panelists, however, express criticism of the view that the problem is too big to handle, calling such an outlook unproductive and self-defeating: "There are too many people who believe that nothing can be done, and that's a contagious mentality." These leaders suggest that programs should be offered in a realistic light, in terms of scope and what they hope to accomplish.

(3) *In its approach to the problems of the underclass, this generation of business leaders can be characterized primarily as pragmatic, and secondarily as compassionate.* They have grown up to accept and to expect the societal responsibility of raising the standard of living for the poor. However, they place a premium, in all their undertakings, on efficiency and financial success and make similar demands of governmental efforts. Consequently, they have little appreciation for the anti-poverty programs of the Great Society or the current welfare system. Their criticism does not stem from any resentment or absence of compassion, nor do they take issue with the programs' goals. Rather, they perceive current efforts as wasteful and ineffective. As one participant expresses his criteria for evaluating these programs, ". . . the question really is 'Will it work?' not 'Is it right?' " This type of pragmatism pervades the focus groups.

In order, then, to persuade baby boom executives to support proposals dealing with poverty, it will be necessary to answer the questions, "Will it work?" and "Can it be done economically?" Compassion is secondary.

(4) *The young business leaders have a personal desire to do something about the underclass, but are critical of the business community's failure to recognize a connection between the growing group of unskilled workers and business's need for skilled workers.* They explain that business is unwilling to commit resources to problems of the poor because the underclass is perceived as having very little to do with corporate success or failure. Participants conclude that, as long as this view prevails, corporate assistance to the poor will be motivated solely by charity or a corporate sense of social responsibility.

However, some participants recognize that companies are occasionally forced to make the connection between the ever-expanding underclass and their own future, most notably when they have difficulty filling job openings. One executive tells about how difficult it has been to find a secretary with basic reading and writing skills. Another notes that the inadequacy of local public transportation makes it virtually impossible for those who cannot afford a car to commute to areas outside the city, where many jobs are available.

Most participants speculate that as corporations realize the growing underclass's direct impact on business, they will act. Among the ideas mentioned are job training programs and day care centers. Specifically cited are corporations that have chosen to retrain their own workers so that they will become more productive employees, and companies that establish on-site day care facilities to attract and hold valuable employees.

Discussion participants conclude that the only thing that can be counted on is a corporation's desire to act in its own financial best interest. As one young leader observes, "There are some cases where you might say that businesses have involvement because they have a higher consciousness level, but I think the motivating factor with business is the bottom line." This reality must play a critical part in the decision-making process of designing public policy programs that involve the private sector.

(5) *These leaders believe that the federal government cannot do everything; in fact, they are wary of programs that claim to do too much. They perceive the federal government, local government and business community as each having its own specific strengths.* Therefore, programs that are well-defined and that have goals especially suited to the talents and strengths of the program implementors, will get the most support from this group of business leaders. One participant comments, "I think, perhaps, that the Johnson administration tried to do too much, too fast. And too much of it was oriented toward the public sector." Participants tend to see the federal government as suited to tackling macro/long-term issues; the local government as suited to micro/short-term issues; and the business community as best for special projects.

Business leaders explain that the federal government, by its nature, is able to afford a long-term view, and is thus the appropriate resource for programs that will have delayed benefits. One participant notes, "The government can take the real long view. The government doesn't need the immediate payback, because the government is us, all the people, not just one corporation more than other corporations, but equally spread out over everyone."

They suggest that local government is better suited, because of its scope, to address community problems of narrower breadth, such as establishing centers for the homeless or homes for teenage mothers.

The business community is seen as very unlikely to be willing to assume any *responsibility* for addressing problems of the underclass, but it is perceived as willing to take on special projects if it gets an incentive from the government. Participants note that the rules of capitalism make it difficult for private enterprise to spend money on programs when the payoff is viewed as remote or intangible. Private companies are therefore more likely to commit themselves to projects that promise immediate returns.

(6) *This group is fearful of inefficiency and huge administrative costs. Thus, the programs most appealing to the business community emphasize management skills and business acumen.* Leaders cast serious doubts on the federal government's ability to be efficient. They have a much stronger faith in the performance of the private sector, and tend to think that anything private business can take on, it should take on. As one business leader comments, "There is no understanding of how to solve problems in the government. You need goals, strategy and tactics—that's how you solve problems. If you give me a problem, I can give you a solution. That's what I do." A recurring theme of our political surveys, that voters want a pro-consumer candidate with managerial experience, surfaces in these discussions. The (probably unattainable) ideal for these young leaders is to find a private corporation with a social conscience like the government's to administer the anti-poverty program. In describing the appeal of Ronald Reagan's campaign message, one participant says, "There is a lot of tightening up that can be done. The problem is, they assume it can all be done that way. The tightening up part has got to continue."

As a solution to the problems of the government's inefficiency and the private sector's unwillingness to assume responsibility, projects emphasizing a public-private partnership are very appealing to participants. Not surprisingly, these business leaders believe that government-created financial incentives will be critical to the development and encouragement of private sector involvement in projects to alleviate poverty.

A few participants, cynical about government's efficiency and productivity, suggest allowing business both to structure and implement programs, with governmental advisory boards. Most see the need for government to establish a financial motivation to which business could respond: "If you want to see private sector involvement, then you create the profit motive—some sort of tax credit or other incentive—but don't go to them and ask them to provide the service on a nonprofit basis because in 15 years it is going to make the world a better place to live."

(7) *In considering issues of the poor, a major sticking point for the participants is whether future policy emphasis should be on the short-term or long-term set of goals.* All participants think both are important, but they recognize that limited resources and political realities can inhibit the successful realization of either set of goals. When forced to prioritize between short- and long-term projects, participants become frustrated, and tensions arise between those who prefer to take

immediate action and those who want to look toward the future. One participant, fed up with endless planning sessions, complains: "I think we sit around sometimes and create more problems just talking about all the possible ramifications. Find them shelter, get them health care, get them fixed up, then deal with some of the longer-term problems." Another participant specifically comments, "[I would] like to find links between the long-term and the short-term."

These executives define short-term strategies as those that cope with immediate problems, such as job training for working-age individuals seeking employment and assistance for people who need food and shelter. Long-term goals include more preventive measures, such as early childhood nutrition and education programs. This is a war that must be fought on two fronts: the short-term involves basic training and retraining for those already in the work force and the long-term involves programs for the very young aimed at combating future entries into the ranks of the impoverished.

Long-term solutions are often the first to be abandoned, because short-term solutions are easier to see and react to. People are most likely to act in response to a crisis: for example, they are moved by specific human tragedies portrayed in the media. Second, programs with long-term goals involving significant social change are more difficult to plan and require a disruption of the status quo.

(8) *Child care emerges as an ideal public program because it meets both short- and long-term goals.* In the short term, child care programs help alleviate problems faced by dual-career parents and single working parents, allowing them to leave their homes and get jobs. They also help families that need two incomes. The long-term benefits include teaching children positive values; keeping them off the street; developing self-esteem in children and parents; and delivering health care, nutritional food and education. Child care programs can serve as models for developing other programs to address the needs of the poor.

(9) *Education is another investment everyone agrees is worthwhile.* These future business leaders understand that breaking the cycle of poverty by reaching children at a very early age is critical to any long-term strategy. Participants are willing to spend their tax dollars on public schools, and they accept that the rewards will not be immediate. Their view of education is as pragmatic as their general approach to the problems of the underclass. Education is discussed in terms of providing occupational training, life skills and a positive work ethic, not in terms of promoting the liberal arts and higher education. As one executive explains, "[We need] programs for the poor that don't focus on just handing out welfare, that focus on creating esteem, building

job skills, building readiness. That [requires] focusing on education which doesn't shoot for the mediocre, or for the average [and focusing on education leads to] focusing on . . . family values."

(10) *Any group that wants to create consensus on a social agenda for the underclass must concentrate on spreading the word about successes that government programs have achieved.* It must counteract the negative reactions the business community has had toward many social welfare programs in the past. After the dinner briefings, in which they learned about some past governmental successes, participants seemed more optimistic about what can be accomplished through governmental programs. As mentioned earlier, the emotional edge of the discussions also became more keen. Despite the sense of resignation expressed by a few participants, the prospects of at least some success seemed to spark in these leaders a greater motivation to make an effort, and a greater sense of a personal stake in its outcome.

FOCUS GROUP QUOTES

In the next six months, either George Bush or Michael Dukakis will take the oath of office. What do you think is the biggest challenge they face?

The total lack of a real quality public education system—when you look at the issue of drugs or homelessness, it stems back to a lack of what happened in elementary school. We are not educating our youth. And with the money and wealth we have here, to not invest in our future . . . FOCUS GROUP #3

I listen to these guys talk and I tend to agree with them. But I see another problem, the issue of the creation of service-related jobs. We're creating service jobs by the thousands overnight: People who flip hamburgers, who sweep floors and any kind of occupation that provides a service to someone else that you get minimum wage for. And there are kids out there making thousands of dollars selling drugs who will not accept $3.35 an hour. Kids who can make more money in the streets will not go to school, either. There are no jobs for graduates. They get stuck in occupations that are less than what we had when we came out. We have more. In my business, out of 32 customer service agents, 70% have college degrees; they can't find other work. I think it's a problem. All our wealth is going overseas. FOCUS GROUP #3

Probably the structuring that is going on internationally is such that we can not only get ahead, but probably more so stabilize the situation, to be able to train, to retrain, and educate the population so that a continually evolving economy is effectively fed with people, and at the same time that they can get the jobs that they need to. FOCUS GROUP # 1

People are living longer and health care is becoming more expensive. I think that this is an issue that I believe we have to deal with today. FOCUS GROUP #2.

I agree with all of the [discussion] about the economy—and certainly about foreign affairs—but I am concerned in terms of poverty, and particularly with education, because that, I think, has the seeds of the most danger than anything else in our society. FOCUS GROUP #2

We have, as a country, lost the articulation of a sense of responsibility to each other. In fact, now we start to look at our people as an inconvenience. These homeless people are kind of a problem that we are stepping over, and there is no one articulating that we have a responsibility to one another. FOCUS GROUP #2

I'm talking about providing shelter and health care and subsistence for the people who are in need right now, preparing the system for the jolt that is going to hit with another recession. FOCUS GROUP #4

I agree [with providing for the needy]. But at the same time, how are you going to fund it? There is a lot of talk on the Democratic side about programs like that that really have disappeared under Reagan. But at the same time, the whole economy is looking at the budget deficit. We're in a tenuous mood and I don't think [poverty programs] will get support. I think the economy is on a very fine line right now. FOCUS GROUP #4

Obviously, the deficit is the number one domestic problem, but how does [a president] cope with that, in the face of pent-up demand for programs that . . . have eroded in the last eight years? Clearly there is a recognized need that there is going to have to be some involvement from the federal government. FOCUS GROUP #4

How are you going to solve these problems?

I would look to economic development as the centerpiece, but it is not related simply to investment issues; it is related to people issues— specifically, focus on education, focus on somehow highlighting family values. FOCUS GROUP #1

Somehow, I think you need to have programs which cause people (particularly among the underclass) to take actions which provide role models, that provide the environment in which the kind of values that I think are important, and generally are important, can be developed. That [means] programs for the poor that don't focus on just handing out welfare, that focus on creating an esteem, building job skills, building readiness. That [requires] focusing on education which doesn't shoot for the mediocre or for the average; and [focusing on education leads to] focusing on a whole range of issues that spring from education, in my view, family values. FOCUS GROUP #1

I think the problem . . . is one of defending the short versus the long run. The issue of restructuring values in the society is not just basic education. It is not something you say you are going to change right away. You have to start and assume that it is a very long-term structural kind of change. FOCUS GROUP #1

I really do believe that if we address some of the basic social issues, not just the homeless, *per se*, but also some of the larger issues, the homeless issue, for instance, could be remedied relatively easily. FOCUS GROUP #2

The homeless—in many ways, that whole situation is our society in two right there. Looking at all the reasons that a person may end up in that situation, they all lead back to our current economic situation, and decisions and policies that came out of the '60s, many of them. FOCUS GROUP #2

It seems to me that what we are saying is that government is being run like a business. Businessmen are very shortsighted, too. They are looking to see how management is going to stay in power and keep a buy-out from occurring and keep the shareholders happy. There is much too much focus on short-term issues. FOCUS GROUP #2

We spoke of people being hip, cool, square, with-it, in terms of conformity. In 1965–75, it was a different view, a period of rebellion. Everything was described in terms of I, mine, my, me. Are we going into a new period in America, or is it just a continuation of the '80s yuppies, more of individual achievements? Is there anything different we're going to see in terms of the '90s?

As a nation we're drifting back to basics. I think we experimented with different lifestyles in society. And I think that time frames, time spans seem to have shortened every day; the time it takes us to learn has shortened. As a result of that, as a people we tend to learn and go through lifestyles or experimentation faster. So I think we've learned and decided to go back to some basics. FOCUS GROUP #3

The anti-war or civil rights movements, etc., weren't [about] "me" or "my." I think that is epitomized in the Michael J. Fox show of the Reagan years, where everything Reagan touched turned to gold. Meese would never be confirmed in this day and time. But Reagan was the Teflon president, and Meese was confirmed without much challenge at all. At the same time, Michael J. Fox was on TV every night, saying how much money he was going to make, and making fun of his parents for having social consciences. FOCUS GROUP #3

There's a change. One thing is the college campuses are changing again. They're not all taking courses and trying to get the best grades to get a Harvard M.B.A. or into Harvard Medical School, and worrying about how much they'll be making when they get out, or which job pays the most money. They're worrying about riots in South Africa, the Peace Corps and things that were popular when I was on a college campus. I think the real test is going to come from the people in the generation that went through the '60s and early '70s, as we move into more leadership positions—whether we benefited having come from that, benefited from the quick fix of the Reagan years, which was extreme economic gratification for those from middle class or upper middle class backgrounds. FOCUS GROUP #3

I became more aware of social problems around high school and college—that time period. Now, I'm more concerned about practical things: the need for a strong economy. While that was not at all the case when I was younger, I'm not sure that the world has changed as much as that I've gotten older, and now my friends live in the suburbs and raise families and are more concerned with traditional values. FOCUS GROUP #4

I see a much more pragmatic approach to things. The question really is, "But will it work?" not, "Is it right?" The homeless are such a problem, lying out on the street; it demands a solution. While the ultimately more serious problems, long-term—like education—get short shrift. FOCUS GROUP #4

There is not an attempt to bind us together as a society. In fact, there is a glorification of the individual, which has reflected itself in really a deterioration of our business ethics, a deterioration of common cause and certainly over the last eight to ten years there has been a deterioration of the social fabric. FOCUS GROUP #2

Basically, there is nothing kind of pulling us together. In fact, we are being divided. The rich are being sort of set against the poor. Interest groups, I think the political system we have, has become more balkanized over the last 25 years. FOCUS #2

It will be a revolutionary generation. We will make structural changes in governance, in the way we govern. FOCUS GROUP #2

I think we'll be remembered for disaster—the generation that couldn't deal with problems. All our money will go to pay interest on the debt. It will take a crisis to make this generation change. FOCUS GROUP #2

My pessimism says we'll be remembered as the generation that handed our power over to the Pacific Rim countries. It will be the decline of the American empire. FOCUS GROUP #2

Would our society be any different today if Lyndon Johnson's ideas—and I am taking Lyndon Johnson as symbolic—if those things had been done? Would it make any difference today to us? Is there any way in which we reap benefits out of equal opportunities?

I think it has tended to make this country more conservative because, I think, there is a perception among a large portion of the population that those sorts of spending programs were not very successful, and were not a very efficient use of public funds. FOCUS GROUP #1

The space program . . . was very effective. I think spending programs and national purpose programs like that tend to be very effective when a large segment of the country views there to be a crisis of some kind, whether it is a world war or the Russians dominating space. [If] you get the whole national will behind it, a program like that tends to be very effective. If you look at employment-related programs, and recognize the fact that 94% of the people in the country have jobs, those sorts of spending programs that don't have broad popular support just don't seem to be as effective. FOCUS GROUP #1

Is there something about which you'll look back at your bosses or your parents and say, "Boy, they made some really great decisions and we're reaping the benefits of those decisions?" Or will it be the reverse—"Boy, they didn't make good decisions and we're paying for it now?"

The federal government made the decision [not investing enough in education]. It's really funny, in a way, for the Reagan administration to totally pull out of the education business. And then they got a secretary whose job it was to dismantle the Department of Education. And now he's on the news all the time talking about how terrible education is, but the federal government's not putting any emphasis on it. And I believe it is a national issue; it's the most important issue for any level of government to worry about our educational progress. If you saw the five-year update on the "Crisis" report yesterday, talking about how we made progress but we've still got a long way to go . . . And those are investments in our future [for which] we won't see a payback; it won't increase any of our take-home pay. In fact, it might decrease our take-home pay. FOCUS GROUP #3

Johnson's decision to create the war on poverty was a terrible decision, because the actual output of that was to take all these talented black college graduates and put them in. Their talent, their skills—they wasted away. And when the federal funds ran out, so did they. They were gone. I think the black community today suffers from that decision. FOCUS GROUP #3

I guess it is sort of a subtle point. I think that establishing programs and creating a demand, pulling everyone up through programs, historically has not proved to be effective. It is inefficient and it tends to be counterproductive. As a result of these programs, you tend to set up . . . counter-incentives and you end up with results that sometimes are counter to what the good intentions are. FOCUS GROUP #1

I think perhaps the Johnson administration tried to maybe do too much too fast, and too much of it was oriented toward the public sector. There might be a role for the private sector in some of these efforts. FOCUS GROUP #1

Tell me the two decisions that you think we have to make in terms of the next four years, decisions that will cause your kids to tell me, when I assemble them, "Hey, old Dad or Mom, that was a great decision."

Education, to me, is key. We discuss the homeless or the hard-core unemployed, and we realize that in terms of the kind of jobs that attract the hard-core unemployed who suffer from illiteracy are dwindling so fast, and that America is proceeding to have such a small manufacturing base as its economic base, that without education, we are going to be absolutely no place. We can't look at everything on a profit basis, but [we need to examine] how that profit basis turns around and regenerates and addresses some of those socio-economic issues of hard-core significance in the country. FOCUS GROUP #3

I want to underscore education. I also find it strange that some say that you can't throw money, you can't throw resources at a problem and solve it. I happen to think that you can throw money and resources at it, and it will go a long way toward solving the problem. FOCUS GROUP #3

Society should guarantee people jobs. Without a guarantee of jobs, education means nothing. What needs to happen is that people in corporate America, both big and small, need to come to some type of decision as to where the job search will be, what kind of jobs we will need. That's the only way the education system can focus on how to train people for jobs. FOCUS GROUP #3

Is there a program you would fight to the death for?

WIC is probably the most cost-effective social welfare program that exists. It is a relatively small program, but it goes back to some of the issues that we have been raising. FOCUS GROUP #1

Are you going to use the resources available to address the most immediate needs, such as immediate food and housing for people, or are you going to use the money to solve the problems so that people can get jobs, so that they can get an education, so that they can get into the system somehow? I think that there is a resistance in the general population to these programs that do more than provide for immediate relief, aid relief and don't take care of the problems. I think that many of the programs that we are talking about take care of immediate needs. FOCUS GROUP #1

I think everybody here agrees that there is some percentage of the population that can't function in a modern society, and that it is a societal obligation that those people should be taken care of. I think, conceptually, you can get conservatives, liberals, people across a broad spectrum to agree. Again, the problem comes when you try to translate that. It is easy to say, but you try to translate that into a program. FOCUS GROUP #1

Define the underclass.

I would say that it is the class of people who haven't been empowered, either financially or through education, or both, to be able to take control of their own destiny. FOCUS GROUP #4

There are certain incentives that most people operate on. If I had to define the underclass, I would say it's those people for whom those incentives just don't count. They don't believe they have a chance at ever making it to a level where they can get a job with good pay, or get the car they want, or the education they want. They've just given up on the system and quit. They might as well live on Mars as here in terms of the things that actually go on here. There is a complete separation from the culture and the government. FOCUS GROUP #4

Why do we have an underclass?

Because if we didn't have one, we'd have nobody to step on. And very simply, it gets down to the fact that we have an underclass because when you get so busy counting all your money, you forget about the people who don't have any. You don't even know that an underclass exists. FOCUS GROUP #3

I think our welfare system is a reason. We have a welfare system that ensure that we do have an underclass. FOCUS GROUP #3

The economy has a lot to do with poverty levels. Two of these other programs, prenatal care and WIC, have a long-term, as well as a short-term, benefit. Taking a position on return, which I like, this could be a great place for investing money. One thing that I would like to suggest relative to the jobs issue is funneling public funds through private sources in this way: for a certain period of time, an employer will be compensated for the training and the education that they are giving a young person that they're orienting into the workforce. Then let that diminish over a priod of time to where they, eventually, are funding their employee. FOCUS GROUP #1

It is politically acceptable—no one is going to run and get a lot of votes by saying, "I'm going to eliminate the underclass." One of the things that might lead to its elimination would be something I just read in the paper about concern regarding the work force. If everyone is a lawyer or a commodities trader, who is going to make the widgets? FOCUS GROUP #4

It runs counter to the American psyche that people can't reach out of that underclass. I think the vast majority of Americans don't believe that the underclass can't do anything about their situation, that they are trapped down there. And until Americans believe that the underclass can't do anything about their situation, then it will be acceptable. FOCUS GROUP #4

I think there is a difference between a lower class and the underclass. You are talking about people who are working class, who have opportunities to move up. By defining underclass as we do, they have no opportunities to move up. They are an underclass and a permanent underclass. FOCUS GROUP #4

We may disagree, but I just don't see (the homeless problem) as a population explosion issue. I think that it is a social issue, an issue much more than that. . . . I think that it is curable. I don't think that we can erase the whole thing, but I think we can seriously change the face of it if we dedicate ourselves to doing it. FOCUS GROUP #2

So how do we deal with it? Do we deal with it at the governmental level, or do we deal with it at the private level?

First you ask who is doing it, then you ask who should be doing it. And the only reason I say it's governmental is that [government's] influence on the private sector has been the only way the private sector will do anything in that arena. FOCUS GROUP #3

[I am] not saying that I want big government [when I] say the government should do it, but the government does set the framework, the laws and the incentives for the corporations. There are laws, and that means it's government. FOCUS GROUP #3

The reason I say private versus government is that, to me, the government will address these issues, solve these problems and then it's always somebody else's responsibility. What I'm suggesting is that it's got to be private, individual. Obviously, no one person is going to change the welfare system, but I think this election in a sense, will end up being a referendum on that issue: is the government going to solve our problems for us or are we going to do it ourselves? FOCUS GROUP #3

I think it is a fact that economically there is enough to go around. Therefore, it becomes an allocation problem, I guess, which is sort of the cold reality. I think to the extent that you try to mandate allocation, you run into a natural resistance on the part of a good segment of the population. FOCUS GROUP #1

I think the government has to play an important role, but almost a secondary role, an assisting role, a propping up role, setting up the sorts of things that need to be set up in society. And, although this is not very specific, to allow people to feel, as I think people did feel up until probably the last 15 or 20 years, that through their own efforts they have a fair chance, that they can get ahead. If they are willing to put in their effort, they can reap the rewards. FOCUS GROUP #1

It is a very big problem. I also have the sense that it feeds upon itself and grows as far as the effect it has upon everybody else. Therefore, perhaps [we should] change the definition of who is in the underclass. FOCUS GROUP #4

Because the problem in a large part stems from value systems, I think that the problem has to be handled at a much more local level. Federal policy should provide a loose structure and guidance for local programs, which can deal with basic things like community pride and the work ethic. FOCUS GROUP #4

If the underclass includes a large portion of single parent households and [if] we are talking about breaking the cycle, one thing we need to focus on is child care. If you can't get out of the house, how can you get a job? FOCUS GROUP #4

I think it is becoming very clear to big business that they have to take a leadership role. The largest organization of big business here announced that they were going to push for a state tax increase for education, provided there was reform in conjunction with that, precisely because business knows that access to an educated work force is in their own self-interest. FOCUS GROUP #4

The private sector has a tremendous role, because the work force is affected. I'm trying to find a new secretary. The candidates we've received in our office from the public school system are functionally illiterate; and it is not their fault. To find someone who is competent, with basic skills, is really tough. And business is going to be affected by it. FOCUS GROUP #4

Business can apply pressure on the political system, and it can also provide money, directly or through loans. Also, there are some talented financial people who have been outplaced as a result of mergers. We could provide funding for a socially beneficial program by paying outplaced people to apply their resources to the community. FOCUS GROUP #4

Business does apply pressure to the political system. They were partly responsible for reform of the local housing authority. They put pressure on the city to set up a crisis management team. Business realized that if the housing authority goes down, so does business. Another problem is that, as the central business district grows up, it comes up against the public housing. FOCUS GROUP #4

In this society, we are asking women, and men also, to make a choice between family or career. Economic survival depends on two people working. How do you juggle that, and what are the long-term implications of that? To me that is a very real social problem. Implicitly, society has made a choice in favor of work right now, because of the lack of child care services. What does that mean? FOCUS GROUP #2

Health care for the aged . . . doesn't concern me that much because I don't think that we have the ability to solve all of the problems that we have. My concern is more focused toward the long-term. People are living longer, and if they can support and take care of themselves, that is fine. I am more concerned about taking resources and devoting them into education, for example, rather than toward health care, national health care, when there are choices that have to be made. FOCUS GROUP #2

I think we sit around sometimes and create more problems just talking about all of the possible ramifications. Find them shelter, get them health care, get them fixed up and then deal with some of the longer term problems. FOCUS GROUP #2

There is a whole population of people like ourselves who are out in the world where we have to really live by creating results. Yet, if you want to participate in these problems, you can't do it with these government people, because they are only interested in having fundraisers for themselves. FOCUS GROUP #2

If the mayor or the governor were to come to you and say, "What problem do we have to correct," would you say that there is one on which you feel more emphasis should be placed?

We talk about who the poor people are today. I think that we have to recognize that the poor we are talking about today are not the poor we were talking about 20 years ago. We have to forget that mind-set of trying to address the problems of 20 years ago. [Today] we are talking about women, and day care is very important. I see that among people who are working—much less, among those who can't work, who don't have jobs, who don't have the money for child care. It is absolutely critical that any program which is going to address the problem of women provides extensive day care. FOCUS GROUP #1

Day care is probably even a larger issue than just in the poor community. Day care is going to become, because of all the working mothers across the country, a societal issue of how we are raising tomorrow's children. There [should be] funding, certainly at the lower income levels, but with some structuring and some regulation across-the-board, of course. FOCUS GROUP #1

[Day care] is like any other program. It could be very, very inefficiently administered. Any government programs runs that risk. The military program is being inefficiently administered, in my opinion, but it is still there. FOCUS GROUP #1

I want to cover a few areas now. Head Start: Is it a good investment? Was it worth the investment, and why?

It's an excellent investment, because it allows the child to come into an environment that is healthy. . . . as opposed to . . . if the child is alone, a negative environment. So, it may not be a perfect program, but like many of these programs, it helps some. FOCUS GROUP #3

There are two reasons to invest in day care, assuming that the implementation is reasonably effective. One is that it frees up the half of the work force that, to my knowledge, no other country in the world has opened doors to—women—and that is enormously important. And two, assuming it's reasonably effectively implemented, it provides an atmosphere of nurturing, one hopes, and preliminary education for kids that otherwise might not get that, and that pays off for years down the road. FOCUS GROUP #3

Are you saying that government should provide the bulk of the resources for early childhood? Is that the place where you need government to provide the resources?

There is no payoff close enough, from the corporation viewpoint. If society agrees that those services are needed, the corporations can't be expected to do it. They are working for their shareholders with respect to return—not necessarily during this quarter or next quarter, but somewhere within their lifetime. The government can take the real long view. The government doesn't need the immediate payback, because the government is us, all the people, not just one corporation more than other corporations, but equally spread out over everyone. FOCUS GROUP #1

Is it being done for the worker or for the child? It is a benefit for the corporation, because if they offer that kind of benefit, they are going to get the employees of the companies that don't offer that benefit. It is strictly a competitive reason for doing it. FOCUS GROUP #1

If you want to see the private sector involvement, you create the profit motive, and then provide some sort of tax credit or some incentive. Then you have the profit motive in the provision of the service, and you are not coming to a corporation and asking them to provide that service on a nonprofit basis because 15 years from now it is going to make the world a better place to live. It is still a competitive market in which the efficient provider should prevail. FOCUS GROUP #1

[I favor] implementation on the local level, but I still think that there needs to be some sort of national monitoring. FOCUS GROUP #2

I don't believe in putting just one arrow in your quiver. I would have a combination and I would insist on accountability. The advantage of local implementation is that it is closer and people feel more part of the process, but it is impossible to do it without the federal government. FOCUS GROUP #2

We have talked about budget deficits, drugs, a strong defense, education; how do we put it all together and what do we do?

Fortunately, I know most of the people in here, and they're socially responsible people. I deal with a lot of socially irresponsible people on a daily basis, and I try to shed a little light. I go back to the government point of view. There are too many people that are not going to participate unless they're forced into participation. They're not going to give up their almighty dollar. So they've got to be forced. Then when they're forced, the only thing that I have found effective is strictly scare tactics: scare them about the street gangs, scare them about an underclass that is going to continue to get more and more rebellious. Although it's a sad way to have to deal with human beings, it's the only way I've found to work with a lot of the corporate people that I deal with on a day-to-day basis. FOCUS GROUP #3

I think the solution is not all that radical, in terms of limits on service to the government. Create an environment for the private sector individual to work in the government as well, and get this cross-pollenization [started], either formally through government service or by creating an environment where private sector individuals and government sit down and form partnerships, so that everyone comes to the table with the same kinds of abilities. FOCUS GROUP #3

I think this is part of the problem of the presidential campaign, that we have no leaders on the scene, it seems, that can put forward a vision. In the corporate world we're dealing with current results, and in terms of the long-range, a vision statement. Where do you start with some kind of vision statment for society? I don't know how you start, other than with quality of life around the people. And then, you must begin to lay out those items underneath, in priority, that drive toward that quality of life within our society—the fundamental things. FOCUS GROUP #3

It's not that hard, it seems to me. In the corporate world we can say, "Here's our vision; here's where we want our company to be 20 years from now." Therefore, with this particular project, if the long range doesn't support that, cut it out. We're not getting a vision from the national leaders about what we want this country to look like, and why. If they do present one that happens to be rather radical, the media comes after them—drastically—because the media has not thought the whole matter through, and therefore cuts its down before the idea gets off the ground. FOCUS GROUP #3

I kind of like the idea about the whole industrial end of it playing a greater part of the education, to create a better society, plus the programs that are in place that we could improve on at the other end of the infancy level, the pre-school level. FOCUS GROUP #1

Joint public and private cooperative efforts have to be leaned on more. I think the focus must be on both sides, both the public sector and the private sector, in designing the programs. FOCUS GROUP #1

I guess I am not sure I see corporate America playing much of a role in the early childhood part. It seems to me, that is the sort of program that can be more of a government-directed program. I think if it is handled right, you get a shot at getting some sort of consensus in the country that it is wise to spend a certain amount of dollars for that. I think that the second component of it is more about jobs skills, taking teenagers in adjunct programs, or junior high school and high school programs, where there is a much more immediate payoff for corporate America. FOCUS GROUP #1

Somehow you have to motivate business to get involved. If it takes incentives, tax incentives, then that is the route to go. Whether it is on a local level, or whether it is on a national level, something has to happen to motivate businesses to move in that way. There are some cases where you might say that businesses have involvement because they have a higher conscience level, but I think the motivating factor with businesses is the bottom line: if I am going to get something out of it, then I will do something about this. FOCUS GROUP #2

Money needs to be spent on these issues, but [we have] to say, "Is it money well-spent?" If you look at [it from] the angle of how it is spent: administration, utilization . . . I think there are a lot of well-intentioned people who have no idea. Are our dollars caught up in the bureaucracy of government? Are there bad programs? Are there good programs? Maybe funding of programs should be halved, but should be done better. FOCUS GROUP #4

You have to realize the underclass is not homogenous. So, helping someone who is homeless (and therefore part of the underclass) who was dumped out of a state mental health facility because there was not money there for that person—obviously, that's far different from dealing with a 16-year-old unwed mother who can be trained, who can have a future. So you've got to make those distinctions when you're talking about individual programs. [Concerning] the second part of your question, obviously I think George is all wrong on that. There has to be a reexamining of federal spending, pronto, and there has to be attention paid to areas that have been ignored and allowed to fester over the last eight years. I'm skeptical that you can do that by shifting money that is already allocated within the budget. FOCUS GROUP #4

Does anyone want their taxes raised?

There is a certain part of the Reagan message that appeals to me. There is a lot of tightening up that can be done. The problem is they assume it can all be done that way. The tightening up part has got to continue. That is what appeals to a lot of people about Dukakis. He admits that that is an important part of the agenda, but it is probably not enough. The Democrats need to concentrate on tightening up before they even think of raising taxes. FOCUS GROUP #4

DISCUSSION AFTER DINNER BREAK

What have you learned? What is different? What do we need to address?

I am left with a sense of frustration as to how we solve these problems. FOCUS GROUP #2

I guess I come away uplifted. I think that here is a relatively affluent group, the supposedly "me generation," and I think that there is a reservoir of fundamental values that we all share. I really did get a sense of a common feeling that something should be done. There were different levels of outrage as you read those sheets. FOCUS GROUP #2

Clearly we differ—largely because we are all so inexperienced in how to implement the solutions—but I think that we share a common sense of objective. I think that we probably could articulate a common vision of what a good society should be. FOCUS GROUP #2

In the one-and-a-half hours before dinner, pre-school and day care may have come up once, twice. After less than a half-hour of speech, all of a sudden almost everyone here mentioned, "We've got to focus on pre-school." So, again, to emphasize the awareness: most of us were very surprised by these statistics. The country doesn't know. I think if you told the country these numbers they'd have the same reaction we did. But no candidate is up there saying, "This is what's going on in our country." FOCUS GROUP #4

I'm somewhat overwhelmed by the data, to start with. Obviously, I agree with the idea that the future is in the children, the education. They have to be put in a position to receive it. FOCUS GROUP #3.

What distresses me is that it almost sounds like you have to cross off the rest of the problem, wait till these people grow up. But what do you do with everybody who's older? What concerns me believing in education and everything, is that there are other problems of the underclass, which we have not addressed. FOCUS GROUP #3

The elderly have a very, very effective lobbying group, and children cannot lobby for themselves. And, therein is one of the real major differences. FOCUS GROUP #3

I think there is a crisis, a crisis for the underclass. I don't think people are really trying to sell the message that we've got a problem here that affects us all—in the pocketbook, in one sense and in a much greater sense. Maybe Kennedy couldn't have been elected now because of what went on in his personal life, but [we need] someone who can convince people that "it's not what your country can do for you." It's not how many tax breaks it can give you, and how big it can let your company get, and how rich it can let you retire, but "what you can do for your country." FOCUS GROUP #3

I wonder if there is a better vehicle for sharing successful programs. I wonder if people are focusing on the replication of these model programs. FOCUS GROUP #4

It's the idea of breaking the cycle. If you can get kids away from that atmosphere of "there is no way out" at an early age, get them out almost immediately and give them hope, you've broken the cycle. I was amazed. I thought the American education system was not good; I had no idea. Your statistics are frightening. FOCUS GROUP #4

The statistics that we heard tonight—I was appalled. Certainly I had an indication that they were out there, but not to that extent. As soon as they get filtered down through society, and things continue to get worse, people will begin to scream louder and louder. I just hope it isn't too late. FOCUS GROUP #4

We need to respond and we need to think in terms of the long-term and the short-term. We have to understand that there are diverse needs of the underclass, and we are going to have to prioritize how we respond. And if the way to mobilize people is around the children, let's do it. FOCUS GROUP #4

FOCUS GROUP
MODERATOR'S GUIDE

I. Overview

  A. Challenges of today—for the United States⁻

    1. What would you say are the biggest challenges facing America over the course of the next five to ten years?—Is our greatest challenge international or domestic?

    2. Where is America falling behind? Why are we falling behind?

    3. Let us say that the next president of the United States comes to you and says he wants to run for office on the slogan, "A president who prepared ahead." What would you tell him he must do? What does the success of Bush, Dukakis and Jackson tell us?

  B. Challenges for your company

    1. What do you feel is the major challenge facing your firm? How is it different from the national challenge? (well-trained work force)

    2. Good investments your company made ten years ago?

      a. How do you know?

      b. How long to find out?

  C. Decisions of the '60s and '70s:

  Thinking about the decisions over the course of the past 15 to 25 years that have been made by the federal government—

    1. Which ones have helped us and made America better?

    2. Which ones were investments that paid off as we look back?

    3. Which decisions have been the worst and have cost us in the long run?

  D. Values of the '90s:

    1. What is your perception of what the mood of the '90s will be?

2. Will the '90s be more like the "Me Decade" or more like the activism of the '60s?

II. The Underclass

A. Who, what, why?

1. Define the "underclass"—who are they? How big a problem is poverty in the U.S.?
2. Why do we have an underclass? What is the reason for the underclass? Is it growing or shrinking? What is the major cause of poverty?
3. How much can America do about this problem?
4. What should we be doing about this and who should be doing it—government or corporations?
5. What were the smart things we have done in the past? What were the unwise things we did in the past? What programs worked? Which ones wasted money? How much is long-term and how much is short-term?

B. A look at the government programs

1. What government human programs do you think work? What are the success stories? Where has the government spent its money wisely?
   a. Immunization
   b. Day care
   c. Head Start
   d. Prevention of teenage pregnancy
   e. Women and Infant Care programs—prenatal
2. Which ones were a good idea but did not work? Which ones were just too expensive for the return on the dollar spent?
3. If you were entrusted with the responsibility of evaluating social programs, how would you decide which ones worked and which ones did not? What questions would you want answered? How would you investigate?
4. Suppose the next president turns to you and says, "Figure out how to balance the budget and invest wisely in the human programs." How would you answer the call? What would you do on specific programs? What would be the optimal design of a poverty reduction program?

C. Connection to business

1. What if all human programs were cut by 50% to meet other needs. How would this affect business, if at all?

2. How do these programs help business? Does it make any difference?
3. What is the role of business? What should business be achieving or doing? What is their responsibility:
   a. Charity
   b. Corporate responsibility
   c. Investment in own future
4. Three things you would recommend to your business.

D. Pre-break for Dinner
What question would you like our expert to address?

III. A review of the problem

A. What was learned
   1. What are the main things you learned? What stood out in your mind? What is important?
   2. Where did you find that new information helped to change your opinions?
   3. What points did not ring true? What questions were left unresolved?
   4. Where do we get the best bang for the buck?

B. Where to go from here
   1. What must be done?
   2. Who should be doing it?
   3. What would you do to get other businesses involved?
   4. How optimistic do you feel about the future?
      a. When we meet five years from now, what will be different?
      b. Twenty years from now, what will we remember about this generation?

ABOUT THE AUTHORS

JAMES COMER is Maurice Falk Professor of Child Psychiatry, Yale Child Study Center; Director, School Development Program, Yale Child Study Center; and Associate Dean, Yale Medical School. He received his M.P.H. from the University of Michigan School of Public Health. He has written numerous articles and books, his most recent, *Maggie's American Dream,* New American Library/Dutton, 1988. He has lectured at numerous universities, medical schools, and scientific associations both in the United States and abroad. He has also been a consultant to the Children's Television Workshop, and the Public Committee on Mental Health. He is a regular contributor to *Parents Magazine.*

CAROL EMIG is director of the Kids Public Education and Policy Project (KIDSPEPP), a joint project of Family Focus and The Ounce of Prevention Fund in Chicago. She has been a staff assistant in the Bureau of Human Rights and Humanitarian Affairs in the U.S. Department of State, a research assistant to former First Lady Rosalynn Carter, and a consultant to nonprofit organizations. She received an M.P.P. from the John F. Kennedy School of Government at Harvard University. She has written several articles about national legislation on children's issues.

STANLEY GREENSPAN is clinical professor of Child Health and Development and Psychiatry at George Washington University Medical School. He also is a supervising child psychoanalyst at the Washington Psychoanalytic Institute. Formerly he was chief of Mental Health Study Center and Clinical Infant Development Program at the National Institute of Mental Health. He is the author of several books and numerous articles.

JAMES GARBARINO is president of the Erikson Institute for Advanced Study in Child Development in Chicago. Prior to joining the Erikson Institute, he served on the faculty of the College of Human Develop-

225

ment at Pennsylvania State University, and was director of the Maltreatment of Youth Project at the Center for the Study of Youth Development, Boys Town. He received his Ph.D. from Cornell University. Dr. Garbarino has authored and edited numerous articles and books. The most recent is *The Future As If It Really Mattered*, Bookmakers Guild, 1988.

ROBERT HALPERN is a professor at the Erikson Institute for Advanced Study in Child Development in Chicago. Prior to that he was an adjunct associate research scientist at the School of Public Health, Columbia University, and project director of the *Cross-Project Evaluation of the Ford Foundation's Child Survival/Fair Start (CS/FS) Demonstration*. He also is a consultant to the Committee on Prenatal Care Outreach, Institute of Medicine, National Academy of Sciences. He received his Ph.D. from Florida State University. He is the author of numerous articles and papers. The most recent is "Community-Based Early Intervention Programs: The State of the Art" in *Handbook of Early Intervention*, edited by Shankoff and Miesels, Cambridge University Press, 1988.

GEORGE MILLER represents the Seventh U.S. Congressional District in Northern California. Prior to his election to the U.S. House of Representatives in 1974, he was a legislative aide to California's Senate Majority Leader and was a practicing attorney. His responsibilities include serving as Chairman of the Select Committee on Children, Youth and Families of the U.S. House of Representatives and Chairman of the Water and Power Resources Subcommittee of the Interior and Insular Affairs Committee. As a high-ranking member of the Budget Committee, Congressman Miller is a member of the Budget Process, Defense and International Affairs, Income Security, and State and Local Government Congressional Task Forces.

JUDITH MUSICK is vice-chair of The Ounce of Prevention Fund in Chicago. Founding executive director of the Fund, she is now a Visiting Scholar at Northwestern University, and on the faculty of the Erikson Institute for Graduate Training in Child Development. She received her Ph.D. from Northwestern University. She is author of numerous books and articles. She is currently writing a book on the psychological aspects of early childbearing.

SARA ROSENBAUM is director of the Child Health Division of the Children's Defense Fund in Washington, D.C. Prior to this, she was a senior health specialist at the Children's Defense Fund, and a staff attorney at the National Health Law Program. She is currently a member of the American Public Health Association and is a member of several other professional societies and organizations. She received her J.D. from Boston University Law School. Her most recent article is "Maternal and Child Health" in *The Women's Economic Justice Agenda: Ideas for States*, 1987.

LISBETH BAMBERGER SCHORR is director of the Harvard University Project on Early Intervention to Break the Cycle of Disadvantage, and Lecturer in Social Medicine, Harvard University Medical School. Prior to this she was adjunct professor of Maternal and Child Health, University of North Carolina, and Chairman of the Select Panel for the Promotion of Child Health. She is a member of the National Forum on Children and Their Families of the National Academy of Sciences, and the Board of Mental Health and Behavioral Medicine of the Institute of Medicine. Her newest book, co-written with Daniel Schorr, is *Within Our Reach, Breaking the Cycle of Disadvantage*, Double-day/Anchor, 1988.

ELEANOR STOKES SZANTON is the executive director of the National Center for Clinical Infant Programs in Washington, D.C. Prior to this, she was a research associate at Steiger, Fink and Kosecoff. She received her Ph.D. from the University of Maryland. She is a member of and a consultant to many boards and panels, including the Family Resource Coalition in Chicago, and the Education for Parenting organization in Philadelphia. She is principal author of *Infants Can't Wait*, NCCIP, 1986.

BERNICE WEISSBOURD is president of Family Focus in Evanston, Illinois. She is also a contributing editor of *Parents Magazine*. She serves as president of the Family Resource Coalition and is president of the American Orthopsychiatric Association. She has written several articles and books, the most recent one, as co-author, *Family Support Programs*, Yale University Press, 1985. She also has served as a consultant to public television shows and film makers.

INDEX